Managing Educational Tourism

ASPECTS OF TOURISM

Aspects of Tourism is an innovative, multifaceted series which will comprise authoritative reference handbooks on global tourism regions, research volumes, texts and monographs. It is designed to provide readers with the latest thinking on tourism world-wide and in so doing will push back the frontiers of tourism knowledge. The series will also introduce a new generation of international tourism authors, writing on leading edge topics. The volumes will be readable and user- friendly, providing accessible sources for further research. The list will be underpinned by an annual authoritative tourism research volume. Books in the series will be commissioned that probe the relationship between tourism and cognate subject areas such as strategy, development, retailing, sport and environmental studies. The publisher and series editors welcome proposals from writers with projects on these topics.

Other Books in the Series

Classic Reviews in Tourism
Chris Cooper (ed.)
Dynamic Tourism: Journeying with Change
Priscilla Boniface
Journeys into Otherness: The Representation of Differences and Identity in Tourism
Keith Hollinshead and Chuck Burlo (eds)
Marine Ecotourism: Issues and Experiences
Brian Garrod and Julie C. Wilson (eds)
Natural Area Tourism: Ecology, Impacts and Management
D. Newsome, S.A. Moore and R. Dowling
Progressing Tourism Research
Bill Faulkner, edited by Liz Fredline, Leo Jago and Chris Cooper
Tourism Collaboration and Partnerships
Bill Bramwell and Bernard Lane (eds)
Tourism and Development: Concepts and Issues
Richard Sharpley and David Telfer (eds)
Tourism Employment: Analysis and Planning
Michael Riley, Adele Ladkin, and Edith Szivas
Tourism in Peripheral Areas: Case Studies
Frances Brown and Derek Hall (eds)

Other Books of Interest

Global Ecotoursim Policies and Case Studies
Michael Lück and Torsten Kirstges (eds)

Please contact us for the latest book information:
Channel View Publications, Frankfurt Lodge, Clevedon Hall,
Victoria Road, Clevedon, BS21 7HH, England
http://www.multilingual-matters.com

ASPECTS OF TOURISM 10

Series Editors: Chris Cooper (*University of Queensland, Australia*), Michael Hall (*University of Otago, New Zealand*) and Dallen Timothy (*Arizona State University, USA*)

Managing Educational Tourism

Brent W. Ritchie

with Neil Carr and Chris Cooper

CHANNEL VIEW PUBLICATIONS

Clevedon • Buffalo • Toronto • Sydney

To Maria and my family

Library of Congress Cataloging in Publication Data
Ritchie, Brent W.
Managing Educational Tourism/Brent W. Ritchie with Neil Carr and Chris Cooper.
Aspects of Tourism: 10
Includes bibliographical references
1. Students–Travel. 2. Foreign study. 3. Tourism.
I. Carr, Neil. II. Cooper, Christopher P. III. Title. IV. Series.
LC6681 .R58 2003
370.116–dc21 2002015590

British Library Cataloguing in Publication Data
A catalogue entry for this book is available from the British Library.

ISBN 1-853150-51-2 (hbk)
ISBN 1-853150-50-4 (pbk)

Channel View Publications
An imprint of Multilingual Matters Ltd

UK: Frankfurt Lodge, Clevedon Hall, Victoria Road, Clevedon BS21 7SJ.
USA: 2250 Military Road, Tonawanda, NY 14150, USA.
Canada: 5201 Dufferin Street, North York, Ontario, Canada M3H 5T8.
Australia: Footprint Books, PO Box 418, Church Point, NSW 2103, Australia.

Typeset by Florence Production Ltd.
Printed and bound in Great Britain by the Cromwell Press.

Contents

Contributors

Thomas G. Bauer, School of Hotel and Tourism Management, The Hong Kong Polytechnic University, Hung Hom, Kowloon, Hong Kong, China (hmthomas@inet.polyu.edu.hk). Thomas Bauer, PhD, is an assistant professor in Tourism in the School of Hotel and Tourism Management at the Hong Kong Polytechnic University. He has been involved in tourism education for the past 14 years and has developed a special interest in tourism in Antarctica. To date he has visited the region eleven times as a researcher, lecturer, guide and Zodiac driver.

Brock Cambourne, Centre for Tourism Research, University of Canberra, ACT 2601, Australia (bxc@comedu.canberra.edu.au). Brock Cambourne is the Deputy Director of the Centre for Tourism Research at the University of Canberra. He has undertaken a range of tourism research and consultancy projects including the development of destination master plans, an analysis of educational tourism in the ACT and a number of major market research programmes for tourist attractions with a focus on the edu-tourism market. He is also co-editor of two books *Wine Tourism Around the World: Development Management and Markets* and *Food Tourism Around the World: Development Management and Markets.*

Neil Carr, Department of Tourism and Leisure Management, The University of Queensland, 11 Salisbury Road, Ipswich, Qld 4305, Australia (n.carr@mailbox.uq.edu.au). He holds a PhD from the University of Exeter and his research focuses on the influence of social relations on leisure and tourist behaviour, gendered leisure spaces and the holiday behaviour of children and young adults. He has published extensively in journals such as the *Annals of Tourism Research, Tourism Geographies, Tourism Management* and *World Leisure,* amongst others.

Eleanor Cater, Chumbe Island Coral Park, P.O. Box 3202, Zanzibar/ Tanzania (chumbe@zitec.org). Eleanor is a project manager for the Coral Park, which is on the UN list of Protected Areas. In 2000 Chumbe was declared a laureate of the UNEP Global 500 Forum and was chosen to represent Tanzania at the EXPO2000 Hannover, Germany. In 2001 Chumbe was awarded the Condenast Traveller Ecotourism Destination of the World Award and was declared the Green Hotelier of the Year by the International Hotel and Restaurant Association.

Chris Cooper, Department of Tourism and Leisure Management, The University of Queensland, 11 Salisbury Road, Ipswich, Qld 4305, Australia (c.cooper@mailbox.uq.edu.au). Chris is Professor of Tourism and Head of School of Tourism and Leisure Management at the University of Queensland, Australia. As well as having degrees in geography and experience in the travel industry, Chris has been influential in the development of the tourism subject area and has worked with the World Tourism Organization in this area. He is currently a member of the WTO's business and education councils. His research interests are in the development of tourist resorts, education and training for tourism, and the knowledge management of tourism research.

Duane Coughlan, Menlo Consulting Group, 105 Fremont Ave, Los Altos, CA 94022, USA (dcoughlan@menloconsulting.com). Duane is research manager at Menlo Consulting Group, a specialist market research company for the global travel and tourism industry. Duane has had many years experience undertaking consultancy research, including research on the school excursion market in Australia. Prior to his current position Duane worked at the University of Canberra (Australia) as the Deputy Director for the Centre for Tourism Research and at the University of Otago (New Zealand) as a junior research fellow and a PhD candidate.

Ngaire Douglas, School of Tourism and Hospitality Management, Southern Cross University, NSW 2480, Australia (ndouglas@scu.ed.au). Dr Ngaire Douglas is a senior lecturer in the School of Tourism and Hospitality Management, Southern Cross University, Lismore, NSW. She is the author, co-author and editor of a dozen books, numerous journal articles, book chapters and monographs on various aspects of tourism in the Pacific Asia region and is editor-in-chief of the multi-disciplinary journal *Pacific Tourism Review*. Research interests include histories of tourism, tourism development in Southeast Asia and the South Pacific, tourism imagery and cruise tourism.

Pam Faulks, Centre for Tourism Research, University of Canberra, ACT 2601, Australia (pamelaf@comedu.canberra.ed.au). Pam Faulks is a

Research Officer with the Australian Governor General's Office in Canberra, Australia. Prior to this she was a Researcher at the Centre for Tourism Research and Cooperative Research Centre for Sustainable Tourism at the University of Canberra, where she worked on a range of projects including educational tourism to Australian Capital Territory, visitor satisfaction studies and a range of strategic event evaluations. Ms Faulks is currently undertaking a Masters by research examining the 'seniors' tourism market.

David A. Fennell, Department of Recreation and Leisure Studies at Brock University, St Catherines, Ontario, Canada (dfennell@arnie.pec.brocku.ca). Dr Fennell's main research focus is ecotourism, which he has explored for many years. As a consequence of his involvement in this area, David has undertaken research and conducted workshops in many different countries. He is the author of *Ecotourism: An Introduction*, a general text on ecotourism and *Ecotourism Programme Planning*, which examines ecotourism from a systems planning perspective. David is also the editor of the *Journal of Ecotourism*, which is in its second year of circulation. Other research interests include carrying capacity, tourist movement in space and time and ecological impacts.

Heather Hardwick, Menlo Consulting Group, 105 Fremont Ave, Los Altos, CA 94022, USA (hhardwick@menloconsulting.com). Heather Hardwick is a senior consultant with Menlo Consulting Group, a market research and strategy consulting firm that serves the travel and tourism industry exclusively. She has a strong background in market analysis and has assisted travel providers with a wide range of projects involving strategic planning, market assessment, branding and positioning, and product development. Ms Hardwick has particularly strong expertise in the educational travel segment, having conducted extensive research and authored studies on this growing segment. She is a frequent speaker at travel industry events and conferences. Ms Hardwick holds a BA from Stanford University.

Janet Hughes, Cultural Heritage Research Centre, University of Canberra, ACT 2601, Australia (Janet.Hughes@nga.gov.au). Janet Hughes trained in Materials Conservation at the University of Canberra where she is currently completing her PhD, researching the deterioration and preservation of historic sites in Antarctica. Two of Janet's four visits to Antarctica have been aboard tourist ships and her observations of visitors' interests and behaviour patterns led to several research papers on the impacts of tourism on Antarctic historic sites. This experience demonstrated that visitor issues must be included when developing management plans for these sites. Janet is currently the Head of Conservation at the National Gallery of Australia in Canberra.

Laura Lawton, Department of Health, Fitness and Recreation Resources, George Mason University, Prince William 1 (Room 312, Mail Stop 4E5), 10900 University Bvld, Manassa, VA 20115, USA (llawton@gmu.edu). Dr Laura Lawton is an assistant professor of tourism and events management in the Department of Health, Fitness and Recreation Resources at George Mason University, Virginia, USA. She received her PhD in tourism management from Griffith University, Gold Coast, Australia in 2002. Dr Lawton specialises in tourism management, resident perceptions of tourism and tourism within protected areas. She is the co-author of the second edition of *Tourism Management*, published by John Wiley.

Teresa Leopold, Masters Candidate, Department of Tourism, University of Otago, P.O. Box 56, Dunedin, New Zealand (resa_leopold@hotmail.com). Teresa has undertaken research on the marketing of memorials as well as industrial-based research on visitor satisfaction as part of her BA (Hons) Degree in Tourism Management from the University of Brighton. She is currently writing a Masters at the University of Otago on dark tourism in Southeast Asia. This research is set within the context of developing a classification system for dark tourist attractions, identifying appropriate marketing methods, commodification, education and authenticity.

Jo-Anne Lester, School of Service Management, University of Brighton, 49 Darley Road, Eastbourne BN20 7UR, United Kingdom (J.A.Lester@bton.ac.uk). Jo-Anne Lester worked in the tour operating and cruise ship industry for several years before joining the University of Brighton as a lecturer in Travel and Tourism. She holds a Masters Degree in Tourism Management and her teaching interests lie in the cruise ship industry and photography and tourism.

Graham A. Miller, University of Westminster, 35 Marylebone Road, London NW1 5LS, United Kingdom (G.Miller01@westminster.ac.uk). Graham's main research interests are in the development of indicators to measure the progress of the tourism industry towards greater sustainability. This has led to examinations of the attitudes of tourism companies to corporate responsibility and of consumers to sustainable tourism products. More recent research has questioned the level of ethical instruction tourism students receive. Related work has explored the accessibility of tourism establishments in the UK for the disabled consumer and the adherence of the industry to the recent Disability Discrimination Act, as well as considering the role of charities within the tourism industry.

Richard Mitchell, School of Tourism and Hospitality, La Trobe University, Bundoora, Victoria 3086, Australia (richard.mitchell@latrobe.edu.au). Richard Mitchell is Senior Lecturer in Tourism Marketing at Latrobe University (Melbourne, Australia) and he is nearing completion of his PhD thesis on the consumer behaviour of New Zealand winery visitors (University of Otago, Dunedin, New Zealand). Along with several publications on wine and food tourism, Richard has completed a number of tourism consultancy projects both in New Zealand and Australia. His other research interests include learning as a motivation for travel, rural landscapes, tourism psychology and destination marketing.

Carleen Mitchell, c/o: Richard Mitchell, School of Tourism and Hospitality, La Trobe University, Bundoora, Victoria 3086, Australia (richard.mitchell@latrobe.edu.au). Carleen Mitchell, a trained chemist, holds a certificate of wine production and has worked on a number of environmental research projects in New Zealand and Australia. While her main career focus has been in the area of environmental chemistry, in recent years her strong personal and professional interest in wine production has seen her work expand to include several wine tourism consultancy projects and teaching wine tourism and business, an area which she intends to continue in the future.

Sara Muñoz Gonzalez, Panama 2, 2A, Majadahonda, 28220, Madrid, Spain (saraibalu@hotmail.com). Sara graduated from the University of Brighton with a BA Honours Degree in International Tourism Management in April 2001. Her dissertation research focused on educational tourism, for which she produced a study on 'The Role of English Language Schools in Eastbourne's Tourism Industry and Economy'. She is presently working in the development team of Madrid Xanadú, the first Leisure and Shopping centre of the Mills Corporation in Europe.

Mark Priddle, Australian National University, Canberra, ACT 0200, Australia (mrpriddle@hotmail.com). Mark is currently completing his Masters Degree in Marketing Communication at the University of Canberra whilst working as a marketing and development officer for the university. His research interests are in services marketing, event management and sustainable tourism development. He has a keen interest in international education and hopes to undertake further research on educational tourism with particular reference to its effects on Australia.

Charlotte Vogels, Menlo Consulting Group, 105 Fremont Ave, Los Altos, CA 94022, USA (charlottevogels@hotmail.com). Charlotte has studied International Tourism Management and Consultancy at the Breda

University of Professional Education in the Netherlands. She conducted her internship period at Menlo Consulting Group, who specialise in market intelligence and strategy consulting for the global travel and tourism industry. Additional to extensive travel experience in Europe, the Americas and Asia, Charlotte has previous working experience in the travel and education industry. At present, she gives lectures and develops curricula on the subject of sustainable tourism for several universities in the Netherlands.

Maree Walo, School of Tourism and Hospitality Management, Southern Cross University, NSW 2480, Australia (mwalo@scu.ed.au). Maree is the Internship Co-ordinator for the School of Tourism and Hospitality Management at Southern Cross University. Her 20 years management experience in the tourism and hospitality industry was primarily in the areas of food service/catering, conference and events and resort management. Maree holds a Masters by Research from Southern Cross University. This research investigated the relationship between internship and students' management competency development. Maree has several diverse research interests including events management, sport tourism, cuisine tourism, tourism education, graduate career development and co-operative education issues. She is a member of the World Association of Cooperative Education.

David Weaver, Department of Health, Fitness and Recreation Resources, George Mason University, Prince William 1 (Room 312, Mail Stop 4E5), 10900 University Bvld, Manassa, VA 20115, USA (dweaver3@gmu.edu). Dr David Weaver is Professor of Tourism and Events Management in the Department of Health, Fitness and Recreation Resources at George Mason University, Virginia, USA. He is a specialist in ecotourism, sustainable tourism and destination life-cycle dynamics, and has authored or co-authored five books and over 50 refereed articles and book chapters. Dr Weaver is also the editor of *The Encyclopedia of Ecotourism*. He has held previous appointments at Griffith University (Australia) and the University of Regina (Canada).

Clare Weeden, School of Service Management, University of Brighton, 49 Darley Road, Eastbourne BN20 7UR, United Kingdom (C.H.Weeden@bton.ac.uk). Clare Weeden is a Senior Lecturer in the School of Service Management at the University of Brighton. She specialises in the marketing of tourism but her wider research interests include consumer psychology and cruise tourism. Clare is currently completing PhD studies examining the role of personal values in cognitive consumer behaviour and tourism.

Josette Wells, Tourism Program, University of Canberra, ACT 2601, Australia (jmw@comedu.canberra.edu.au). Josette is a senior lecturer and programme director of the Bachelor of Tourism Management at the University of Canberra, Australia. She has a particular interest in historical tourism research, but has also published in the area of tourism education, addressing curriculum and professional issues in tourism higher education. Among her other research interests are tourism marketing and entrepreneurial education in tourism.

Preface

A number of authors and commentators have noted the apparent interest amongst consumers for educational holidays. This interest has led to the provision of tourism products with some form of learning or education as an integral component. Examples include special interest holidays, including ecotourism and cultural heritage tourism, as well as specialist educational holiday providers and operators, such as Elderhostel, Odyssey Travel, Linblad Cruises and the Disney Orlando Institute. However, despite the apparent growth in these two areas of tourism, little research has been conducted on educational forms of tourism and the integration of learning experiences within tourism. Yet for some tourism niche markets, such as ecotourism, learning and education are identified as important aspects to the experience.

Similarly, a number of authors have noted the growth in provision of education, especially offshore or foreign educational experiences such as language schools, university and college tourism as well as school excursions and field trips. To date little has been written about their tourism impacts or issues surrounding the management of this tourism market segment. It is hoped that this book contributes in some small way to the study of both types of educational tourism and their sub-segments. It is hoped that by discussing and exploring educational tourism greater interest and understanding of this form of tourism will occur, perhaps stimulating more research in the field.

The book does not profess to cover the multitude of educational tourism types – as Smith and Jenner (1997a) note, broadly speaking all types of tourism can be viewed as educational. Instead the book highlights key market segments and sub-segments and explores key themes associated with the management of educational tourism, which may be explored in greater detail by other authors/researchers or in a second edition of this book! Authors made contributions in a variety of countries and settings, yet the book highlights a range of similar themes and issues. Understanding educational tourists, the educational tourism industry and the impacts and issues of educational forms of tourism is critical if these forms of tourism is to be managed effectively and efficiently. The book aims to be accessible to not only academics and students but also the tourism and education industry. Therefore, the book consists of case studies and exhibits or displays to help highlight key issues and themes through the use of relevant and timely examples.

Acknowledgements

I would like to acknowledge the support and assistance of various individuals and organisations who have helped turn the idea of this book into reality. First I would like to thank the book series editors, Chris Cooper and C. Michael Hall, for providing the opportunity to write this book, even though the process was more difficult than was anticipated. Thanks should also go to the University of Canberra for their financial support in the form of a University Research Grant that helped support some of the research conducted for this book. Thank you to Duane Coughlan who helped develop the initial idea, but through circumstances was unable to complete the book with me.

I would also like to thank a number of people for their support and encouragement in completing the book. Thanks go to staff at the University of Canberra, including Trevor Mules, Josette Wells, Niki Macionis, Brock Cambourne and Helen Ayres. University of Brighton colleagues and staff such as Paul Frost, Steven Goss-Turner, Nigel Jarvis, Graham Shephard, Peter Burns, Cathy Palmer, Thrine Hely, Jo-Anne Lester, Harvey Ells and Chris Dutton have also been very supportive and encouraging.

Special thanks go to organisations who have helped supply information concerning educational tourism, including the Canadian Tourism Commission, the Schools Educational Tourism Committee in Canberra, especially Gary Watson and Brian Weir, Elderhostel, the Menlo Consulting Group, the British Trust for Conservation Volunteers and Tourism Concern. A big thank you also goes out to all of the individual contributors from all parts of the globe who have written either case studies or exhibits for the various chapters. Also thank you to those authors and colleagues who supplied photos to help illustrate the book, including Janet Hughes, Ngaire Douglas, Thomas Bauer and Paulette Cowles. I should acknowledge the support of the publishing team at

Channel View for their assistance, hospitality and patience throughout this process. Finally, thanks to my family for their love and support, and to my partner Maria who has to put up with my constant ranting about tourism!

B. W. Ritchie
London
July 2002

Copyright Permissions

The author and publisher would like to thank the following individuals and organisations for allowing reproduction of the following items within this book.

- Janet Hughes for Plate 3.1.
- Thomas G. Bauer for Plate 3.2.
- Canadian Tourism Commission for Figure 1.1.
- Belhaven Press, London for Table 2.1.
- Addison Wesley Longman, Australia for Table 2.2.
- Routledge, London for Table 2.3.
- Elsevier Science for Figure 2.2 and Table 6.3.
- Paulette Cowles for Plate 2.1.
- Channel View Publications for Table 6.1.

Chapter 1
An Introduction to Educational Tourism

Introduction

The growth of both education and tourism as industries in recent decades has led to growing recognition of these industries from both an economic and social perspective. As Roppolo (1996: 191) notes, 'as countries become more interdependent, their success, growth and economic prosperity will largely depend on the ability of two industries – education and tourism – to create the avenues necessary to support international exchange and learning'. The changes in the tourism industry over the last two decades coupled with the changes in education have seen the convergence of these two industries with education facilitating mobility and learning becoming an important part of the tourist experience. Smith and Jenner note that educational tourism has generated little excitement to date from the tourist industry and this is reflected in the gathering of research and data. They note that 'very little research has been done because this segment is not seen as warranting it, yet because little research has been done, the industry is unaware of the true size of the segment' (Smith & Jenner, 1997a: 60). Roppolo (1996) agrees and notes that there are many areas yet to be examined empirically concerning the links between education and tourism.

This chapter begins by exploring relationships between education, tourism and educational tourism, first with a section to assist the reader in understanding tourism (definitions of tourism and the growth of this sector) and education (definitions of education and learning and the growth of education and lifelong learning). The chapter then discusses educational forms of tourism by providing a brief history and an outline of how educational tourism may be conceptualised or understood. The chapter argues that a systems and segmentation approach to understanding educational tourism is useful and concludes that, although educational tourism is a broad and complicated field with limited past research, the importance of this area of tourism is likely to grow due to trends in both the tourism and education sectors.

Understanding Tourism

Tourism is one of the fastest growing industries taking place in both developed and developing countries worldwide. The growth of tourism has been fuelled by the growth in leisure time combined with an increase in discretionary income and a desire to escape and engage in holidays both domestically and internationally. Definitions of tourism vary with respect to whether the definition is from a supply-side (industry) or demand-side (consumer) perspective. As Smith (1988: 181) has noted, 'there are many different legitimate definitions of tourism that serve many different, legitimate needs'. Moreover, many of the tourism definitions vary due to the organisation or individual trying to define tourism and to their motives. However, there are commonalities between many of the definitions.

Former tourism definitions stated that a minimum of a 24-hour stay was required to be considered a tourist. However, this has been modified to an overnight stay, which, according to Weaver and Oppermann (2000: 28), 'is a significant improvement over the former criterion of a 24-hour stay, which proved to be both arbitrary and extremely difficult to apply'. If a person's trip does not incorporate at least one overnight stay, then the term excursionist is applied (Weaver & Oppermann, 2000). This definition can be applied to both international and domestic travellers. For example, international stayovers (or tourists) are those that stay in a destination outside of their usual country of residence for at least one night, while international excursionists (or same-day visitors) stay in an international location without staying overnight. Furthermore, a domestic stayover (or tourist) is someone who stays overnight in a destination that is within their own country of residence but outside of their usual home environment (usually specified by a distance of some kind). Domestic excursionists (or same-day visitors) undertake a similar trip but do not stay overnight.

Smith (1988) believes that it is difficult to determine the precise magnitude of the tourism industry due to the absence of an accepted operational definition of tourism. Nevertheless, the tourism industry has been defined as an industry that 'encompasses all activities which supply, directly or indirectly, goods and services purchased by tourists' (Hollander, Threlfall & Tucker, 1982: 2). Hall (1995: 9) believes that the following three factors emerge when examining the myriad definitions concerning the tourism industry:

- the tourism industry is regarded as essentially a service industry;
- the inclusion of business, pleasure, and leisure activities emphasises 'the nature of the goods a traveller requires to make the trip more successful, easier, or enjoyable' (Smith, 1988: 183); and
- the notion of a 'home environment', refers to the arbitrary delineation of a distance threshold or period of overnight stay.

However, McIntosh *et al.* (1995: 10) take a more systems-based approach when defining tourism as 'the sum of phenomena and relationships arising from the interaction of tourists, business suppliers, host governments, and host communities in the process of attracting and hosting these tourists and other visitors'. This definition includes the potential impacts that tourists may have upon the host community, and also includes 'other' visitors such as students.

The above discussion illustrates that there are many different components to defining tourism, which range from tourists themselves, the tourism industry and even the host community or destination. A number of authors view tourism therefore as an integrated system of components (Gunn, 1988; Leiper, 1989; Mathieson & Wall, 1982; Mill & Morrison, 1985; Murphy, 1985; Pearce, 1989), which generally have a number of interrelated factors:

- a *demand side* consisting of the tourist market and their characteristics (motives, perceptions, socio-demographics);
- a *supply side* consisting of the tourism industry (transport, attractions, services, information, which combine to form a tourist destination area);
- a tourism *impact side* whereby the consequences of tourism can have either direct or indirect positive and negative impacts upon a destination area and the tourists themselves;
- an *origin–destination approach* which illustrates the interdependence of generating and receiving destinations and transit destinations (en route) and their demand, supply and impacts.

According to the World Tourism Organization (WTO, 1999) tourism is predicted to increase with future tourist arrivals growing to 1.6 billion by the year 2020 at an average growth rate of 4.3%. Despite the effect of external factors such as the Asian Economic Crisis in the late 1990s and the September 11 incident in 2001, tourism growth appears to be assured. According to the World Travel and Tourism Council (WTTC, 2001) tourism currently generates 6% of global Gross National Product and employs one in 15 workers worldwide. It is predicted that by 2011 it will directly and indirectly support one in 11.2 workers and contribute 9% of Gross National Product worldwide (WTTC, 2001).

The growth of tourism has spread geographically with the market share of tourist arrivals reducing in Europe and increasing in the Asia-Pacific area, which has the fastest growth rate of world tourist arrivals. There has also been a growth in tourism to developing countries with their share of tourist arrivals and expenditure increasing especially in destinations such as Eastern Europe, South America, the Middle East and Africa. Tourists are now more than ever travelling further in search of new and unusual experiences.

However, the growth of tourism on a worldwide scale, coupled with the search for new destinations and experiences, has added to the questioning of tourism impacts and calls for more sustainable or 'alternative' types of tourism. The problems associated with mass tourism and the ability of tourism to transform destinations and impact negatively upon host communities is well recognised (Fennell, 1999) and there is a move toward more 'soft', 'sustainable' or 'alternative' forms of tourism. Since the 1980s the tourist marketplace has become increasingly specialised and segmented resulting in the growth of niche markets such as rural tourism, ecotourism, adventure tourism and cultural heritage tourism. Furthermore, a number of educational and learning experiences within tourism appear to be increasing (CTC, 2001), while travel and tourism experiences specifically for study or learning also appear to be increasing (Roppolo, 1996), illustrating the potential for educational forms of tourism.

Understanding Education and Learning

Education has been defined as 'the organized, systematic effort to foster learning, to establish the conditions, and to provide the activities through which learning can occur' (Smith, 1982: 37). The key word 'learning' indicates some form of process. As Kulich (1987) states, learning is a natural process which occurs throughout one's life and is quite often incidental, whereas education is a more conscious, planned and systematic process dependent upon learning objectives and learning strategies. Education therefore can be considered as consisting of formal learning through attending classes, language schools, and so on, or participating in further, higher or work-based education.

Nevertheless, despite the presentation of definitions, authors such as Kidd (1973) and Smith (1982) believe that there is no precise definition of learning, because it can refer to a product (where the outcome is important), a process (which occurs during learning) and a function (the actual steps to achieve learning). Therefore, from these observations it becomes clear that educational tourism may be viewed in a similar way, as a product, process and function. In other words as a product the emphasis is on the outcome of the learning experience (such as a university degree for international university students). While viewing it as a process or a function the focus is on the means to an end (Kalinowski & Weiler, 1992). For instance, if learning is itself defined as an end, then the experience may be focused upon mastering or improving knowledge of what is already known about something (such as a trip to a marine biology station to learn about marine biology). Furthermore, if learning is derived as a means to an end, then, according to Kalinowski and Weiler (1992), the focus is to extend or apply previous study; for example, travelling to an ancient monument after studying the monument. Thus from these definitions it can be seen that travel for educational purposes can be a diverse and complicated area of study.

There appears to be a contemporary transition from an industrial to a knowledge-based or learning economy and society with an increasing emphasis on extending learning beyond initial schooling (OECD, 2001). The reasons behind a drive to extend learning beyond schooling is so that individuals, communities and countries are able to better adjust themselves to current and future changes, and are more likely to contribute to society through increased innovation, business development and economic growth. Another rationale behind the drive for education and lifelong learning is to provide a more inclusive and fair society by making education more accessible, particularly to less privileged members of society (DFES, 2001). Generally speaking education and lifelong learning are said to encompass 'all learning activity undertaken throughout life, with the aim of improving knowledge, skills and competence, within a personal, civic, social and/or employment-related perspective' (European Union, 2001).

Since the 2001 general election the British government has created the Department for Education and Skills and a State Minister for Lifelong Learning and Higher Education. The aims of the Department for Education and Skills (2001: 5) are to help build a competitive economy and inclusive society by:

- creating opportunities for everyone to develop their learning;
- releasing potential in people to make the most of themselves; and
- achieving excellence in standards of education and levels of skills.

Their objectives to achieve their aims are to:

- give children an excellent start in education so that they have a better foundation for future learning;
- enable all young people to develop and to equip themselves with the skills, knowledge and personal qualities needed for life and work; and
- encourage and enable adults to learn, improve their skills and enrich their lives.

Similarly, the Enterprise and Lifelong Learning Department (ELLD) of the Scottish Executive is responsible for economic and industrial development, tourism, further and higher education, student support, and skills and lifelong learning in Scotland. ELLD promotes lifelong learning through policy development and funding for further adult education and higher education in Scotland.

The policies of Western governments toward lifelong learning, as seen above, combined with a growth in economic development and prosperity, has seen a rise in the provision of post-secondary education. Coupled with this growth has been an increase in provision of colleges and institutions to cater for the demand for educational qualifications (see Table 1.1). The higher education market (or third level enrolment) is also expanding rapidly as income levels rise in the developed world, thus allowing for greater expenditure on education by parents. As Table 1.2 notes, the USA had 14.4 million students in higher education followed by Russia with 4.5 million and Japan with 2.8 million students enrolled in higher education (Smith & Jenner, 1997a). UNESCO (1995 in Smith & Jenner, 1997a: 64) estimates suggest that in 1980 a total of 30% of young people in the developed world were in higher education, rising to 40% in 1991 and predicted to be 50% by early 2000. This would mean a total of 79 million enrolled in higher education in the year 2000 rising to 97 million in 2015 and 100 million in 2025.

Furthermore, Roppolo (1996) notes that educational institutions will need to incorporate international experiences into their curriculum in light of the growing interdependence of countries, providing benefits to both students and the tourism industry. In the United States foreign students enrolled in higher education institutions has risen from 311,000 in 1980–81 to 481,000 in 1997–98 (Institute of International Education, 1998). This is partly due to economic prosperity but also the relaxation in border and visa controls and social changes in generating countries allowing the development of student exchange programmes. In the United States from the 481,000 foreign students a total of 57.9% in 1997–98

Table 1.1 Estimated population, enrolment and teachers in the world, 1980, 1990, 1996 ('000s)

Item	*World total*[1]		
	1980	*1990*	*1996*
Population, all ages[2]	4,447,090	5,281,986	5,767,443
Enrolment, all levels	857,052	980,993	1,127,901
First (primary) level[3]	541,444	596,791	661,750
Second level[4]	264,521	315,555	381,890
Third level[5]	51,087	68,647	84,261
Teachers, all levels	38,263	47,083	52,270
First (primary) level[3]	19,046	22,593	24,641
Second level[4]	15,368	19,352	21,535
Third level[5]	3,848	5,138	6,093

Notes:

1. Enrolment and teacher data exclude the Democratic People's Republic of Korea.
2. Estimate of midyear population.
3. First level enrolment generally consists of elementary school, grades 1–6.
4. Second level enrolment includes general education, teacher training (at the second level), and technical and vocational education. This level generally corresponds to secondary education in the United States, grades 7–12.
5. Third level enrolment includes college and university enrolment, and technical and vocational education beyond the high school level. There is considerable variation in reporting from country to country.

Because of rounding, details may not add up to totals.

Source: Adapted from United Nations Educational, Scientific, and Cultural Organization, Paris, 1998 *Statistical Yearbook* (this table was prepared August 1999 in OECD, 2000)

were from Asia, followed by 14.9% from Europe and 10.7% from Latin America. The biggest increase in market share from 1980 to 1998 in the United States appears to be from Asia and Europe, which has grown from 30.3% and 8.1% to comprise 57.9% and 14.9% of the market respectively (Institute of International Education, 1998). This rapid increase in foreign students in higher education is not limited to North America. In Australia the number of overseas students enrolled in higher education institutions has risen by 51.5% since 1994 and over 30% per annum over the period 1994 to 1996 (DEETYA, 1998 in Musca & Shanka, 1998). These

Table 1.2 Number in higher education in selected countries, 1993 ('000s)

Country	*Higher/University pupils*
Germany	1,875
France	2,075
UK	1,528
Spain	1,371
Italy	1,682
Netherlands	507
Russia	4,587
Poland	694
Czech Republic	129
USA	14,473
Canada	2,011
Japan	2,899

Source: Modified from UNESCO and Euromonitor in Smith and Jenner (1997a: 64)

statistics illustrate the economic significance of education and the growth in international students and offshore education.

Language learning, particularly English language learning, has grown rapidly over the last few decades. Graddol (1997) believes that the English language has become the global language, and it is therefore not surprising that the provision of EFL (English as a Foreign Language) courses has grown into a global industry with 1 million people estimated to be learning English as a foreign language (Batchelor, 1998). The United Kingdom views itself as a unique destination for language learning provision, yet the competition for this £2 billion market is intense with the United Kingdom attracting over half of the market (640,000 students) in 1998 (McCallen, 2000). Claims have been made that English Language Teaching (ELT) is Britain's seventh largest export industry (Education and Training Export Group, 1998) and is therefore seen as an important economic sector.

Growth in domestic and international school excursions has also increased over the last few decades. As Cooper notes in Case Study 4.1 changes in the curriculum in Europe have encouraged students to learn outside of the normal school environment and a number of school excursions both domestically and internationally have facilitated travel and tourism for primary and secondary schoolchildren. However, similar to the higher education and EFL market, little research has been conducted on this market segment and data is sparse. There is little recognition of the needs of these educational travellers and how to manage this form of tourism at destinations.

In summary, there appears to be a growth in tourism and an increase in 'alternative' tourism experiences that appear to include a growing number of educational and learning elements. This may be partly due to the growth and promotion of lifelong learning and further/higher education amongst Western countries, combined with a search for postmodern tourist experiences and travel to new and exciting destinations. The growth of offshore education, foreign language learning and school excursions involving travel is also evident. The need for continued education and keeping pace with technological change has fuelled the growth of education and lifelong learning. The growing potential market for the travel and tourism industry amongst schools, universities and further educational institutions is one that should not be ignored and needs to be better understood by the tourism industry. However, to date the interrelationship between both types of educational tourism (travel for purposeful study or education, and travel incorporating elements of learning) have not been comprehensively explored or researched.

Educational Tourism

Brief history of educational tourism

Despite the recent attention paid to tourism and education as industries, travel for learning and education is not a new concept. Travelling in search of either academic qualifications or broad general learning and observation predates our times by several centuries. Smith and Jenner (1997a) suggest that tourism broadens the mind, and thus all tourism may be considered educational. However, they acknowledge that there are smaller, more identifiable, market segments within the broad educational tourism field, which will be discussed within this and subsequent chapters. Nevertheless, Smith and Jenner (1997a) note that the concept of travel for education and learning is a broad and complicated area, which explains why tourism academics and industry have to date largely ignored this field.

The Grand Tour was seen as the beginning of cultural and educational tourism, undertaken initially by scholars and aristocratic British youth as part of their education during the seventeenth, eighteenth and much of the nineteenth centuries (French *et al.*, 2000; CTC, 2001). The purpose behind the Grand Tour was to teach and civilise participants through a series of study tours lasting up to several years in European destinations such as France, Switzerland and Germany. Participants were taught foreign languages, fencing, riding, dancing, and foreign affairs. Visiting continental universities and other aristocrats, accompanied by an entourage of tutors and servants, was commonplace during this time, especially for emerging English scholars. As Hibbert (1987: 14) notes, 'there were few English scholars of the time who did not go to Italy for some part of their education'. In fact scholars were one of the first groups of tourists, and as Kaul (1985 in Theobold, 1998: 7) notes, 'the English, the Germans, and others, travelling on a grand tour of the continent, came to be known as tourists'.

As Towner (1996: 115) correctly states, from very early on travel for education and learning could take place either formally or informally depending on individual motivations and the type of experience demanded. He suggests:

> the spatial patterns of the Grand Tour passed through two stages; from a quest for a formal acquisition of practical training and social skills at specific educational centres to a broader and more informal social and cultural education that was best attained at the main courts and social and artistic centres in Europe.

However, the cost of undertaking the Grand Tour at this point in history was not economical. Despite this, participation moved over time from being solely an activity of the upper class and wealthy elite, to the bourgeoisie, and later to the lower class and mass market (Gee *et al.*, 1997). Furthermore, due to a reduction in available time and money, the bourgeoisie and lower class had to shorten their trips and hence activities and the number of destinations and settings visited were intensified, leading to an increase in more general sightseeing (Steinecke, 1993), and therefore more informal learning through travel. By the mid eighteenth century an estimated 15,000 to 20,000 British tourists travelled abroad (Towner, 1996: 98). As the destinations of the elite changed in order to avoid the mass market, so interest in and visitation to alpine regions increased. The latter phases of the Grand Tour in the eighteenth and early nineteenth centuries contributed to the discovery of the Alps, which were avoided during the earlier periods of the Grand Tour, resulting in an increased scientific interest in the mountains. An increase in travel to the Alps for educational purposes resulted in many mineralogical, geological and geomorphological discoveries, which were made public through guest lectures and publications in scientific journals and periodicals (Steinecke, 1993).

According to Burkart and Medlik (1981), following on from the initial travel for education and learning, travel existed to satisfy travellers' curiosity about the way people lived at home and abroad. In later years the tradition of the educational value of travel facilitated the development of study abroad as a legitimate component of tertiary education in Europe and later the United States (Kalinowski & Weiler, 1992). Education and learning has more recently become an increasingly important and recognised component of travel activity and travel experiences (see CTC, 2001), with an increasing amount of tourist activity involving some form of either formal or informal education and/or learning. Despite this, little research has examined educational tourism or the links between tourism and learning/education and various educational tourism market segments.

Conceptualising and researching educational tourism

Educational tourism has been discussed by very few tourism academics. The major discussion of this form of tourism was undertaken by Kalinowski and Weiler (1992) and more recently by Wood (2001). However, both Kalinowski and Weiler (1992) and Wood (2001) have taken perhaps a narrow view of this form of tourism by discussing primarily adult extension programmes or adult study tours and cultural educational tourism. As the Canadian Tourism Commission (2001) note, educational or learning forms of tourism can be viewed along a continuum ranging from 'general interest learning while travelling' at one end to 'purposeful learning and travel' at the other (see Figure 1.1). They also note that learning travel programmes can be organised independently (informally) or through affiliated or unaffiliated groups (formally).

From this discussion it is evident that there are more potential segments of educational tourism which may become more prominent due to the growth of education. One example or type could be of a 'tourism first' segment of educational tourism whereby travel is a primary motivating factor and purposeful learning is secondary. But the question arises as to what extent do particular 'education first' segments comprise educational tourism? By 'education first' or purposeful segments this author refers to school excursions, language schools and university/college student experiences. This group is primarily motivated by education and learning but may be classified as tourists even if they are not perceived to be tourists or if tourism is not their primary motivation. Nevertheless, even though

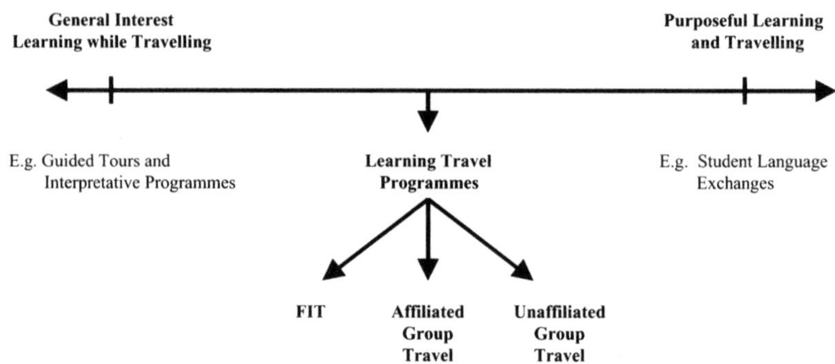

Figure 1.1 The learning/travel continuum
Source: Modified from CTC (2001)

they may not view themselves as tourists, they have tourist impacts and regional development implications, even if their motivations may be substantially education-related. In fact on some excursions language school students learn through travelling and visiting cultural tourist sites. So what then constitutes educational tourism? Similarly to other groups and segments of tourism, classifying educational tourism is a difficult and complicated process.

Figure 1.2 provides a model illustrating a number of potential educational tourism market segments and the relationship between education, tourism and the changing external environment. Although a relatively simplistic model, the reader can see that educational tourism may consist of:

- General travel for education (or 'edu-tourism') and adult or seniors' educational tourism, where some form of education or learning is an important (and often motivating) part of the tourist experience. In this book they will be referred to as 'tourism first' educational tourism experiences or products and are discussed in Chapters 2 and 3.
- University/college students' and schools' tourism (language schools, school excursions and exchange programmes), whereby tourist experiences may be secondary to the educational aspect or intentions and may be considered 'education first' educational tourism experiences or products. These are discussed in Chapters 4 and 5.

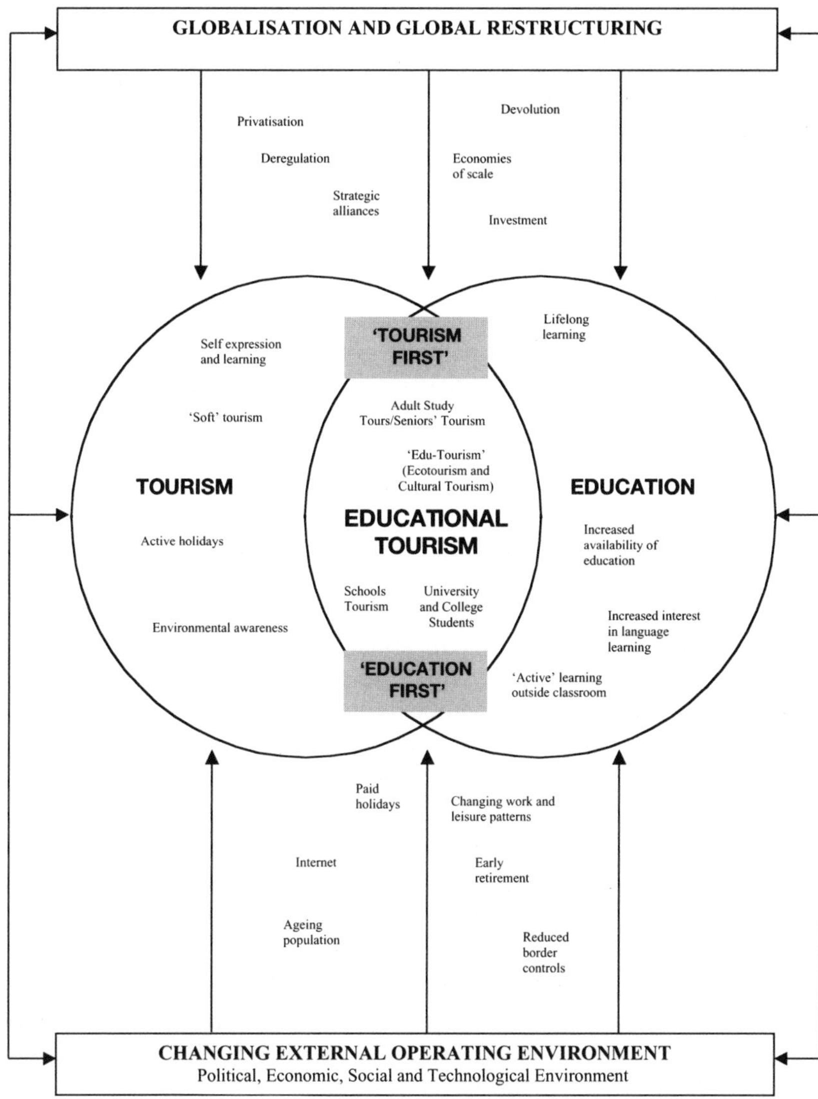

Figure 1.2 Conceptualising educational tourism: a segmentation approach

Nevertheless, in both instances, although tourism or education/learning may be primary or secondary motives, both of these groups can be considered tourists and have distinct tourism-related impacts and needs. Some impacts or opportunities may not be being fully realised or leveraged by the tourism industry as segments may not consider themselves to be tourists and the industry itself may also not view them as a viable tourist market. This point has been discussed by several previous authors (Bywater, 1993a; Cooper, 1999; Ritchie & Priddle, 2000; Seekings, 1998).

In terms of conceptualising educational tourism, Figure 1.3, using a systems approach, illustrates the educational tourism market system. It illustrates the elements and settings that combine to provide the educational tourist experience and helps to conceptualise potential research avenues, including from the demand (or consumer perspective):

- educational tourist demographics, motivations, perceptions and resulting travel behaviour;
- educational tourist personal impacts resulting from their experiences; and
- the interrelationship of factors within or between these groups.

From a supply (or product perspective) research avenues could include:

- the nature of the primary educational tourism product;
- managing and marketing structures for educational tourism;
- the resource base for educational tourism;
- destination impacts related to educational tourism; and
- the interrelationship of factors within or between these groups.

The supply of learning vacations can be diverse with a wide range of potential services and suppliers at a variety of locations. The Canadian Tourism Commission (2001) notes two main components to the supply side of educational tourism: the primary tourist product and secondary or support elements. A variety of organisations combine to form the primary educational tourism experience, including:

- *Attractions and events* which provide the venue for learning experiences (e.g. parks, historic sites, zoos, bird and wildlife sanctuaries and archaeological dig sites).
- *Resource specialists* who are responsible for delivering the learning component of these vacations (e.g. employees, curators, interpreters, lecturers, storytellers, researchers and academics).
- *Affinity travel planners* from organisations who help plan and develop learning programmes for travellers (e.g. special interest groups, conservation organisations, universities and language schools),

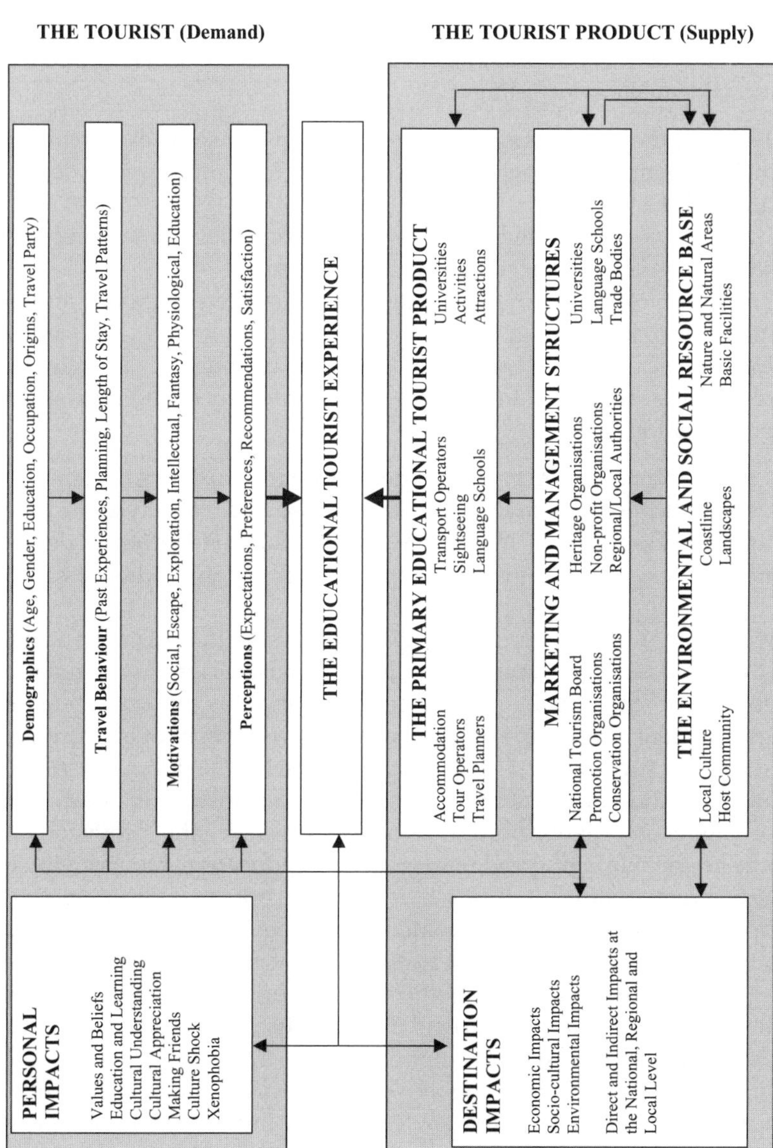

Figure 1.3 The educational tourism market system

- *Tour and receptive operators* who package experiences for customers and organisations and provide destination expertise, local knowledge, escort services and marketing services.

However, secondary suppliers or support services are also required for educational travellers including:

- *Transportation* such as cruise, bus and train transport as part of an independent trip or package, including travel to and from the departure point.
- *Hospitality services,* including catering, recreation, entertainment, social activities and accommodation options.
- *Travel services,* including travel agents, insurance companies, travel media and advertising.
- *Destination marketing organisations* who operate at a national, regional or local level to promote educational travel and tourism to potential tourists.

It is the combination of primary and secondary suppliers which will create the educational tourist experience consumed by travellers. The continued development of innovative partnerships and product development is critical to the future of the educational tourism industry (CTC, 2001).

However, as the model and CTC (2001) illustrate, the diversity of the market and the fact that many are not tourism businesses or may not see tourism as their 'core' business could constrain the effective management and development of this type of tourism. The involvement of educational establishments such as universities, language schools, cultural heritage organisations and conservation organisations illustrates this point. The diverse range of organisations that are involved in the provision of product and the marketing and management of educational tourism illustrate the fragmentation of this sector and the potential difficulties in developing collaborative arrangements between organisations. This diversity and these difficulties can restrict the potential benefits for destinations, the tourism industry and educational tourists. This illustrates the complexity of educational tourism and the usefulness of a systems approach to understanding it.

Despite the obvious differences between the various potential segments of educational tourism, some parameters concerning the nature of educational tourism can be identified (see Figure 1.4). The figure notes that educational tourism experiences can differ due to length of time, tourist intention, motivation, preparation, level of formality and the various

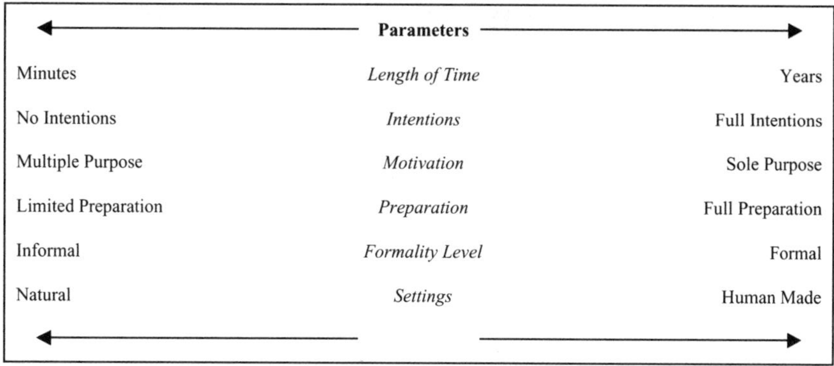

Figure 1.4 Parameters of educational tourism

settings where the educational tourist experience can be undertaken. For instance, an educational tourist experience could consist of a 30-minute visit to a museum, or a three-year degree undertaken partly in a foreign country. Similarly, tourist intention and motivation may differ, for example from a holiday where the sole purpose is educational (such as a cruise with Swan Hellenic) to a beach vacation in Florida with a side trip to an educational attraction (such as the Disney Orlando Institute).

Motivation and intentions may also dictate the level of preparation for an educational holiday, with greater preparation required for an educational study tour to the Inca ruins and limited preparation for a visit that may be organised by a tour guide. This aspect of preparation is directly related to the level of formality within the experience. The learning component of the travel experience can be formally organised by a tour operator, guide or attraction, or it can be organised by the individual independently and informally within a variety of cultural, natural or human settings. As Kalinowski and Weiler (1992: 17) state in regards to educational travel:

> [it] can serve a wide variety of purposes, such as satisfying curiosity about other people, their language and culture; stimulating interest in art, music, architecture or folklore; inspiring concern for natural environments, landscapes, flora and fauna; or deepening the fascination for cultural heritage and historic places.

As Kalinowski and Weiler (1992) also note, educational travel can comprise a diversity of activities and experiences sought by educational tourists, as well as a variety of settings and products supplied to these tourists. Kalinowski and Weiler (1992: 17) further explain that educational tourism goes 'beyond a curiosity, interest or fascination for a particular topic. It involves a travel experience in which there is organised learning, whether that be formal or experimental.'

Educational tourism: Towards a definition

From the above discussion, a definition of educational tourists and educational tourism can be developed. For the purposes of this book, an educational tourist (or educational stayover) may be considered as:

> a person who is away from their home town or country overnight, where education and learning are either the main reason for their trip or where education and learning are secondary reasons but are perceived as an important way of using leisure time.

An excursionist (or same-day educational tourist) is:

> a person involved in any educational/learning activity or excursion, which does not include an overnight stay away from their home destination, and for whom education and learning is seen as an important way of using leisure time.

Therefore, educational tourism can be defined as:

> tourist activity undertaken by those who are undertaking an overnight vacation and those who are undertaking an excursion for whom education and learning is a primary or secondary part of their trip. This can include general educational tourism and adult study tours, international and domestic university and school students' travel, including language schools, school excursions and exchange programmes. Educational tourism can be independently or formally organised and can be undertaken in a variety of natural or human-made settings.

Understanding Educational Tourism Through Segmentation

As well as the general trend toward experiential and educational travel, or edu-tourism (Holdnak & Holland, 1996), educational tourism can consist of many different market segments and sub-segments including international and domestic university students, international and domestic schools' tourism, and adult education or extension programmes.

These segments can be examined based upon tourist motivation toward formal education and qualifications, whereas learning vacations and travel for nature-based or cultural learning may be considered a form of 'tourism first' educational tourism.

Therefore, this book takes a segmentation and a systems-based approach to discussing the concept of educational tourism from both 'tourism first' and 'education first' perspectives. In particular, segmentation can help researchers and industry further understand and manage consumers and the tourism industry, in this case educational tourists and specific educational tourism types. Segmentation is splitting a population down into sub-groups or segments based on similar characteristics, needs and buying behaviour (Swarbrooke, 1995). Or as Mill and Morrison (1985: 423) state, it is where 'people with similar needs, wants and characteristics are grouped together so that an organisation can use greater precision in serving and communicating with its chosen customers'. The three main types of segmentation are demographic and socio-economic (age, gender), geographic (where they live) and psychographic (attitudes and opinions).

Demographic and socio-economic segmentation

Key factors such as age, gender, income, employment and education are often important and interrelated determinants of demand which often change over time. For instance, age can play an important role in the types of activities and experiences that appeal to an individual while on holiday. Generally, the older one becomes the fewer the recreational activities participated in and the more passive the activities become (Manning, 1983; Devlin, 1993). Mill and Morrison (1985) believe that younger travellers have a higher tolerance for all types of new experiences and are thus likely to be more adventurous and 'active' travellers. Despite this and the growth of adventure tourism, very little research has been undertaken to examine the youth market. However, the youth market is discussed in more detail in further chapters of this book concerned with schools and the university/college educational tourism market (Chapters 4 and 5). During the middle years, as a person's travel career develops, there is a greater desire to travel in groups, according to McIntosh and Goeldner (1986). In later years immobility threatens activities which need physical exercise, such as climbing and hiking, and tourists may begin to seek out organised tours. However, as Weaver and Lawton note in Case Study 2.1 older ecotourists can, and may prefer, to keep mentally active, with older respondents (those 65 or older) more likely to prefer interpretation, to pursue pre-experiential learning and to seek mentally challenging experiences within ecotourism.

Gender has been known to influence vacation and activity choice. For the purpose of this book and Chapter 2, previous studies have noted that males and females have different preferences and needs and therefore seek different types of activities and types of vacations. Within cultural heritage tourism females prefer visiting art galleries while more men visit museums in London (Sogno-Lalloz, 2000). Weaver and Lawton, in Case Study 2.1, note that females are more likely than males to want to seek on-site learning and to express the belief that ecotourism has made them more environmentally responsible. Chapter 3 also notes that the ageing population and changing socio-demographics will lead to a greater number of single women participating in vacations and adult study tours.

In general, the higher one's income, the greater the number of recreational activities participated in (Manning, 1983). However, a greater income does not necessary allow for greater spending of money on tourism and travel-related products. Discretionary income, which is income left after expenditure on fixed items, is a more appropriate measure of potential demand for travel and tourism products. Richards (1996) notes that the growing 'new middle class' is directly responsible for the growth in cultural heritage tourism in Europe since the 1970s. Similarly, it has been the expansion of the middle class that has been responsible for the growth in nature-based and educational ecotourism marketed by middle-class organisations such as the International Ecotourism Society. Income, employment and education are often interrelated, with higher educationally qualified individuals securing more highly paid jobs. One way of examining social class is to classify individuals into socio-economic groupings.

However, demographic and socio-economic variables cannot alone predict if people will indeed travel or what experiences they may seek. If couples have young children this affects their travel decisions substantially and therefore income, gender and education are meaningless. The stage of family lifecycle is an important part of segmentation and influences travel decisions greatly, as does where people live and their psychographics. The age of the family structure and children often impact upon travel decision making. However, marketers must consider the changes that are occurring and will continue to occur within the social environment and their effects on tourism demand and behaviour. Some of the changes include:

- an ageing population base creating a growing seniors' and adult education market (discussed in Chapter 3);
- the postponement of children to later in life or the decision not to have children;
- double-income couples with no children (often called DINKS);
- greater numbers of single-parent families;
- couples with children who have grown up and left home (often called 'empty nesters'); and
- the increase in gay or lesbian couples.

These social factors and changes further complicate the lifecycle concept and its relevance, and subsequently need to be considered for any educational tourism marketing or management strategy.

Geographic segmentation

Geographic segmentation uses the basis of geography (climate, location) to develop market segmentation strategies. Research on tourist motivation has previously outlined that it is often associated with 'escape' from one destination to another, whether this is to a different rural, urban, alpine or coastal environment. Some authors have noted how the rural environment attracts urban visitors who are looking to escape, while the development of European coastal tourism has been driven by European workers looking for a summer 'escape' from their home environment. However, Richards (1996) identified that cultural tourists in Europe tend to be both travelling from and visiting predominately urban destinations, noting that the type of destination may not be as important as 'escaping' from the so-called normal or usual home environment.

Often travel for school excursions may also be a result of climate. A school ski trip to the French Alps, or an adventure tourism safari in Africa are two examples. Other examples include language school students from the Northern Hemisphere travelling to the Southern Hemisphere during their winter break to learn English, whereas the proximity and status of England to European countries may be reason enough to encourage English Language learners from Spain and France.

Psychographic segmentation

Buying behaviour and tourist demand (including educational tourism) are also influenced by sociological and psychological or mental forces. As

Middleton and Clarke (2001: 116) note, 'some individuals are mentally predisposed to seek adventure, enjoy the risks and active vacations ... some seek environmental qualities often represented in ecotourism, while others seek the self-development associated with cultural tourism'. In order to improve the prediction and segmentation process for products, including tourism, researchers and marketers have more recently used psychographic variables in conjunction with demographic and geographic variables to identify target markets and develop products to suit their preferences and needs. Defined broadly as lifestyle patterns (Beane & Ennis, 1992 in Blamey & Braithwaite, 1997), psychographics is an all-encompassing term for many psychological concepts, including values, attitudes and personality characteristics.

The Stanford Research Institute in the USA pioneered the measurement of values, attitudes and lifestyles (VALS) in the late 1970s by dividing the population into nine different segments based upon these factors. Measurement was based on Maslow's hierarchy of needs and wants, and has since been used internationally. In the UK, Synergy Consulting divides the population into three groups using a variation on the VALS methods (see Middleton & Clarke, 2001). Other countries such as Australia (with the Roy Morgan Value Segments) also undertake tracking research on psychographic segments and their propensity to purchase goods and services, including tourism. A discussion of this occurs in Case Study 3.1 with regard to wine tourists and education/learning.

Segmentation and educational tourism sub-segments

Segmentation in any discussion of educational tourism is an important consideration. This book discusses particular segments of the educational tourism market throughout the subsequent chapters. Moreover, within each potential educational tourism segment, sub-segments and groups exist which may have more of a propensity and preference toward education and learning within their tourist experiences (such as 'specific cultural tourists'), or may have quite different needs and preferences (such as international language school students compared to domestic school excursion students). It is therefore important that we consider these segments and sub-segments as to their characteristics, needs and preferences and how to best manage the educational tourism experience. Classifying all educational tourists as homogeneous only simplifies any examination of this type of tourism.

The importance of a special interest dictates the types of experience tourists seek and the type of product and setting which should be supplied to satisfy these tourists. Research in the cultural tourism field has illustrated the different segments of cultural tourists who have a tendency towards learning and education as they have higher educational qualifications (see Richards, 1996; Silberberg, 1995 in Chapter 2). Similarly, there are distinct segments of ecotourists to whom learning and education are important aspects of their trip compared to other ecotourists (see Case Study 2.1 and Chapter 2). This can also be seen in research examining wine tourists and their motives and perceptions, including education and learning (see Case Study 3.1).

A segmentation-based approach to understanding types of educational tourism and sub-segments within this particular area is not only useful for examining the demand side of the educational tourism market system and personal impacts, but also the supply side and the providers of educational tourism experiences.

Book Structure

An increasing number of studies have taken place in the field of educational tourism (for instance, Kalinowski & Weiler, 1992; Weiler & Kalinowski, 1990), and of the travel characteristics of international and domestic university students (for instance, Chadee & Cutler, 1996; Field, 1999; Hsu & Sung, 1997; Sung & Hsu, 1996). Research has also been undertaken on school excursions in the United Kingdom (Cooper & Latham, 1985, 1988, 1989) as well as in Australia (Coughlan & Ritchie, 1998; Coughlan & Wells, 1999; Coughlan *et al.*, 1999). Further educational tourism research has been conducted on participants attending private schools (Coventry, 1996; Moser & Kaspar, 1990) and language schools (McCallen, 2000; Goldberg, 1996; Muñoz Gonzalez, 2001).

However, none provide an integrated picture of educational tourism generally, and the challenges associated with the marketing, managing and planning of this form of niche market. Many of these educational tourism segments have differing motivations, perceptions and ways in which they are satisfied, which have both education and tourism implications for those involved with the marketing, management and planning of educational tourism experiences. This book discusses the demand and supply elements, as well as the marketing and management implications of the educational tourism segments, while also highlighting underlying relationships and themes related to educational tourism as a whole. Due to this large scope, this book hopes to provide an introduction to the concept and issues surrounding educational tourism types. It has also restricted the concept of educational tourism to the segments outlined below and does not discuss conference tourism or other potential forms of educational tourism such as technical visits.

The second section of this book will discuss the major educational tourism segments, including:

- general educational tourism with an emphasis on ecotourism and cultural heritage tourism (for both the youth and adult market);
- adult and seniors' educational tourism;
- international and domestic schools' tourism; and
- international and domestic university/college students' tourism.

The third section begins by highlighting the growth in knowledge-based industries, including education, and the use and role of educational tourism for destination marketing and regional development. The use of educational forms of tourism for marketing and regional development has seen the growth of collaborative arrangements at international to local level, as organisations attempt to overcome diversity and fragmentation. This section concludes by discussing the underlying themes and similarities between the educational segments, their impacts and management, and will examine the potential future direction of educational tourism with emphasis on technological innovations.

Conclusion: The Management of Educational Tourism

This chapter has introduced the concept of educational tourism and discussed some reasons for the growth in educational tourism types, including a brief history. The chapter has also attempted to conceptualise educational tourism and proposed a systems and segmentation approach to understanding this complicated area. Subsequent chapters will examine educational tourism using a segmentation approach and key themes and issues in the management of educational tourism will be discussed. It is hoped that in this way the book will provide insights into educational tourism and stimulate further research by academics and interest from the industry itself, both of which are required to adequately manage the growth of educational tourism segments.

Chapter 2

Exploring Nature-based and Cultural Educational Tourism

Introduction

As discussed in Chapter 1 the growth of tourism and the development of more specialised and segmented markets, combined with a desire for postmodern and more experiential travel, has seen a growing demand for educational tourism. Despite the potential importance of education and learning within tourism experiences, to date little specific research or inquiry has examined the relationship between education, learning and tourism. This is somewhat surprising considering that some tourist experiences such as ecotourism attempt to instil knowledge and environmental ethics in participants.

This chapter begins by discussing the demand for educational holidays or 'edu-tourism' within the global tourist industry and the reasons for this increased demand. The chapter then examines the two largest tourist segments where education and learning are important components, namely nature-based tourism, or ecotourism, and cultural heritage tourism. Within these two major market segments the demand, supply of product, impacts and management issues for this 'tourism first' form of educational tourism are considered with respect to both youth and adult market segments.

Demand for General Educational Travel or 'Edu-tourism'

As outlined in Chapter 1, globalisation and other global changes have impacted upon the nature of both the education and tourist industry resulting in many changes over the last 50 years and these factors will continue to impact upon the future of education, tourism and educational tourism. More recent social changes have influenced the type of tourist and their resulting motivation, demand and ultimately the supply of tourist products. Similarly, the increased desire for education and learning has also dramatically increased the demand for educational travel and tourism. This section outlines the changing trends toward educational holidays or vacations and the more recent impacts this has had on the tourism industry. The following section then examines educational tourists' demand characteristics.

An emerging desire for education and learning in travel?

Krippendorf (1987) outlined a framework for the changing composition of the Western tourist market (see Table 2.1) from 1986 to the year 2000, which illustrates the changing travel motivations of tourists, from more passive activities and 'liberation', toward learning or broadening horizons and being creative while on holiday. The changes that have been occurring in the tourist marketplace over recent decades have caused the rise of what has been termed 'new' tourists or 'new' tourism (Poon, 1993), similar to Krippendorf's (1987) predictions of a changing tourist market.

The 'new' tourist is often perceived to be:

- better educated;
- more culturally aware and attuned to the natural environment;
- more curious and analytical;
- often seeking not only knowledge of the world, but also self-knowledge; and
- more active in their tourism participation.

These social changes and trends have generated new demand patterns for travel and tourism and changing product needs. As Martin and Mason (1987: 112) state:

> social change has a major influence on the shape of the tourism market. Shifts in population structure, and changing social values and lifestyles, will combine with increased leisure time and disposable incomes to determine the amount and nature of holidays and travel.

The growing trend towards involvement and participation in travel and tourism has been described by some as the 'active vacation'. Smith and Jenner (1997a) agree with this trend and note that not only are increasing numbers of travellers being involved in active holiday or vacations, but also this activity is more likely to be educational in nature. One of the main trends emerging in tourism appears to be the development of a new 'leisure–education hybrid', according to Smith and Jenner (1997a), whereby education is becoming an important part of the leisure

Table 2.1 The changing composition of the Western tourist market

Market segment	*Travel motivations*	*% of market*	
		1986	*2000*
Work-orientated (live for work)	Recovery – rest, doing nothing, passivity, being served, switching off; and Liberation – no duties, no worries, no problems.	10–20	≈10
Hedonistic life-style (one works in order to live)	Experience something different, explore, have a change; Have fun, enjoy oneself, play; Being active, together with others; Relaxation without stress, do as one pleases; and Nature, enjoying proximity with nature, and interact with environment.	~60	45–60
'New unity of everyday life' (reduced polarity between work and leisure)	Broaden one's horizons, learn something; Introspection and communication with other people; Come back to simpler things and nature; Creativity, open-mindedness; and Readiness for experiments.	20–30	30–45

Source: After Krippendorf (1987); Weiler and Hall (1992)

environment, creating new demand for leisure products which have an educational or learning component.

A 1988 study by the National Tour Association, the largest tour organisation in North America, noted that 93% of respondents believed the opportunity to learn while travelling was an important consideration in their choice of travel (in Ayala, 1995). This has also been noted by other authors who suggest that 'a lot of tourists are eschewing veg-out trips in favour of vacations where notepads may be more important than swimsuits' (Baig, 1994: 112), and where working holidays blur the distinction between work and leisure (see Krippendorf, 1987 and Table 2.1). The trend that Baig (1994) refers to is the growth of special interest holidays that involve some form of learning or education as an important component.

Special interest and alternative tourism

Special interest tourism is defined by the World Tourism Organization (1985: 3) as 'specialised tourism involving group or individual tours by people who wish to develop certain interests and visit sites and places connected with a specific subject. Generally speaking, the people concerned exercise the same profession or have a common hobby.'

Read (1980: 195) defined special interest tourism as:

> travel for people who are going somewhere because they have a particular interest that can be pursued in a particular region or at a particular destination. It is the *hub* around which the *total* travel experience is planned and developed.

In other words the special interest itself often dictates the planning and development of travel to a particular destination. However, this depends upon the importance of either the activity or setting as motivating factors. Sometimes the activity is more important than the setting while at other times the setting is more important than the activity, and sometimes the setting and activity are equally important.

Special interest tourism is also known as *serious leisure*, or leisure where participants are able to find personal fulfilment, enhance their identity, and express themselves, as opposed to casual or un-serious leisure (Stebbins, 1982, 1996) and more sedentary pursuits. The special interest tourist tends to seek durable benefits such as self-actualisation, self-enrichment, recreation or renewal of self, self-expression, social interaction and sense of belonging, and also seek lasting physical products of the activity (Stebbins, 1982, 1996), including education and/or learning. They also often require a special knowledge, skill or training in order to pursue their chosen activity (such as birdwatching, cooking or art), and they tend to be part of an established 'career path' in pursuing their interests. These travellers have also developed a unique ethos based on norms, beliefs and principles associated with a particular chosen activity. Special interest tourism can include cultural heritage tourism and eco-tourism that places an emphasis on interaction with the natural environment.

Helber (1988) reported a trend towards 'experience orientated' holidays with an emphasis on action, adventure, fantasy, nostalgia and exotic experiences; while Read (1980) suggests that the term special interest travel should be discarded and replaced by the notion of REAL travel, or travel that would be a:

- **R**ewarding,
- **E**nriching,
- **A**dventuresome,
- **L**earning experience.

In particular, there has been an increasing interest in heritage tourism, including the natural and cultural environments, which has education and learning as a central component.

Recent changes in the demand side of tourism may have led to an increasing interest in education and learning as a significant part of tourism and travel experiences. In some instances, education may be the key motivating factor for travel, while in other cases education or learning may be secondary but still make an important contribution to the travel experience. In particular, the rise of 'new' tourism and special interest holidays which involve a component of education and learning (such as cultural heritage tourism and ecotourism) have influenced the nature of tourism, its settings, the tourism industry, and its resulting impacts on the individual traveller and the host destination. The following sections of this chapter examine these changes and impacts, and their resulting implications.

Educational tourist motivation, demand and behaviour

In examining the characteristics of tourists researchers have become increasingly aware that not all tourists are homogeneous. This fact becomes even more important considering the more recent development of special interest tourism and niche markets within tourism. Even within specific segments there are sub-segments with quite different preferences and travel behaviour that may require different forms of product and experiences. In some ways their motivations and perceptions determine this.

The motivations for travel and tourism usually arise due to some need to escape from the home environment or from the burdens of daily life; these have been noted as 'push' motives (Krippendorf, 1987). Similarly, education is often perceived as an escape from the burdens of everyday life and is increasingly being undertaken in leisure time (Cross, 1981). One of the other categories of motivation has been described as 'pull' motives, which can determine the location to which people travel after being subjected to 'push' motives.

In terms of general tourist motivation, Gray (1970) noted that motivations for pleasure travel were either associated with a desire for natural attractions, climate, relaxation and rest (which he termed 'sunlust'), or associated with 'wanderlust'. According to Gray (1970: 87) wanderlust is 'that basic trait in human nature which causes some individuals to want to leave things with which they are familiar and to go and see at first hand different exciting cultures and places'. Wanderlust tourists seek foreign cultural experiences and have an interest in built and cultural attractions, while travel is seemingly undertaken for some form of educational or learning purpose. Crompton (1979), in outlining his motivations for travel, also identified education as a central motivating factor. However, other authors have identified that an interest in cultural heritage and the customs of a destination could be considered cultural motivations (also possibly comprising important components of education and learning). Subsequently, social motivations such as the pursuit of hobbies, continuation of education and learning could also be viewed as educational motives for travel. Iso-Ahola (1983) noted that tourism can provide an outlet not only for escaping or avoiding something, but also for seeking something which provides intrinsic (inner) rewards such as self-fulfilment, education and learning. This is perhaps best illustrated by the previous discussion concerning special interest tourism. Table 2.2 indicates the many motivational factors that exist for travel and where educational tourist motives may exist (the author's emphasis is noted in italics).

Furthermore, a number of authors in the field of tourist motivation have acknowledged that education and learning can be an important part of tourist motivation, while other authors identify educational opportunities and educational tourism in their writing and research (see Dowling, 1997; Page, 1995; Ryan, 1991; Swarbrooke & Horner, 1999). Although many writers identify educational tourists, little comprehensive discussion of this type of tourism has taken place.

The scope of education and learning motivations illustrates the diverse scope and breadth of the general educational tourism market segment, and the potential difficulties in examining and measuring this segment and its sub-segments. The transient nature of tourists poses problems with research (Page, 1995), while research concerning specific segments of tourists is even more problematic. Despite the reported growth of educational tourism, explicit research is rare and statistical data is sparse (Bywater, 1993a; Smith & Jenner, 1997a), making it difficult to examine the demand and exact nature of educational tourism. This difficulty and lack of information is in part due to the nature of general travel for

Table 2.2 Motivations of the tourist and educational motives

Motivational category	*Specific motivations*
Physical	• Refreshment of body and mind • For health purposes • For participation in sports • Contact with an outdoor way of life
Cultural	• *Curiosity about foreign countries, people, culture and places* • *Interest in art, music, architecture and folklore* • *Experiencing specific cultural events*
Social	• Visiting friends and relatives • *Meeting new people* • Seeking new friendships and relationships • Travelling for travel's sake • Prestige and status • Fashion • *Pursuit of hobbies* • *Continuation of education or learning* • Seeking of business contacts and pursuing professional goals • *Conferences and meetings* • Strengthening family bonds
Spiritual	• *Visiting places and people for religious reasons* • *Travelling as part of a pilgrimage* • *Travelling to 'find oneself'* • *Contact with nature*
Fantasy	• Personal excitement of travel • 'Anomic' – escaping from one's own permanent social environment • 'Ego-enhancement' – sensual indulgence (both real and imagined) • Wish fulfilment

Note: Italics indicate author's emphasis.

Sources: Mathieson and Wall (1982); Pearce (1982); Mill and Morrison (1985); Murphy (1985); Goodal and Ashworth (1988); McIntosh and Goeldner (1990); Ryan (1991); Weiler and Hall (1992); Page (1995), modified after Hall (1998)

education and learning, or 'edu-tourism', compared to more identifiable market segments such as schools' tourism or university and college students' tourism (discussed in subsequent chapters). Difficulties also exist with the crossover between educational tourism and other tourist types and products such as cultural heritage tourism and ecotourism. The difficulty in classifying tourists is an issue noted by Richards (1996: 270) who states that cultural tourists often consume cultural attractions as part of a wider tourism experience (such as a beach holiday) and may not be driven solely by cultural or learning motives.

Supply of Educational Travel Experiences: Natural and Cultural Heritage Tourism

This section of the chapter will examine two main special interest tourist products (natural and cultural heritage) that have increasingly involved education and learning as an important component of the tourist experience for both youth and adult educational tourism markets (explored in Chapters 3 to 5). Particular emphasis is placed on the educational or learning components of these tourist products and their resulting impacts and management issues.

Ecotourism definitions and market characteristics

Ecotourism has recently emerged as a visible and potentially major segment of the tourism industry (Wight, 1996), which involves visiting and experiencing quality natural heritage environments and protecting them from harm or destruction (Orams, 1995a). The term 'ecotourism' has arisen from a greater interest in the natural environment from consumers, as well as concern from industry and government about the negative impacts that 'mass' and 'hard' tourism can generate (Valentine, 1993).

As with many other components of tourism and sustainable tourism, academics and industry have grappled with how to define ecotourism and what exactly constitutes an ecotourism product. As Fennell (1999, 2001) notes, the proliferation of definitions of ecotourism and operators has created difficulties for the ecotourism sector, yet the reasons for this proliferation are unknown. The problem in developing a consensus over the definition of ecotourism is derived from the way in which individuals perceive ecotourism and this has been a contentious issue. Many commentators, and indeed industry operators, view ecotourism in either a passive or active sense (see Orams, 1995a; Page & Dowling, 2002).

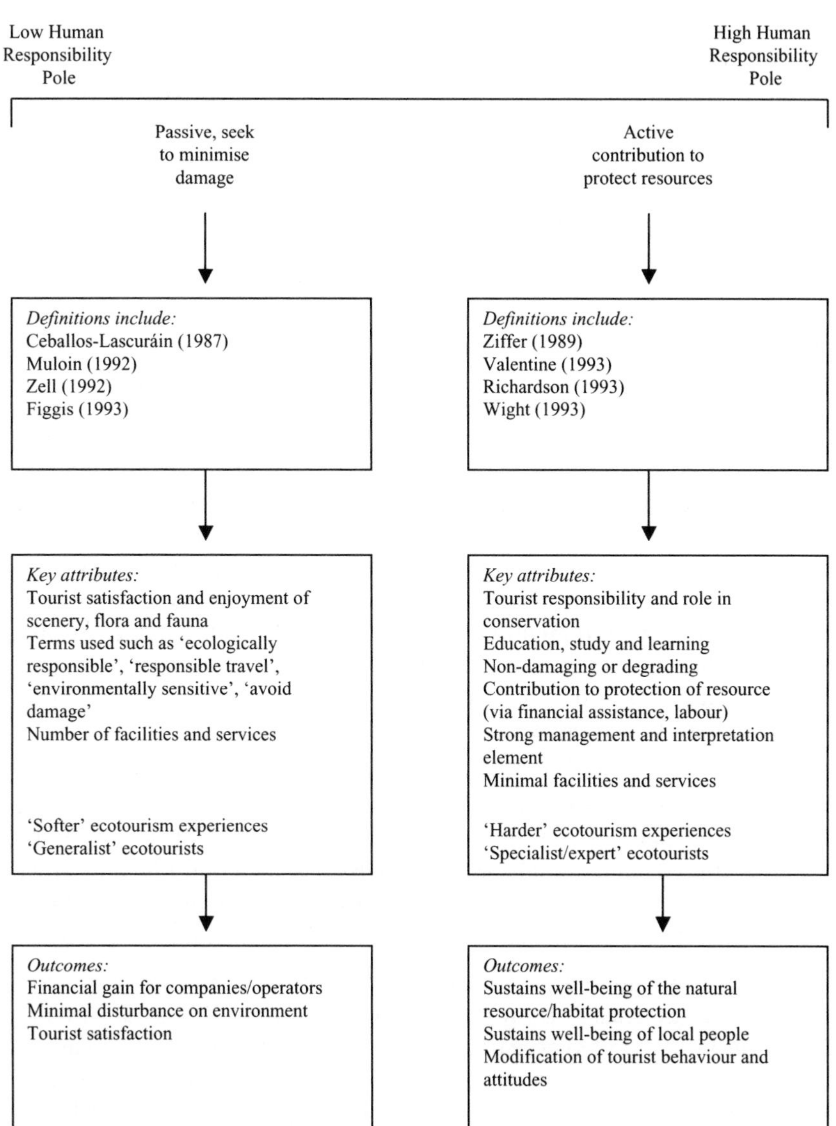

Figure 2.1 Competing paradigms, definitions, attributes and outcomes of ecotourism

Sources: After Duffus and Dearden (1990); Orams (1995a); Fennell (1999); Weaver (1999)

In passive or active definitions of ecotourism, the dominant paradigm views ecotourism through a framework of human responsibility toward the environment and the ecotourism client. Therefore, passive definitions involve passive approaches, including low human responsibility toward the environment and low responsibility toward instilling education, learning and conservation values in ecotourism clients. At the other end of the spectrum, active definitions involve more active approaches, including high human responsibility toward the protection of the environment and educating clients (see Figure 2.1). This educational process is best illustrated by working holidays organised by environmental charities such as The British Trust for Conservation Volunteers and Raleigh International (see Turner *et al.*, 2001 and Exhibit 2.1).

With respect to education and learning, these terms are often applied to more active definitions and views concerning ecotourism. Authors have noted that education, learning and even modification of behaviour after a vacation are important concepts and outcomes from a true or pure ecotourism experience (see Figure 2.1 and Table 2.3). Orams (1995a: 5) comments that 'an objective of ecotourism experiences should be to attempt to move the visitor experience beyond mere enjoyment to incorporate learning and to facilitate attitude and behaviour change' through the use of interpretation (see Exhibit 2.2). In fact, in Australia the former Office of National Tourism acknowledged the importance of the educational element in ecotourism. They commented that:

> Ecotourism is seen as ecologically and socially responsible, and as fostering environmental appreciation and awareness. It is based on the enjoyment of nature with minimal environmental impact. The educational element of ecotourism, which enhances understanding of natural environments and ecological processes, distinguishes it from adventure travel and sightseeing. (ONT, 1997 in Hall, 1998: 291)

Many authors agree that educational components of ecotourism experiences distinguishes it from other forms of tourism (Page & Dowling, 2002), yet little detailed research has been conducted on the educational element of ecotourism. Buckley (1994) notes that educating individuals is a defining criterion of ecotourism, while Eagles (1997) suggests that ecotourism involves travel focusing on discovery and learning about wild, unnatural environments. As Page and Dowling (2002: 67) note, 'ecotourism education can influence tourist, community and industry behaviour and assist in the longer-term sustainability of tourist activity in natural areas'. However, as ecotourism broadens in its acceptance and responsible tourism increases, the need for education and minimisation

Exhibit 2.1

Working holidays organised by environmental charities

By Graham Miller

Capitalising on the public's increased leisure time in order to fill the omnipresent need for funds, charities have developed volunteer strategies as ways of turning leisure time into fund-raising, labour and awareness opportunities. Working holidays in the UK have been operating for over 30 years, providing both the young and old with the opportunity to make a difference within their communities. Such charities that operate within the tourism industry do so to fulfil goals of education, scientific research and conservation. Many of these charities grow from a natural history background with scientists or nature enthusiasts as members and, because of their origins, bring a credibility and respectability to their cause and receive substantial sums in grant aid. In recent years, however, they have been using their scientific expertise to yield profits from wildlife holidays led by natural history experts, conservation work, consultancy and lectures. These projects bring in money and increase a charity's independence from government and trusts, enabling it to be more outspoken in campaigning should a need arise. These holidays translate the message of the 1980 IUCN (World Conservation Union) World Conservation Strategy in which the sum of individual environmental achievement was heralded to represent a major impact on the conservation of culture and environments.

Working holidays appeal to the growing numbers of tourists concerned with the protection of habitats and ecosystems and with achieving an educational component to their holiday choice. The types of holidays promoted by these charities encourage people to take practical action to conserve and understand their environment by providing a true 'hands-on' learning experience and thereby allowing people to make a positive contribution to all aspects of environmental preservation. As volunteerism is central to the environmental movement, the link with providing holidays has been a natural one and, while the holidays have retained the element of voluntarism, the focus of the work of the charities has shifted necessarily as the challenges have changed. Thus, the focus today is increasingly on providing an organised, fun, learning experience directed at 'hard-core' or dedicated nature tourists and is characterised by a higher claim to meet ecotourism criteria than the larger operators.

At the forefront of conservation working holidays in the UK is the acronymic organisation TOC H, as well as The National Trust and The British Trust for Conservation Volunteers (BTCV). Sustrans (a charity committed to the task of developing a UK-wide cycle network) also organises weekend projects to help in building the National Cycle Network, but these take place on a much smaller scale. The holidays are all similar in that people 'vacation' in very basic conditions yet amidst beautiful surroundings to work extremely hard completing their project. As none of these organisations operating in the UK uses the working holidays as a method of raising funds for their causes, the holidays are inexpensive and the volunteers provide a vital workforce for the charities.

However, charities operating within the tourism industry are not confined to working within the UK. Raleigh International is a UK charity which operates conservation and development working holidays abroad. Yet, the motivations behind Raleigh are somewhat different from other charities operating working holidays in the UK. Launched formally in 1984 as an international youth development organisation, Raleigh focuses on personal growth and sees conservation and research as a means to achieving this. To date Raleigh International has taken over 21,500 people from 80 different nations on 179 expeditions in 36 different countries, including, most famously, Prince William on his gap year before university. Raleigh estimates that the volunteers have contributed nearly 3.8 million hours of work on the various expeditions, the equivalent of the complete working lives of more than 40 people. While Raleigh focuses on young adults (17–25) it is possible to engage in Raleigh expeditions beyond this age, but all volunteers must pass an assessment weekend in which commitment, motivation and teamwork skills are tested. Successful volunteers then face a daunting challenge of raising up to £3000 in sponsorship for their expedition and thus provide Raleigh's most important source of funding. Often working with other charities such as Save the Children Fund (SCF), World Wide Fund for Nature (WWF) or Surgical Eye Expeditions (SEE), international projects are also planned, funded and executed with governmental organisations in each country, commonly the national parks authority. Raleigh usually operates ten expeditions per year in its attempt to contribute to the development of youth worldwide.

In addition to the expeditions, Raleigh has added a programme for 'At-Risk' young people to help to develop the confidence of those deemed socially excluded. The programme has received sponsorship from the Millennium Commission and claims a great deal of success in using the expeditions to change the lives and outlook of this group of people. Raleigh also uses its experience in organising developmental expeditions to deliver corporate training events. These programmes have attracted major UK and international companies to develop teamwork and the events can be UK-based or conducted abroad, more in the style of the expeditions.

of visitor impacts will perhaps increase. Therefore, better quality visitor education and interpretative programmes will be required to educate the ecotourist and local community.

Similar to other tourist typologies, academics and researchers have attempted to categorise or profile ecotourists based on their characteristics, such as their demographics, motivations and perceptions, and on the basis of the setting, experience and group dynamics (Fennell, 1999). Like general tourists, ecotourists are not one homogeneous group that have similar characteristics and motivations. There are so called 'hard' or 'soft' ecotourists who have different values, motivations or reasons for travel and therefore can seek quite different experiences, activities and settings to fulfil these motivations. Differentiation can be made based on visitors being considered either 'specialists', 'experts' or 'generalists' (Boyd & Butler, 1993 in Wight, 1996; Duffus & Dearden, 1990). 'Specialists' or 'experts' are generally smaller in number yet high in previous experience and knowledge concerning particular flora or fauna. Because of their small numbers they place little pressure on the environment and conduct themselves with minimal impact. Yet 'generalists' are less ambitious, higher in number, more demanding of facilities and require greater management and interpretation, according to Duffus and Dearden (1990). Some authors (Ayala, 1996; Ryan *et al.*, 2000; Weaver, 1999) note the growing convergence between ecotourism and mass tourism, which creates substantial challenges for natural area managers and an obvious need to understand the demands of a changing market place.

Wight (1996) notes the confusion surrounding the characteristics of ecotourists with differing findings evident from research. A number

Table 2.3 A comparison of ecotourism and nature tourism definitions

Main principles of definition[a]	*Definitions*														
	1	***2***	***3***	***4***	***5***	***6***	***7***	***8***	***9***	***10***	***11***	***12***	***13***	***14***	***15***
Interest in nature	✓	✓			✓	✓	✓	✓		✓	✓			✓	✓
Contributes to conservation			✓		✓	✓	✓	✓	✓	✓			✓	✓	✓
Reliance on parks and protected areas	✓		✓		✓	✓		✓	✓				✓	✓	✓
Benefits local people/ long-term benefits			✓		✓	✓	✓		✓				✓	✓	✓
Education and study	✓	✓	✓			✓					✓			✓	✓
Low impact/non-consumptive					✓							✓	✓	✓	✓
Ethics/responsibility				✓					✓	✓					✓
Management					✓			✓			✓				✓
Sustainable								✓			✓			✓	✓
Enjoyment/appreciation	✓				✓									✓	
Culture	✓				✓									✓	
Adventure		✓													
Small scale												✓			✓

1 Ceballos-Lascuráin (1987); 2 Laarman and Durst[b] (1987); 3 Halbertsma[b] (1988); 4 Kutay (1989), 5 Ziffer (1989), 6 Fennell and Eagles (1990); 7 CEAC (1992); 8 Valentine (1993); 9 The Ecotourism Society (1993); 10 Western (1993); 11 Commonwealth Department of Tourism (1994); 12 Brandon (1996); 13 Goodwin (1996); 14 Wallace and Pierce (1996); 15 The present study.

Notes: [a] Variables ranked by frequency of response. [b] Nature tourism definitions.

Source: Fennell (1999: 41)

Exhibit 2.2

Ecotourism, education and interpretation

By David A. Fennell

The background for our understanding of how education links to ecotourism may be traced to two rather widely accepted streams: outdoor education and environmental education. Briefly, there appears to be general consensus that outdoor education is fashioned *in* the outdoors, *about* the outdoors (outdoor resources/skills or as a location and a process with the aim of enhancing existing curricula), and *for* the outdoors, implying the incorporation of leisure pursuits and an associated understanding of stewardship and natural processes (see Ford, 1981). It is not a separate discipline with its own set of prescribed objectives, but rather a vehicle from which to examine a number of disciplines including science, social science, health, recreation, physical education, music and language arts. These may occur in a range of different settings, including schools, local parks, museums, historical monuments or other heritage attractions, provincial/state parks, national parks, wildlife areas, zoos, and so on. On the other hand, environmental education is focused on the natural and social sciences, particularly ecology, political science and economics (Nowak, 1972). The focus on these disciplines is evident in the following goals and objectives of environmental education as endorsed at the 1987 UNESCO–UNEP International Congress on Environmental Education and Training in Moscow (UNESCO–UNEP, 1988):

Goals:

- To foster clear awareness of, and concern about, economic, social, political and ecological interdependence in urban and rural areas.
- To provide every person with opportunities to acquire the knowledge, values, attitudes, commitment and skills needed to protect and improve the environment.
- To create new patterns of behaviour of individuals, groups and society as a whole towards the environment.

Objectives:

- *Awareness.* To help social groups and individuals acquire an awareness of and sensitivity to the total environment and allied problems.
- *Knowledge.* To help social groups and individuals gain a variety of experiences in, and acquire a basic understanding of, the environment and its associated problems.
- *Attitudes.* To help social groups and individuals acquire a set of values and feelings of concern for the environment, and the motivation for actively participating in environmental improvement and protection.
- *Skills.* To help social groups and individuals acquire the skills for identifying and solving environmental problems.

Interpretative programmes and techniques are the mechanisms used by guides and other service providers for the purpose of transferring information to ecotourists (Weiler & Ham, 2001). Interpretation and education may thus be differentiated on the basis of the former acting as a means by which to convey the meaning of something through explanation or exposition, while the latter is the knowledge derived from the experience (Knudson *et al.*, 1995). Tilden (1967) writes that interpretation is an educational activity which aims to reveal meanings and relationships through the use of original objects, first-hand experience, and by illustrative media, rather than simply to communicate factual information. While the factual 'scientific' information is essential (e.g. information on botany, animal behaviour, and so on) to the experience, it is the art form used to transmit this information that is the catalyst which makes the interpretation event happen. The interpreter may thus rely on music, imagery, metaphors and various props to communicate the desired information.

Of concern is the fact that, although there is a natural link between ecotourism and environmental education, there is decidedly little research on appropriate methods (Kimmel, 1999). This is echoed by Orams and Hill (1998) who write that, although there appears to be widespread support for education programmes to minimise ecotourist impacts, little research exists to support such claims. Despite this fact, various models of interpretation and environmental education have emerged in the literature, which have been geared towards ecotourism. In their research on education to control ecotourists in a wild dolphin feeding programme, Orams and Hill (1998) found that formal, structured education programmes were successful at curbing inappropriate behaviour. A model developed by Forestell (1993) suggests that there are three stages to consider in understanding and modifying the behaviour of ecotourists:

- a dynamic disequilibrium (pre-contact stage);
- managing cognitive dissonance (contact stage); and
- resolution of cognitive dissonance (post-contact stage).

This model was subsequently modified by Orams (1995b), also in the context of a marine environment. In other research, Masberg and Savige (1996) suggest that the interpretative planning process often does not include mechanisms for ecotourist input in many parks and protected areas. Their Ecotourist Needs Assessment (ETNA), allows for the collection and inventory of information from ecotourists, in addition to the information amassed by planners and advisors, which may be collectively analysed, synthesised and built into an effective interpretative plan.

It was not too long ago that education and interpretation programmes were treated as secondary functions within parks and protected areas. This was due largely to park funding schemes which were more centralised and which appeared to be less visitor-management oriented, due to shrinking budgets. However, new funding schemes based on the implementation of 'user pays' practices, tiered pricing systems for locals, international visitors and tourist operators, for example, recognise that, as a form of revenue, ecotourists have tremendous potential to pay for many park operating costs. In order to maximise visitor numbers and visitor experiences, interpretation and education programmes may thus have a renewed function within the park. As such, innovative methods and models should continue to emerge with the intent to support what appears to be a stronger focus on learning in the travel destinations and experiences sought by tourists.

of studies have reported that ecotourists are older than average tourists, while other studies report that they are younger. Wight (1996) believes that all age groups are interested in taking an ecotourism vacation, but that experienced ecotourists are generally older than general consumers. Yet studies differ with respect to whether ecotourists are in the majority males or females. This could be partly due to the overlap of ecotourism experiences with outdoor recreation participation. For instance, Wight (1996) found that participation varied by activity, with males preferring cycling and camping while females preferred hiking. In addition, ecotourism clients have also tended to be highly educated and of higher than average incomes (Wight, 1996), although this may change as the market broadens and ecotourist profiles evolve over time.

Profiling ecotourists or tourists who are interested in combining travel with learning and education can help in understanding the wants and needs of ecotourists for suppliers who provide educational tourism products, such as ecotourism and cultural heritage tourism (see for example Case Study 2.1). Profiling segments of ecotourists and the ratio of ecotourists to each profile or segment can assist in the product development and provision of suitable infrastructure and satisfactory experiences. However, despite the advantages of understanding the ecotourism market and the lucrative nature of the market, little is known about the profile of ecotourists (Blamey & Braithwaite, 1997).

A segmentation analysis conducted in Australia on international ecotourists provided interesting information on the profiles and characteristics of the ecotourist market. A total of three clusters were found and labelled clusters A (35% of the sample), B (15%) and C (50%). Blamey and Hatch (1998) noted that the first segment (A) had a general interest in nature-based tourism, the second segment (B) appeared more interested in rest and relaxation in a natural setting, while the third segment (C) were strongly motivated by many aspects of nature-based tourism. The results from this segmentation exercise of Australian ecotourists are outlined in Table 2.4.

The table and results illustrate that segment C ecotourists were more dedicated and after 'harder' ecotourism experiences, while segment A ecotourists were more interested in undertaking novelty and learning experiences. Segment B were more interested in escaping their environment and in rest and relaxation within a natural setting. Segment Cs were young, participating in a greater number of tours for educational purposes but for a shorter period of time than other segments. They undertook more activities than other segments and the main determinants of their satisfaction were related to minimisation of tourism impacts and

Table 2.4 Motivations, demographics and trip characteristics of Australian ecotourist segments

Segment	*Proportion*	*Motivations*	*Demographics*	*Trip characteristics*
Segment A	35%	• to see and experience something new • to be close to nature • to have an educational or learning experience	• more likely to be female • middle-aged (40–49 years)	• 2.6 nature-based tours (2 for education) • 2.7 nights on each tour • activities undertaken • desire more time at sites, quality sites and helpful staff
Segment B	15%	• escaping tourism masses • escaping towns and cities • rest and relaxation	• more likely to be female	• 3.2 nature-based tours (3 for education) • 3.7 nights on each tour • few activities under-taken
Segment C	35%	• to have an educational or learning experience • to be close to nature • a different or unique way of experiencing nature • to see wildlife in detail	• male and female • younger (20–29 years)	• 3.4 nature-based tours (3 for education) • 2.4 nights on each tour • more activities under-taken • desire tourism impact management and small tour numbers

Source: Adapted from Blamey and Hatch (1998)

small tour numbers (Blamey & Hatch, 1998). Segment As were more likely to be female and middle-aged and undertook the least number of trips but more activities than segment Bs. However, their satisfaction determinants were centred around the quality of the site, the amount of time spent at the site and the helpfulness of staff. Segment Bs were also more likely to be female and undertook a reasonable number and duration of trips during their holidays, but, perhaps because of their motivations for rest and relaxation, they undertook fewer activities. This kind of research can assist the ecotourism industry in developing educational components and interpretation to meet the needs of 'harder' or 'softer' ecotourists who may have different education and learning requirements.

Cultural heritage tourism definitions and market characteristics

Cultural heritage is culture that is valued by society and therefore transmitted from one generation to another. Often cultural heritage involves the packaging of the past for consumption by individuals (locals, tourists) so that they might become aware and learn to appreciate human history. Tourism has been identified as being able to assist the funding, preservation and regeneration of cultural heritage. In some instances tourists directly contribute to the preservation of cultural heritage, through visitor entry fees or donations at cultural sites such as historic properties and cathedrals. Heritage tourism has been viewed as 'tourism centred on what we have inherited, which can mean anything from historic buildings, to art works, to beautiful scenery' (Yale, 1991 in Garrod & Fyall, 2000: 683).

The World Tourism Organization (1993: viii) states that cultural tourism is 'small, well-managed, educational and frequently upmarket tourism ... involving music, the arts and ethnic exchange'. Cultural heritage sites' and museums' roles are to collect, conserve and protect cultural objects/artefacts and to display them for scholarship, education and/or pleasure (Law, 1993). The ability of tourism to conserve and educate through heritage is well known, yet many heritage managers do not even consider themselves to be in the 'tourism business' (Croft, 1994 in Garrod & Fyall, 2000). The role of education and learning is of fundamental importance to the delivery and experience related to cultural heritage tourism. The increasing desire to preserve culture and present it for locals and visitors to learn and enjoy has led to the increased provision of cultural heritage product; however some studies note that tourists may not be so interested in learning or in educational experiences at cultural heritage attractions, despite the claims from some heritage managers.

'Museums will stand or fall not only by their competence to care for collections but also by their ability to care for people ... they will need to be market-orientated if they are to survive' (Cossons, 1995 in Middleton & Clarke, 2001: 348). Understanding this market involves research to identify the profile of visitors and interpret their needs and desires. The consumption of heritage is closely associated with certain social groups and in particular the 'new middle class' (Richards, 1996). Merriman (1991 in Richards, 1996) showed that frequent museum visitors in the United Kingdom predominately come from higher-status groups and tend to be well educated. Despite the problems with using social class to segment tourists, the propensity to visit heritage and cultural attractions appears to be dictated to some extent by social class. Nearly two-thirds of ABs visit cultural/heritage sites compared with 48% of C1s, 30% of C2Ds and 20% of Es (Sogno-Lalloz, 2000: A34). Museums are often visited by those who can understand their content and the cultural aspects that are within them are perhaps a direct reflection of class divisions. Research discussed by Richards (1996: 270) indicates that the socio-economic profile of visitors to museums and other heritage attractions has hardly changed in the last 30 years, but demand has grown due to a growing 'new middle class' with high levels of education and income.

Research in Europe indicates that cultural heritage visitors are highly educated with 80% gaining some form of tertiary education and almost a quarter with some form of postgraduate qualification (Richards, 1996). In addition, market research on over 7000 visitors to London museums and galleries notes that a large majority of regular visitors hold postgraduate qualifications while only a minority of those without formal education go to these places (Songo-Lalloz, 2000). Furthermore, Songo-Lalloz (2000) notes that those who have degrees from lower socio-economic groups and those who use technology regularly are more likely to visit museums and galleries, suggesting that an *attitude toward learning* and a *readiness to learn* are more important than social class and educational characteristics in determining who visits such sites. With regard to age, research in London has shown that visitors to museums and galleries are more likely to be middle aged (Songo-Lalloz, 2000). Also, museums tend to attract more men, who are first-time or low-frequency visitors either visiting alone or with an adult-only party, while galleries attract more women, who are younger and from higher social classes and tend to visit alone (Songo-Lalloz, 2000).

Using data from a European survey Bonink and Richards (1992) identified tourists who had travelled specifically to visit particular cultural attractions and who stated that the attraction was either an 'important' or a 'very important' motivating factor for their destination choice. They also identified 9% of all tourists as 'specific cultural tourists', corresponding to the 'specific cultural tourists' noted by an Irish Tourist Board (1988) study and the 'culturally motivated tourists' identified by Bywater (1993b) who comprise about 5% of the market. This market was found by Bonink and Richards (1992) to contain more frequent consumers of cultural heritage attractions and also had a higher level of total tourism consumption with nearly twice as many short breaks undertaken in the 12 months prior to surveying. This small sub-segment of 'specific cultural tourists' is perhaps illustrated in the case of the newly opened and very successful Tate Modern Art Gallery in London. From a total of 5.25 million visitors, making it now the world's top gallery for modern art, only 100,000 (perhaps specifically motivated) actually paid to see the first major international exhibition, 'Century Cities' (Kennedy, 2001).

High levels of consumption of cultural heritage at home are also more likely to lead to high levels of culture consumed on holiday, according to Richards (1996) and Hughes (1987). The connection between home and holiday motives can be further explained by examining the employment patterns of cultural tourists. Employment patterns of European cultural tourists illustrate that 22% were employed in heritage, performing arts or visual arts compared to 13% of 'general cultural tourists' and 29% of 'specific cultural tourists'. Furthermore, a clear link was discovered between the employment sector and respondents' cultural tourism consumption patterns. As Richards (1996: 272) notes:

> those working in 'heritage' were more likely than other respondents to visit museums and heritage centres while on holiday, and employment in the visual or performing arts was also correlated with a higher level of visits to visual or performing arts attractions on holiday.

Other findings from the study on the segments of cultural tourists in Europe discovered that many of the 'specific cultural tourists' are younger, more likely to be self-employed and in possession of a high level of cultural capital and knowledge related to their employment in the cultural industries (Richards, 1996).

The provision of ecotourism product

As discussed earlier in this section, the type of ecotourism product differs depending on who is defining ecotourism, what ecotourists desire and what is provided to ecotourists to consume. For instance, in Kenya and Costa Rica, two destinations where the natural environment is an important part of the tourist product, Weaver (1999) notes that the majority of ecotourism in these two countries is undertaken by 'passive' ecotourists. Ecotourism product may include, according to Swarbrooke and Horner (1999: 233):

- wildlife safaris in East Africa;
- journeys up the rivers of Borneo to see native villages;
- visits to endangered rain forests;
- natural history walking holidays in the mountains of Europe;
- outback trips in Australia; and
- whale-watching holidays to New England or New Zealand.

The type of product offered differs depending on the characteristics of those tourists who demand different types of ecotourism experiences, whether they are single-day excursions to a national park or two-month journeys through the Amazon rainforest. Some may be working holidays organised by conservation charities (such as The British Trust for Conservation Volunteers, discussed previously), while other holidays may include more luxury (such as the ecolodge experience in Case Study 2.1). As some authors note there are many niche markets within ecotourism itself and the market is not homogeneous (Page & Dowling, 2002; Wight, 2001).

As a result of the search for exotic locations and the improvement in transport and communication, tourists are increasingly searching out new tourist destinations. Subsequently, ecotourism experiences have broadened from Western countries to include less developed countries such as Costa Rica, Belize and Kenya, which now rely heavily on ecotourism for their growth and development. Furthermore, research and writing has focused on ecotourism in the developing world (see for instance Cater, 1994; Weaver, 1998, 1999). Weaver (1999) notes, in examining Eagles' and Cascagnette's (1995 in Weaver, 1999) case study work, that a total of 62% of case studies involved less developed countries, indicating increased academic and industry interest in ecotourism in the developing world. This is perhaps not surprising considering that many ecotourists travel from developed countries to less developed countries (Cater, 1993), yet questions remain concerning the impacts and local benefits.

The variety of ecotourism product has expanded considerably over the last decade, with some authors noting that some ecotourism operators are experiencing business problems as competition intensifies in order to take advantage of the greening of the tourism marketplace (Hall, 1998; Lew, 1998). Some operators at the passive end of the ecotourism definition are using ecotourism as a selling tool and are perhaps more concerned with sustaining profits than the environment, creating commercial and image problems for more 'active' ecotourism operators.

Types of ecotourism product differ depending on the country visited and the motivations and type of ecotourist. However, ecotourism activities such as wildlife observing, trekking and hiking appear popular in some destinations as do participating in local culture and jungle excursions (see Jenner & Smith, 1992). Furthermore, many ecotourists do not participate in an ecotourism vacation provided by a tour operator as they may be independent travellers seeking ecotourism experiences (Wight, 1996). This illustrates the diversity of the ecotourism sector and that ecotourist demand for educational experiences can vary. Issues associated with the provision of ecotourism product include the importance of interpretation for educational tourists and managing the growth and proliferation of ecotourism experiences.

Interpretation

It is obvious, as Fennell noted earlier in Exhibit 2.2, that, although there is a natural link between ecotourism and environmental education, there is little research on appropriate methods of interpretation and little research on how it can help minimise ecotourist impacts. This could be in part due to the debate about whose role and responsibility it is to educate tourists (Weiler, 1993 in Turner *et al.*, 2000). Interpretation is essentially an educational activity of transferring information to visitors to natural and cultural sites. As noted earlier in the case of Australian ecotourists, although education and learning were less important than other motivational factors, 69% of visitors rated them as important or very important (Blamey & Hatch, 1998). Additional questions were asked of these individuals and Table 2.5 outlines their responses.

The research illustrated that being provided with information or learning about the natural environment and the geological or even historical context of the natural environment was important for Australian ecotourists. The provision of interpretation and the development of suitable programmes or packages to offer ecotourists are therefore critical. The Canadian Tourism Commission (CTC, 2001) notes that successful educational tourism experiences should be high quality, authentic, experiential and have interactive learning activities. A total of 86% of learning travel providers in Canada report that educational programming is part of the core experience (CTC, 2001: 35). In examining the educational component of non-profit organisations and tour operators in Canada the CTC discovered that tour operators are offering more experiential learning and research experiences. A total of 46% of tour operators offer experiential components to their products compared to 30% of non-profit organisations, while 25% provide research experiences compared to 5%

Table 2.5 Importance of various learning experiences for Australian international ecotourists (%)

Learning experience	*A*	*B*	*C*	*D*
Seeing and observing animals, plants and landscapes	76	21	3	<1
Being provided with information about biology or ecology of species/region	40	44	9	3
Being provided with information about the geology or landscapes of the area	38	32	18	4
Learning about the cultural and/or historical aspects of the area	40	34	10	9

Note: A = Very important, B = Important, C = Neither important nor unimportant; D = Unimportant.

Source: Adapted after Blamey and Hatch (1998: 47)

of non-profit organisations. However, in the case of Canadian educational tourism providers, the lecture still dominates as the most-used method of passing information to educational tourists, with 66% of tour operators and 63% of non-profit organisations favouring this method of delivery (CTC, 2001: 36–7).

This illustrates the importance of the tour guide or specialist lecturer in providing a quality educational ecotourist experience. Yet despite this, the role of the tour leader or tour guide in providing interpretation for learning has not been thoroughly examined (Weiler & Davis, 1993), particularly in the field of ecotourism. Weiler and Davis (1993) note that the tour guide plays a host of different yet complementary roles to provide a quality experience for tourists. In using Cohen's (1985) model on the role of tour guides, Weiler and Davis (1993: 97) note that tour guides act as:

- *tour managers*: organising and entertaining the tour group;
- *experience managers*: acting as group leaders but also teachers;
- *resource managers*: who attempt to motivate tourists to modify their behaviour and impacts onsite but also promote environmental values and facilitate longer-term change.

Dowling and Field (1999 in Page & Dowling, 2002: 238) note that guides' principle characteristics can be viewed as the 4 'E's:

- Education or knowledge both of the product and the surrounding region.
- Environmental awareness of the natural, cultural and heritage environments.
- An Ethical approach which fosters integrity and honesty.
- Enthusiasm, which can make the difference between an 'average' and an 'excellent' tour guide.

Adequate skills and knowledge are needed by ecotourism guides if they are to provide a quality tourist experience. As discussed earlier, in the case of Australian ecotourists, for some the helpfulness of staff was a key determinant of satisfaction, while for others the ability of staff to minimise the impacts of tourism and provide small tour groups was critical for satisfaction. The education and training of tour guides and leaders is therefore vital.

General tour guide training and environmental education is available through a range of university qualifications at the degree, diploma and certificate level. However, in response to the growing ecotourism market and industry, organisations have developed specific ecotourism training programmes which include tour guide training. Furthermore, many organisations are implementing voluntary accreditation programmes for the ecotourism industry to raise standards and improve the quality of the experience for ecotourists. For instance, the International Ecotourism Society established in 1991 provides short courses and training for ecotourism professionals and businesses which often includes guiding instruction. The Ecotourism Association of Australia (2002) provides an EcoGuide certification, not to train guides however but to assess guides' skills, knowledge, attitude and actions. The EcoGuide Program complements and supports the Nature and Ecotourism Accreditation Program (NEAP), which accredits nature tourism and ecotourism product in Australia.

According to the Ecotourism Association of Australia (2002) EcoGuide certification provides a number of benefits to a wide range of stakeholders:

- Certified guides gain the advantage of an industry qualification and a pathway to nationally recognised formal qualifications that will provide a defined competitive edge.
- Operators gain a simple method of recognising quality guides, a benchmark to use for training purposes and greater product appeal

through employing and promoting the use of bona fide nature and ecotour guides.
- Both guides and operators gain an opportunity to promote guiding services as genuine nature tourism or ecotourism, providing a competitive edge for these niche markets.
- Visitors gain a guarantee of guides who are committed to providing quality nature tourism and ecotourism experiences in a safe, culturally sensitive and environmentally sustainable manner.
- Environmental benefits flow from improved guiding practices that lead to fewer negative environmental and cultural impacts.
- Training providers gain a benchmark of best practice nature and ecotour guiding.
- A potential advantage for protected area managers is the ability to identify operators who employ staff with appropriate training and qualifications when reviewing permit applications in sensitive areas.

As ecotourism experiences continue to increase, an awareness of the needs of ecotourists, especially concerning information and learning needs will ensure the development of more effective programming and interpretation by ecotourism providers.

Managing growth

With an increase in demand for 'active' vacations and a growing interest in the environment, health and fitness comes increasing pressure on natural resources by tourists and recreationalists alike. There are a number of methods which can be used to manage the educational tourism experience so that the resource is protected and visitor experiences are not compromised. One of the options to limit the impacts of tourism upon the natural and cultural resource base is through manipulating visitor flows through the zoning of sites suitable for tourist visitation and impact. Many national parks and marine reserves limit visitor numbers or direct visitors to other more resilient or resistant parts of the national park or reserve.

This approach to visitor management takes into consideration the nature of the resource as well as the likely needs of visitors regarding facilities and infrastructure. However, visitor management strategies at heritage attractions are increasingly being revised as past strategies appear not to be able to cope with either the increased numbers or the increased demands for positive experiences being placed on such sites, according to Hall and McArthur (1998). This is illustrated by the example of the Galapagos Islands, which are struggling to balance the demands

Exhibit 2.3

Tourism and the environment in conflict? Ecotourism in the Galapagos Islands

By Brent Ritchie

The Galapagos Islands are located 1,100 kilometres west of Ecuador off the South American coast. They have unique flora and fauna that have been the object of interest and scientific study for many individuals including Charles Darwin who published *On the Origin of Species by Means of Natural Selection* in 1859. Fauna that live on the Galapagos Islands include marine and land iguanas, tortoises, birds such as flightless cormorants, penguins, blue, red and masked boobies, hawks and finches. The Islands are also used as nesting sites by the waved albatross, frigate bird, tropic bird and the sea turtle.

After gradual colonialisation by farmers from 1846 to 1934, the islands' unique flora and fauna led in 1959 to the islands being designated a National Park by the Ecuadorian government. By 1969 mainstream tourism arrived with the introduction of the first cruise ship visit to the islands, and infrastructure such as roads and cruise landing stages were subsequently created to cater for tourists. Very early on the Ecuadorian government realised that the Galapagos National Park needed a strategy to deal with the increasing numbers of tourists travelling to the islands. In 1973 a team of Ecuadorians and international experts developed the first master plan for the islands which was published in 1974 with the aim of allowing the people of the Galapagos to live in harmony with the environment and to control the level and nature of tourist activity. Part of this included the zoning of activities using a physical/spatial planning approach toward economic activities including fishing and tourism. A number of zones are used to balance the use of the islands with protection of the unique resources, including:

- intensive use zones (25 areas where 90 people could disembark daily);
- extensive use zones (about 16 less interesting sites where 12 people are allowed daily);
- primitive use zones (where a special permit is needed to visit);

- scientific zones (which are visited only for scientific research and by scientific personnel); and
- special use zones (which are located next to colonised areas and can be used by residents although use is controlled).

From the master plan visitor numbers to the Galapagos were restricted to four or five groups of 20 people per day accompanied by a qualified National Park guide or a total of 12,000 visitors per annum. In 1976 Budowski, the then head of IUCN (International Union for Conservation of Nature and Natural Resources) described the Galapagos Islands as an example of how conservation and tourism could work together in a 'symbiotic' relationship, with education and learning a key foundation of this relationship. However, this restriction of visitor numbers was exceeded in 1978, the same year in which UNESCO proclaimed the islands as a 'patrimony of harmony'.

In 1981 another master plan to 1985 proposed a limit of 25,000 visitors per annum which was not exceeded until 1986, very soon after a new master plan, initiated in 1985, increased permitted visitor numbers to 50,000. This limit was again exceeded in 1993 due to improved access to the islands through increased flights from the mainland, cruise ship traffic and ferry transportation, and in 1996 when UNESCO gave the islands Biological Reserve Status as a World Heritage Site visitor numbers were approaching 60,000 per annum. These official statistics have been questioned by the World Wide Fund for Nature, who believe that, in 1986 alone, real visitor numbers were double the 25,000 estimates of the Ecuadorian government at 50,000 visitors per annum (in Jenner & Smith, 1992). As well as this Nolan and Nolan (1997 in Weaver, 2000: 111) note that most visitors to the islands are passive or 'soft' ecotourists with many combining an excursion to the Galapagos with sunbathing and shopping.

Along with the increase in visitors since the 1960s there has been a growth in settlement of the islands which has increased the resident population in search of employment opportunities from 5000 in 1985 to 20,000 in 1995 (see Plate 2.1). Settlers have been involved in a variety of jobs including farming, fishing and the tourist trade. However, conflicts of interest, a lack of tangible employment opportunities and poor pay have generated social problems for settlers and the Ecuadorian government. The government has found itself in a

Plate 2.1 Migrant housing in the Galapagos Islands. The migration of Ecuadorians to the Galapagos Islands and their pressure on the natural environment is posing challenges for the government

Source: P. Cowles

difficult position, where on one hand it wants to protect the natural environment that attracts tourists, but on the other hand needs to create economic development and employment opportunities for local migrants. The increasing pressure and demands from tourists as well as settlers have led to the environmental carrying capacity of some parts of the island being exceeded. Negative impacts such as disturbance to bird life during nesting, erosion, damage to coral and rubbish disposal (see Jenner & Smith, 1992; Weaver, 2000), as well as the difficulty in policing such a large area of the National Park, provide evidence that the environmental carrying capacity has been reached. Similarly, De Groot (1983) and Kenchington (1989) in Fennell (1999: 122) noted that this carrying capacity had been reached in particular because:

- patrol boats do not always control numbers on the island effectively;

- the official limit of 90 tourists on an island at one time is often overlooked; and
- the number of tourists is still increasing as total visitation has not been controlled as it should be.

In 1999 UNESCO stated that the heritage status of the islands was in jeopardy due to the environmental problems experienced, and that heritage status could be revoked. The Galapagos Islands are at a key stage in balancing the protection of the unique flora and fauna with increasing tourist and settler pressures. Budowski may be disappointed that the islands, which were once an example of the symbiotic relationship between conservation and tourism, are now a potential example of tourism and conservation in conflict. Although initiatives have been undertaken to slow the negative direct and indirect impact of tourists, such as the 1998 Special Galapagos Law to restrict settlement and the introduction of a National Park fee for tourists, it is too soon to judge the effects of these 'reactive' initiatives. The future management strategies that the government implements in the coming years will be important not only for the protection of the islands, but also the future sustainability of the local tourist industry.

Note: For a more detailed investigation of tourism in the Galapagos Islands see Weaver (2000).

of visitors and local residents with protection of the natural resource base (see Exhibit 2.3). Some commentators believe that the problems many natural area managers face are due to funding cuts in ecotourism locations, resulting in low re-investment of profits to protect the area against negative environmental impacts. As Weaver (1999: 806) explains, 'there is an agreement that many of the problems identified in the protected areas of Costa Rica and Kenya have their origins in a legacy of chronic underfunding'. This underfunding has limited the budget given to protected area managers and exacerbated their reliance on visitor income and revenue, with an increasing number of visitor entry fees and higher charges imposed by park managers.

If management is not suitable, this can lead to reduction in visitor satisfaction and even the possible destruction of natural resources such as wildlife and vegetation. If this occurs then ecotourism as a tool for nature conservation has not worked. However, the implementation of stringent management techniques and tools (such as pricing, 'user pays' and the development of boardwalks) is required in order to protect the resource and the integrity of the educational tourism experience. Nonetheless, the growing interest in the environment by tourists and the growth of more 'passive' ecotourism experiences provide a distinct challenge to natural area managers in the future.

The provision of cultural heritage tourism product

The cultural heritage product consists of many different forms of attractions, ranging from tangible products (such as buildings), to intangible products (such as folklore, customs and traditions). Some authors such as McCannell (1976, 1993 in Richards, 1996) believe that all tourism is a cultural experience. Cultural heritage plays a major part in the tourism industry worldwide and the importance of cultural heritage to the tourism industry has increased as tourists search for postmodern tourist experiences, subsequently increasing the demand for cultural attractions. In Europe Richards (1996) reports research illustrating a 100% increase in heritage visits in Europe between 1970 and 1991. However, within this 100% increase variation occurs, demonstrating that countries such as the United Kingdom experienced a 200% increase over this period while Italy's was only 18% due largely to a lack of heritage management expertise. Richards (1996) also notes a move away from the 'high arts' such as the theatre and ballet toward general heritage attraction attendance at museums and galleries. Between 1988 and 1992 approximately 700 new attractions opened in the United Kingdom to cater for this growing demand, including heritage centres, museums and industrial heritage attractions (Swarbrooke, 1995). Furthermore, over half the 5552 officially recognised attractions in the United Kingdom in 1992 were historic buildings or museums (Swarbrooke, 1995).

As Olding (2000) notes, in the United Kingdom alone historic properties attracted 79 million visits in 1999, of which 33% were undertaken by overseas visitors. Museums and galleries attracted a further 77 million visits, of which 23% were made by foreign origin tourists. This rapid growth and importance of cultural heritage tourism product is not limited to the United Kingdom. In the USA since the 1960s a new museum has opened ever 3.3 days, so that by the 1980s there were 6000 museums and in 1992 more than 8000 museums open in the USA (see Law, 1993). Some of these museums in both Europe and the USA are becoming increasingly specialised (such as the Sex Museum in Amsterdam and the Design

Museum in London), with some even displaying 'heritage' as recent as the 1960s (Urry, 1990). This increased supply coupled with specialisation has led to some criticism over the rapid expansion of new museums, with the Director of the Dutch Museums Association suggesting in 1993 that criteria should be developed to stop the setting up of 'silly museums' and 'ego-tripping collectors' (in Richards, 1996: 274). This highlights the issues of what exactly constitutes cultural heritage, how it should be preserved and presented for consumption, and to what degree it should provide education or entertainment for visitors.

Furthermore, as noted by several authors (Olding, 2000; Richards, 1996; Silberberg, 1995; Swarbrooke, 1995), there are concerns that the supply of cultural heritage attractions are outstripping current demand, with visits to heritage attractions slowing in the 1990s, providing major challenges for cultural heritage managers. Richards (2001) notes that the underlying assumption of much of the writing is that an increased interest in heritage has led to increased demand for heritage attractions. However, he notes in earlier work that the almost parallel growth of consumption and production experienced in the 1970s slowed in the late 1980s when the increase in new heritage attractions outstripped the growth in heritage visits (Richards, 1996). Interestingly, Schouten (1995) points out that the number of visitors to museums has not increased, but the number of visits has, with visitors increasing the number of their visits over time.

Richards (2001) believes that the growth rate of heritage attraction attendance is related to the growth rate of international tourism in Europe, while other authors note a decline in museum visitation in England and historic house visitation in south-east England (see Markwell *et al.*, 1997; Middleton and Clarke, 1998). Part of this rapid growth in cultural heritage tourism is also due to an increase in heritage funding through lottery grants in the USA and United Kingdom. However, there has been a move away from expanding the available product in some areas toward improving the quality of current product. As Olding (2000: A9) comments regarding the Heritage Lottery Fund in the United Kingdom:

> The Fund has consistently taken a cautious approach to giving grants to new heritage attractions for their own sake: it is a very low priority, for example, to support a new museum. The intention has been to deliver change primarily through underpinning the infrastructure . . . thereby safeguarding the quality of heritage assets rather than adding significantly to the quantity.

Moreover, cultural heritage providers such as museums and galleries are not only competing against themselves but also against many other leisure options and indirect competitors, suggesting that cultural heritage attractions need to understand their market, their needs and preferences and provide a quality and satisfying visitor experience. As Sogno-Lalloz (2000) notes, the number and quality of leisure offerings are increasing making it even more difficult for museums and galleries to capture a share of the market. This is particularly challenging considering that the growth in cultural heritage product may be outstripping current demand patterns.

Three major management implications facing cultural heritage managers are:

- educating visitors through entertainment;
- commodification of cultural heritage; and
- use of interpretation to improve learning amongst visitors.

Entertainment or education?

Garrod and Fyall (2000), in a Delphi study of a panel of owners and managers of heritage in the United Kingdom, discovered that education was the third highest goal of attractions after conservation and accessibility and was rated higher than both relevance and recreation. As Garrod and Fyall (2000: 693) note:

> While the panel recognized that education is more effective if it can be made entertaining, the panel still considered it more important to educate users than to offer them an entertaining recreational experience.

Yet is this what visitors desire and how might this potential conflict between heritage managers and visitors be resolved? Heritage managers are often faced with a dilemma of balancing satisfaction for the majority of general visitors who may desire a recreational experience, with pleasing a smaller proportion of visitors who are after a more intense educational experience that may be more aligned to the views of heritage managers.

Furthermore, museums and galleries often attempt to broaden their audience by expanding their educational charters to maintain a market share of visitors as competition increases. Museums such as the Natural History Museum of London and the Canadian Museum of Civilisation have been accused of 'dumbing down' and treating visitors as less intelligent than they are, thus Disneyfying the museum experience (in Griffin *et al.*, 2000). Some museums and galleries are utilising technology to provide an enjoyable, memorable and educational experience for their

Exhibit 2.4

Education or entertainment? The case of the Museum of New Zealand, Te Papa Tongarewa

By Brent Ritchie

Te Papa is located on the Wellington waterfront and has a vision to provide New Zealanders with exciting ways to explore and reflect on their cultural identity and natural heritage. One major aspect of its mandate is to attempt to increase and broaden the traditional museum audience. This is quite different to the museums of the past, who, according to Schouten (1995), loath catering to the general public. This vision and the way it has been implemented through the museum's display and interpretation of visual arts have been the source for debate and even criticism. However, despite this, visitors have supported the museum, with visitor numbers exceeding the Ernst and Young estimate of 723,000 visitors for the first year of operation within just three months. During their first year a total of two million visitors had participated in Te Papa, with 35% of New Zealanders having visited the museum to date (Te Papa, 2001). Although 39% of visitors were from the Wellington area, a total of 41% were from outside this area and 18% of visitors were international in origin.

Extensive visitor research has been undertaken both prior to and throughout the museum opening, and a close working relationship has been established between the indigenous Maori population and museum management. A total of 93% of visitors have rated their experience as good to excellent and 37% of visitors surveyed were on a repeat visit with 76% of visitors stating that they would revisit the museum in the next 12 months. This repeat visitation is particularly surprising compared to other cultural heritage attractions and is perhaps testimony to the popularity of the museum with the New Zealand public and visitors alike. Themed attractions of a highly experiential nature have been developed, based on audience research to allow for the layering of interpretation. Te Papa won the 'Most Successful Project Implementation Award' and the supreme award of 'Overall Excellence in the Use of Information Technology' at the Computerworld Excellence Awards in 1999. The awards recognised both the contributions that Te Papa's information technology has made to the overall visitor experience and the professional implementation of Te Papa's many technology-related projects. The previous year, Te Papa won the Gold Medal in the prestigious International Multi Media Awards in New York for its interactive computer database *Te Papa OnScreen*, which provides additional information on art exhibits and is anticipated to become a powerful and important interpretation tool in the future (Griffin *et al.*, 2000).

However, this success has not been without its fair share of criticism, which began before the museum opened. Due to the ongoing criticism and debate surrounding the museum the New Zealand Ministry for Culture and Heritage initiated an independent review. Griffin *et al.* (2000: 20) in their review note the problems in developing a museum that attempts to attract and stimulate a broad audience, and note that 'while designed to meet the expectations of multiple target audiences, some museum exhibitions were described to the Review Team as lacking in clarity of intent or not having sufficient regard for the layering of interpretative material'. In particular, criticism was levelled at some exhibitions as being 'too descriptive' and not challenging scientific assumptions, with a need for more 'depth of material'. In particular, art exhibits and information on the artworks are limited, with some critics suggesting that they leave the viewer uninformed and that 'audiences are intelligent enough to deserve more information than is provided' (Griffin *et al.*, 2000: 33). In particular, the exhibition 'Parade' has had extensive criticism over a lack of information, inadequate storyline and appropriateness of art and design objects (Griffin *et al.*, 2000). Griffin *et al.* (2000: 48) note that:

> Te Papa has been criticised heavily, particularly in the media, for being too simple, presenting text and other interpretation that is unchallenging ... most stridently, it has been criticised particularly by some scholars for 'dumbing down', for being like a Disney-style theme park.

These criticisms illustrate the difficulties of balancing an ambitious desire to expand the audience for museums and other cultural heritage attractions while still satisfying 'serious educational users'. Problems exist in developing a mixture of interpretation that satisfies the generalist/populist audience and the art-interested audience. This will become even more difficult as museums and cultural attractions attempt to broaden their appeal and relevance to the public in the future to maintain public funding, justify their existence and expand their educational mandate.

visitors, which has generated substantial debate and even criticism in some instances. One example which has faced both criticisms is the Museum of New Zealand, Te Papa Tongarewa, which opened in 1998 in Wellington (see Exhibit 2.4). Te Papa is dealing with issues directly related to the broadening of their audience and the use of experiential interpretation, including technology.

Commodification or authenticity?

In recent years there has been growing concern expressed about the commodification of culture. Tourism in particular has been identified as a major force here (Richards, 1996: 265) and the commodification of culture has been deplored by some as being shaped to meet political and economic rather than cultural ends (Hewison, 1987 in Richards, 1996). However, others believe that some cultural product developed for tourists may be accepted as authentic by both tourists and the suppliers of that product, and that tourism is the ideal arena to explore culture (see Cohen, 1988; McCannell, 1976). This is an issue that many cultural heritage managers face and it can be seen in the management of former Nazi concentration camps in Germany. The former concentration camps were memorials to soldiers and relatives of the deceased, but as time has passed they are increasingly becoming commodified for tourism purposes, in part due to the changing demographics and needs of visitors (see Case Study 2.2). These changes, coupled with the need for memorials to develop their own revenue streams due to variability in funding, have led to the development of visitor facilities at many memorial sites. As the case study notes, this is providing a substantial challenge to the managers of this particular cultural heritage product.

Interpretation and mindfulness

Similar to interpretation in ecotourism or nature-based tourism, interpretation within the cultural or built heritage field has similar goals to enhance the visitor experience, support conservation and also to encourage appropriate visitor behaviour (Hall & McArthur, 1998). As Moscardo (1996: 378) notes, 'interpretation can play a critical role in sustainable tourism by educating tourists about the nature of the host region and culture, informing them of the consequences of their actions, enhancing their experience and encouraging them to engage in sustainable behaviours'. Learning and education are key concepts related to any form of interpretation.

Moscardo (1996) discusses the concepts of mindfulness and mindlessness and how the combination of visitor factors (such as motivations and desires) and setting factors (such as the packaging and display of heritage)

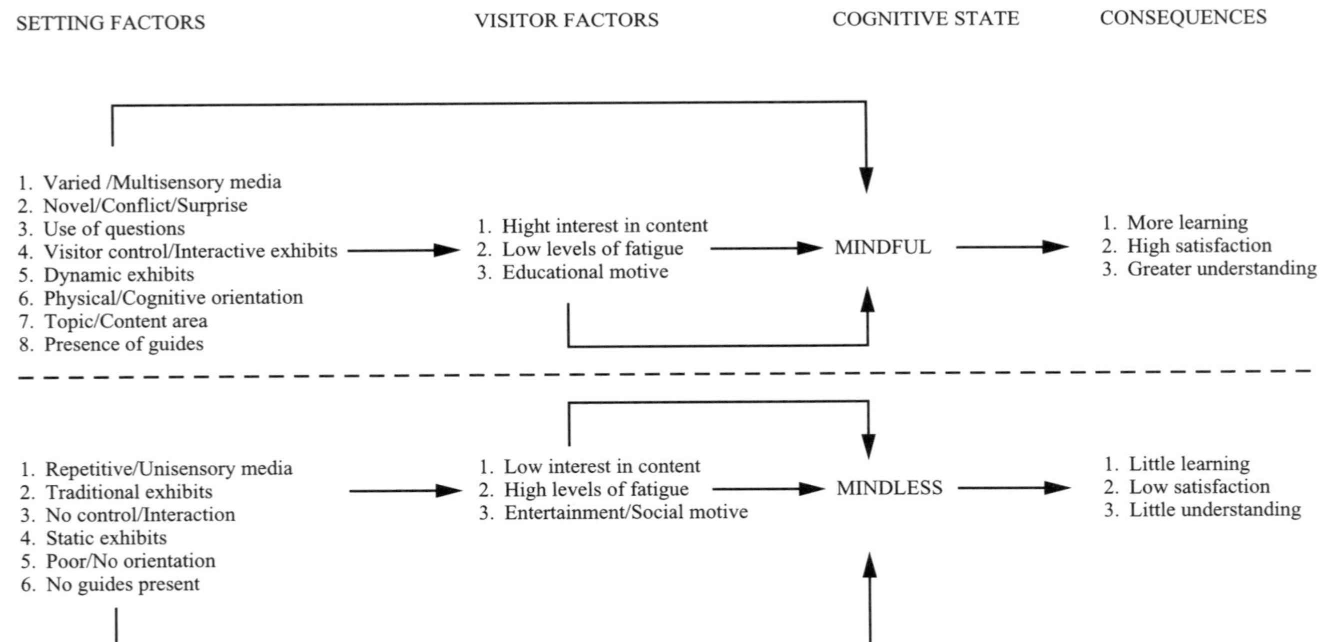

Figure 2.2 Mindfulness model of visitor behaviour and cognition at built heritage sites

Source: Moscardo (1996: 383)

can combine to create a cognitive state which can produce either mindful or mindless responses (see Figure 2.2). A mindless or a mindful cognitive state will impact upon the level of learning for the visitor, the overall satisfaction level and understanding of the material presented.

Mindlessness is said to exist because of routine or boredom due to the construction and design of repetitive or traditional exhibits in heritage settings. A lack of sensory media, lack of interactive exhibits and limited guidance or interpretation may all create a situation of mindlessness for visitors and hinder their overall satisfaction levels. However, the provision of the opposite is said perhaps to lead to an aroused state of mindfulness where individuals have control over their own learning and will gain more understanding of the heritage presented (Moscardo, 1996). Nevertheless, Moscardo (1996) notes that the level and nature of information and interpretation provided may also affect the process, with too much information providing an overload and reduced cognitive performance, and while too little information inducing mindlessness as routine and boredom set in. The effectiveness of mindfulness is also determined by the effectiveness of guides, which was discussed earlier as being an important tool for educational tourism in the ecotourism sector. Nevertheless, Moscardo (1996) also notes that visitor interest and motivation may also induce either a mindful or mindless experience, regardless of the setting factors.

Ecotourism and cultural heritage tourism impacts

Although ecotourism has been defined as a potentially low-impact form of tourism, it is not without impact and can generate significant negative outcomes, as well as positive benefits, without appropriate management. Many definitions of ecotourism stress the need for ecotourism to preserve and even protect the environment (see Brause, 1992; Farrell & Runyan, 1991). The preceding section concerning the definition of ecotourism has already discussed the different ways that ecotourism has been perceived and the controversy that surrounds the use of the term. Moreover, the general nature of tourism as a seasonal activity and the concentration of tourism and ecotourism at key times and locations may increase the potential negative impacts of ecotourism. Impacts can be economic, socio-cultural and environmental and can be a combination of the positive and the negative. As Exhibit 2.5 illustrates with regard to the Eden Project in England, educational tourism attractions not only can have an impact on the economy of a region but also can provide personal benefits to individual visitors and the local or national community.

Exhibit 2.5

The Eden Project

By Clare Weeden

The Eden Project is a visitor attraction in Cornwall, southwest England, which first opened in March 2001. It is located in a former china clay pit, near St Austell, over 34 acres, and showcases plants from all over the world, which are housed in two 'biomes' – the biggest conservatories in the world. These biomes, the largest of which is 240 metres long, 55 metres high and 110 metres wide, house plants from the world's humid tropics, and from the temperate plains of the Mediterranean, southern Africa and southwest USA.

With the Millennium Commission funding half of the £80 million development costs, partnerships were forged with local organisations, including South West of England Regeneration Agency, South West Water and developer McAlpine. However, the bulk of funding came from the EU Regional Development Fund and English Partnerships (the government's regeneration agency) along with an £18m bank loan from Royal Bank of Scotland and NatWest Bank. The Project deliberately pursues this collaboration between the public and private sectors, underlining their philosophy of supportive partnerships and bringing joint ventures to the challenge of regeneration and restoration.

The Project has been an outstanding success, with visitor numbers far exceeding estimates – in its first eight months of operation, a total of 1.4 million people visited the site, making it the fourth most popular 'paid-for' attraction in the UK during 2001. The Project employs local people as much as possible, making a direct contribution to the local economy. The surrounding communities of southwest England have also benefited from the Project's success, with local businesses reporting that the Eden Project has extended the tourist season considerably, with revenues for September and October 2001 up by more that 14%. In fact, the 'Eden Effect' has so far contributed more than £111 million to the surrounding economy (Eden Project, 2001).

From the start Eden was going to be more than just a visitor attraction. For Tim Smit, the creative visionary behind the Project, it was about 'people being able to do something good in the world'. His aim with Eden was to put the fun back into the environmental movement, which he perceived as having become somewhat joyless and worthy, resulting in the public losing interest in the topic.

The supporting belief for this vision was that, without plants, human life would not survive, and Smit felt that people had begun to lose sight of the importance of their relationship with the natural plant world. He wanted the Eden Project to emphasise the serious function of plants, and as a result its core concept is based upon science and research. Although it is first and foremost a visitor attraction, Eden aims to educate and inform the visitor in an entertaining and inspirational manner.

Eden has acted as a catalyst for regeneration, not just for Cornwall as a place to live and work, but also for increasing the visitor's knowledge of the natural world. Its declared mission is 'to promote the understanding and responsible management of the vital relationships between plants, people and resources, leading to a sustainable future for all' and this is at the centre of its activities. It aims to achieve this through supporting a range of science, research and education projects, and working closely with partners to search for real solutions to real problems. Eden's point of difference as an attraction, however, is not limited to local partnerships.

The educational spirit of Eden has established links with schools and universities, not just in the UK but also on a global scale. Conservation projects set up through Eden include supporting research into the revegetation of desertified land on St Helena, encouraging environmental awareness among children and supporting research on beneficial deployment of waste on landfill sites. Eden supports other projects, such as conservation of rare island plants in the Seychelles, community forest programmes in Thailand's mangroves, as well as pioneering work into promoting social inclusion in the UK. Overseas links for these conservation projects are central to the attraction's aims. The Eden experience thus exists on different levels: as a tourist attraction, an educational experience and a serious scientific contributor to understanding the relationship between the natural and the human world.

An example of Eden's educational programme is the 'Feeding Minds, Fighting Hunger' project, an educational initiative for a world free of hunger, centred on annual World Food Day. It aims to engage students and teachers at three levels – primary, intermediate and secondary – in a better understanding of the causes of global hunger and malnutrition. Booklets and other resources are available to teachers, free of charge, either by post or through the website, to help them plan lessons around the relevant topics. These lessons are designed to last 45 minutes while teachers are encouraged to adapt them to local interests and cultures. Each lesson contains suggested activities and discussion points to enable teachers to engage their pupils in an understanding of the global debate.

Eden's serious intent for its educational role is demonstrated through their choice of global partner organisations for this programme. Key partners include UNESCO, the National Peace Corps Association, and the United States National Committee for World Food Day. By linking with such partners Eden ensures its credibility.

The scientific research and the global/local sustainability projects work hand in hand with the educational remit of Eden. The result is a truly sustainable attraction. By appealing to target markets such as scientists and teachers they are sustaining a long-term interest in the Project as an attraction. Without these core activities Eden would be just another tourist attraction, a 'green' theme park, subject to the whims of tourists' trends, and possibly becoming an unfashionable 'white elephant' in a part of the country that already experiences the problems associated with tourism and seasonality.

By cultivating a global audience and creating a worthwhile and valuable platform for debate, Eden is ensuring its own survival in what is often thought to be a fickle, superficial and short-term tourism industry.

Economic impacts

The positive economic impacts of tourism have been widely acknowledged by many governments and global institutions, such as the World Travel and Tourism Council (WTTC) and the World Tourism Organization (WTO), and have been discussed previously in Chapter 1. It is not surprising that the positive economic impacts of ecotourism have also received heightened attention and are often cited as the main reason for the promotion of ecotourism by developing countries, as it provides an attractive investment option and business opportunity (Cater, 1993). While estimates of the economic benefits vary from US$10 billion to well over US$200 billion in 1992 (see Jenner & Smith, 1992; Ceballos-Lascuráin,

1992 in Cater, 1993), other estimates note that anywhere between 1.5% and 25% of world travel could be defined as ecotourism (Whelan, 1991; Giannecchini, 1993). This difference, according to Weaver (1999), is dependent upon the adoption of a broad or 'passive' definition of ecotourism compared to a specialised or 'active' definition. Furthermore, he notes that there is still no solid statistical base for any of the global estimates surrounding ecotourism and in particular assessing the economic impact of 'passive' versus 'active' forms of ecotourism.

Some small-scale local economic opportunities exist for residents located adjacent to parks and ecotourism development. However, a lack of statistical data exists on the impacts of ecotourism on quality of life and residents' standard of living in ecotourism destinations and localities (Weaver, 1999). Generally, though, as Butler (1991) notes, in wilderness areas there is often nothing to spend money on. Weaver (1999) agrees and notes that, despite park entry fees and some limited spending, little direct economic impact exists in Costa Rica and Kenya; however he notes that indirect impacts on other 'non-ecotourism' products may be more substantial and involve more of the local population. Some positive economic impacts are generated for some residents, but most research indicates that only the elite benefit from ecotourism development, particularly in the developing world (see Weaver, 1999).

Foreign developers are often involved in ecotourism projects, particularly in less developed countries which often do not have the domestic capital for large-scale ecotourism investment or development. As Cater (1993) noted in the case of Belize, 90% of all coastal development is owned by foreign companies. Not only can this create social problems and resentment among local people, but also foreign ownership can limit the amount of economic benefit that remains in the host country concerned. Evidence suggests that leakages of up to 80% are not uncommon in many ecotourism destinations due to high levels of importation (Britton, 1982; Shackley, 1993). However, the developing world needs the foreign investment and expertise to modernise its tourist facilities and provide employment opportunities for the local population. This dilemma between foreign ownership, economic development and modernisation is illustrated in the case of the Galapagos Islands.

With regard to the economic impact of cultural heritage tourism, one of the positive outcomes of its development has been the use of this form of tourism to assist with the economic and social restructuring of urban areas. Following the economic restructuring of many regions and the subsequent loss of heavy industry in many industrial and waterfront areas in the 1970s and 1980s, tourism has been perceived as a mechanism to regenerate urban areas through the creation of leisure, retail and tourism space. This process appears almost universal in the developed world. Such a situation led Harvey (1988 in Urry, 1990: 128) to ask, 'How many museums, cultural centres, convention and exhibition halls, hotels, marinas, shopping malls, waterfront developments can we stand?' Similarly, Zukin (1992: 221) observed that the city is a site of spectacle, a 'dreamscape of visual consumption'.

Bilbao in the north of Spain is one such destination that is using cultural heritage tourism as part of an urban development strategy to regenerate the city. The building of a Guggenheim Museum, tourist attractions and hotels are part of a strategy to regenerate the area by attracting tourists and business and creating employment in the city. As Richards (1996) notes, the concepts of culture and economic capital, both useful for regeneration, are intertwined, as demonstrated by the 900,000 visitors that chose to view the Bilbao Guggenheim Museum in 2001. A similar strategy has been developed in many urban destinations throughout the Western world. In Australia, Sydney has also redeveloped its former waterfront area (Darling Harbour) with the use of cultural heritage attractions, including a Maritime Museum, National Aquarium, and The Powerhouse Museum, while its fierce rival Melbourne has developed a similar strategy along its riverside.

In England, destinations such as Liverpool and London have developed cultural tourism attractions along their waterfronts to help regenerate these areas. In Liverpool the Beatles Museum and Liverpool Maritime Museum are located in former warehouses, while in London the South Bank has been recently redeveloped with the imitation Shakespeare Globe Theatre and the Tate Modern Art Gallery, which attracted 5.25 million visitors in its first year of operation. From UK visitors to the gallery 21% cited the building as a major factor for visiting, as it is viewed as an outstanding piece of architecture comprising part of the old bankside power station. However, as Kennedy (2001: 3) rightly points out, many of the people come for the 'experience of viewing the building, as they might visit a theme park, rather than to see the art', although this is disputed by the gallery management. Nevertheless, consultants have estimated that the gallery has provided an economic benefit of £100 million and 3,000 jobs for the local community (Kennedy, 2001).

Environmental impacts

Although 'active' definitions of ecotourism purport that this form of tourism can contribute to conservation and preservation, the majority of studies and research note that, although this can be the case, the reality is often that the tourism and conservation are more often than not in conflict. With increasing numbers of visitors exploring potentially fragile destinations and locations, pressures on the destination can impact both directly and indirectly, with often-interrelated negative environmental impacts that can affect:

- vegetation (through plant collection, trampling and camping);
- water and air quality (through pollution from tourist developments);
- wildlife (through disruption of feeding and breeding patterns, and changes in predator–prey relationships); and
- geological structures (through soil structure modification caused by compaction and changes in chemistry due to waste disposal and erosion of soil).

According to Hunter and Green (1995: 13), the ecological environment is a delicate system which has taken a considerable time to evolve and self-regulate, but it can be destroyed or impacted upon negatively by tourism and tourist activity. For example, mangrove swamps and vegetation have been cleared to make way for coastal resort development in Belize in order to provide facilities for the general ecotourism market (Cater, 1993). Balancing demands between tourists and locals is a difficult process and one that looks likely to continue as tourist numbers and the world population grows.

With the growth in visitor numbers to ecotourism destinations, and the move toward nature-based experiences within mass tourism, the need for facilities and infrastructure will continue to grow. As Cater (1993) notes, as facilities and infrastructure are created to serve for increasing numbers of ecotourists, then the environment will become degraded and resource conflicts will occur more frequently. Similarly, animals will be displaced from their local habitat to make room for tourist developments. Demand for souvenirs, trophies and gifts by nature-based tourists has resulted in the killing of animals and marine life to cater for their needs. This is best demonstrated in African countries where animals have been killed to provide souvenirs for tourists (see Dupuy, 1987 in Hunter & Green, 1995), while in the Pacific Islands Milne (1990) noted similar patterns in the production of marine souvenirs for tourists. However, the increasing involvement of the local population in ecotourism ventures, coupled with education of tourists may lead to a reduction in the killing of wildlife and marine life for tourist purposes.

However, there have been positive impacts associated with the growth of tourism. Sofield (2000) challenges the deforestation crisis and environmental degradation claims made concerning Nepal. He notes that Nepal has one of the better forestry regimes in Asia, with 14% of the country classified as a protected area and with 90% of tourist-related revenue supporting the management of these sites (Sofield, 2000: 229). Shackley (1993) noted that deforestation and competition between residents and tourists for firewood was leading to negative environmental impacts in Nepal, but Sofield (2000) disagrees and illustrates that tourism has not facilitated deforestation, but that in fact initiatives by locals and organisations have led to reforestation and greater cover. In fact, in a review of twenty tourism development projects carried out by inter-governmental agencies, all have components related to countering fuel-wood consumption. Sofield (2000) notes that this may be partly due to the myth of deforestation.

However, although the number of cultural heritage sites has increased rapidly over the last two decades, overcrowding at popular sites is common (see Jenner & Smith, 1992).

Some heritage tourist sites, particularly popular ones such as World Heritage Sites, can be overused, resulting in damage to buildings and landscapes and a reduced educational experience for visitors. Stonehenge in England is one example that has grappled with how to deal with the growth of visitors to the site and surrounding area. The site has been a popular tourist attraction with close to one million visitors. Prior to the 1960s there was no formal management of the site and this led to some destruction and souveniring, which was stopped with the introduction of fences and a more formalised management presence.

However, with the growth in tourist numbers, combined with the motoring age, more car park and tourist facilities were required. Site managers have introduced unique ways to try to provide facilities for car parking and ancillary services without detracting from the Stonehenge experience. First, an underground tunnel allowed access to the site and an entrance fee was raised to discourage an increase in visitor numbers. Future plans in a £155 million project between English Heritage, the Highways Agency and The National Trust are to:

- build a tunnel to hide the traffic and restore the landscape by removing the current visitor centre;

- create a full-sized replica of Stonehenge and a new visitor centre away from the original site; and
- use theme park buggies to carry tourists to and from the site.

Personal impacts

One of the major components of an ecotourism experience is the personal impact that it may have upon tourists. This experience can vary from being simply enjoyable and pleasurable to being an educative experience which challenges ecotourists' behaviour and imparts conservation ethics. The personal impacts will obviously differ due to the type of ecotourism experience offered (passive or active, soft or hard) the type of product consumed (luxury ecolodge, environmental charity) and the motivations of ecotourists themselves (towards learning and education or simply to relax and enjoy the natural setting).

Research conducted on the characteristics of ecotourists visiting Australia showed that an educational learning experience was rated less than important on average, and no more important than 'something to tell my friends about' as a motivating factor (Blamey & Hatch, 1998). Seeing the natural beauty of sites was the main motivating factor, followed by a chance to see or experience something new, seeing wildlife in detail, being close to nature, and undertaking a different or unique way of experiencing nature. These findings, according to Blamey and Hatch (1998), suggest that the most important motivations correspond to stimulation, self-esteem, development and fulfilment motives. Other researchers have identified that, although ecotourists are more sophisticated and educated, they are after all on holiday, and so may not necessarily be interested in learning or education (Geelong Otway Tourism, 1995 in Ryan *et al.*, 2000). Wheeller (1994) agrees and believes that ecotourism is really about massaging our egos as travellers and making us feel good about our consumption patterns. In light of this Wheeller (1994) redefines ecotourism as 'egotourism'.

Evidence from self-defined ecotourists at Fogg Dam in Australia suggests that more 'active' roles claimed by visitors were exaggerated and that visitors sought a 'passive' experience by simply driving over the dam wall and visiting the observation deck rather than undertaking many of the nearby walks (Ryan *et al.*, 2000: 155). The researchers noted that the ecotourism experience was an affective encounter rather than an occasion for participating in cognitive learning. Ryan *et al.* (2000: 157) also noted that, when visitors were asked if they would describe Fogg Dam as an ecotourism experience, nearly all respondents agreed. However, as the authors note:

> why was this, given that 62% of the visitors spent less than 60 minutes there, that about a quarter were unable to list 3 species of birds and a third could not list 3 types of plants in spite of information being provided? (Ryan *et al.*, 2000: 157)

The researchers concluded that the experience at this particular setting is a hedonistic and social activity rather than a learning and educational experience. However, in contrast to this it has been noted that those who take part in ecotourism as part of a larger trip tend to be the least pro-environmental in their attitudes (Uysal *et al.*, 1994). Beaumont (2001), in examining the environmental interest and involvement of ecotourists, discovered that commercial ecotourists (coach day visitors and guests) had stronger ecotourist motivations than the independent groups (day visitors and campers), although less than one-third of them were classified as hard ecotourists. Immediately after their visit it was also these visitors who were the most likely to say that the visit had influenced their conservation views and their behavioural intentions (Beaumont, 2001: 336). The research suggests that those with the lowest environmental interest and weakest attitudes initially will be influenced most through any ecotourism experience, compared to those who may already have strong environmental attitudes.

Although the personal and educational impacts of visits to cultural heritage attractions have been noted there is debate, similar to that of the educational and personal benefits of ecotourism experiences, over the educational value of such visits. Research on visitor motivations suggests that heritage visits are not necessarily motivated by a desire to 'learn about the past'. As Markwell *et al.* (1997: 97) state, 'a widely propagated myth, which has been fuelled by visitor surveys, is that people visit heritage sites to learn, yet studies also show that visitors do not appear to learn very much'. This could be partly attributed to the motivations of heritage visitors and the changing consumption of cultural experiences, with some authors noting that cultural heritage visitors are often after a leisure experience rather than an educational one (Prentice, 1993; Schouten, 1995). Swarbrooke (1996) suggests that the purchasing of cultural experiences is perhaps perceived more as a leisure product than as a cultural experience. Yet longitudinal evidence surrounding the educational motivations of cultural heritage visitors is lacking and there is limited empirical evidence available concerning this issue. What has been noted, however, is the need to try and identify and evaluate the impacts and benefits of cultural heritage on society, including learning and education. David Anderson's (1997) report 'A Common Wealth' reviewed the current activities of museums in the UK as centres for learning and stated that:

> it is not acceptable for museums to justify their existence to a significant degree in terms of their educational value in a society, and yet to be unable to specify what that value is in concrete and practical terms ... most museum directors, if asked to demonstrate that the museum benefits society, would be unable to do so (in Thinesse-Demel, 2001).

So, although some authors believe cultural heritage tourism to be important for learning, education and society generally, limited empirical or longitudinal research has been carried out on visitors' learning and education from such visits.

Conclusion

This chapter has discussed the demand for educational holidays or 'edu-tourism' within the global tourist industry and the reasons for this increased demand. The chapter examined the two largest tourist segments where education and learning are important components of the tourist product and experience, namely nature-based tourism, or ecotourism, and cultural heritage tourism. Within these two major market segments the demand, supply of product, impacts and major management issues for this form of 'tourism first' educational tourism have been considered and discussed. The following chapters examine segments of educational tourism, namely adult and seniors' educational tourism, schools' educational tourism and university/college students' tourism.

Case Study 2.1

Segmentation of educational tendencies among tourist markets: Ecolodge patrons at Lamington National Park, Australia

By David Weaver and Laura Lawton

In 1999, a major market segmentation study was conducted among the domestic overnight patrons of two well-known and adjacent Australian ecolodges (Binna Burra Mountain Lodge and O'Reilly's Rainforest Guesthouse) to identify distinctive sub-sectors among these consumers of a specialised ecotourism product (Weaver & Lawton, 2002). A 16-page questionnaire was sent to a random sample of 3000 patrons (1500 from each facility), from which 1180 valid responses were received. Segmentation was achieved through a cluster analysis of the first section of the questionnaire, which consisted of 37 Likert-type statements that pertained to the actual and intended ecotourism-related behaviour of the respondents. The questionnaire sought to obtain information on the respondents' overall ecotourism behaviour, and not just in relation to their experiences at the two ecolodges. The 37 statements were designed to reflect the core criteria that are now widely associated with ecotourism, including the desirability of educational and learning-related outcomes for participants (Blamey, 1997).

The cluster analysis itself revealed three distinct groups. 'Harder' ecotourists (34%), with their strong support for enhancement sustainability and untouched settings, largely conformed to the expected characteristics of hard ecotourists. The use of 'harder' instead of 'hard' is based on the assumptions that the truly hard ecotourists are more likely to eschew fixed-roof accommodation and other site-related services. In contrast, 'softer' ecotourists (27%) were similar to soft ecotourists in their preference for services, lower commitment to the environment, and tendency to participate in ecotourism as part of a multi-purpose tourism experience. The use of the relative term 'softer' suggests that the true soft ecotourist is likely to be a day-tripper who does not use specialised overnight ecolodge accommodation. The third cluster (40%) were 'structured' ecotourists who emulated the services-preferences of the softer group but had similar environmental views to the harder ecotourists.

Table 2.6 provides the overall and cluster-specific mean responses to six statements in the first section that were directly related to the education and learning criterion of ecotourism. These are listed in descending order based on the overall means on a five-point scale (where 5 = 'strongly agree' and 1 = 'strongly disagree'). Not surprisingly, all groups revealed a strong desire to learn as much as possible during their visits about the natural environment of ecotourism destinations, although the desire of softer ecotourists to do so was significantly lower than that of respondents from the other two groups. These responses were corroborated in the motivations section of the questionnaire, where 'learning about the natural environment' scored 4.04 overall, with the softer group at 3.73 registering significantly lower than the harder (4.17) or structured (4.14) ecotourists. A similar pattern of relationship among the three clusters, but a greater level of ambivalence, was revealed in the statement about

Table 2.6 Education- and learning-related behavioural statement means by ecotourist cluster

Statement	*Overall mean*	*Clusters*		
		Softer	*Harder*	*Structured*
I want to learn as much as possible about the natural environment of the sites that I visit while I am there.	4.04	*3.73*	4.17[3]	4.14[2]
My ecotourism participation has made me more environmentally conscientious.	3.99	*3.66*	4.11[3]	4.11[2]
I learn more about the natural environment on an escorted tour than through travelling on my (or our) own.	3.74	3.75	*3.39*	**4.03**
I prefer ecotourism sites at which the natural attractions are interpreted or explained to me.	3.66	3.65	*3.34*	**3.94**
I try to find out as much about the natural environment of a destination as I can before I actually go there.	3.54	*3.13*	3.75[3]	3.65[2]
I like my ecotourism experiences to be mentally challenging.	3.22	*2.78*	**3.49**	3.28

Notes: All ANOVAs significant at the 0.000 level.

Superscript indicates that this value is not significantly different from the value in the indicated cluster. Bold numbers signify means that are significantly higher than the other two clusters. Underlined numbers signify means that are significantly lower than the other two clusters.

pre-experience, *off*-site learning. Pending further investigation, this may indicate a desire to avoid any pre-empting of the actual experience that could result from assimilating too much knowledge or information in advance. The phenomenon of pre-experience and off-site learning, in general, is a neglected area of ecotourism-related education that requires more research (Weaver, 2001a).

Very different response patterns were evident in questions regarding interpretation, which is a central concept of ecotourism given its function of conveying meaningful and interesting information to ecotourists. Similar outcomes were obtained on statements pertaining to the superior learning outcomes of escorted tours and the preference for mediated sites. In both cases, the structured ecotourists scored significantly higher than the other groups, while hard ecotourists scored significantly lower than the softer or structured clusters. The latter appears to corroborate the conventional wisdom that hard ecotourists tend to prefer unmediated interactions with the natural environment. Yet it must also be borne in mind that this level of preference is relative to the other groups; the actual mean values for harder ecotourists on these two statements (3.39 and 3.34) still indicate substantial support for interpretation.

The statement on ecotourism participation is important in so far as it reflects the outcomes or *post*-experience dimension of the ecotourism-based learning experience. The overall mean of 3.99 indicates that most respondents were positively impacted by their ecotourism participation in terms of their attitudes toward the environment. The extent to which this derives from effective interpretation requires further investigation, though evidence from the Tangalooma Dolphin Feeding Programme on Moreton Island, near Brisbane, suggests the positive role of interpretation in fostering more environmentally aware behaviour (Orams, 1997). Yet, it is somewhat ironic that, while environmental well-being is an inherently serious and challenging topic, the respondents were ambivalent about the extent to which they preferred mentally challenging ecotourism experiences (overall mean = 3.22). Harder ecotourists were more positive in this respect, though not overwhelmingly so (3.49), while softer ecotourists showed the least inclination (2.78). This may attest to the importance of environmentalism-oriented interpretation that avoids a pedantic, heavy-handed approach.

There were no gender differences among the three clusters, while structured ecotourists were significantly older than harder ecotourists. However, to obtain more insight into the influence of age and gender on the responses, the means of the statements were also examined in terms of these variables. As depicted in Table 2.7, older respondents (those 65 or older) are more likely to prefer interpretation, to pursue pre-experiential learning and to seek mentally challenging experiences. Females are more likely than males to want to seek on-site learning and to express the belief that ecotourism has made them more environmentally responsible. While this data indicates that advanced age and female gender are positively related with the desire to seek educational outcomes from ecotourism among ecolodge patrons, these are propositions that require further investigation from other case studies and other ecotourist market segments.

Table 2.7 Education- and learning-related behavioural statement means by age and gender

Statement	*<65*	*65+*	*F*	*M*
I want to learn as much as possible about the natural environment of the sites that I visit while I am there.	4.03	4.11	4.09	3.97
My ecotourism participation has made me more environmentally conscientious.	4.01	3.92	4.06	3.88
I learn more about the natural environment on an escorted tour than through travelling on my (or our) own.	3.70	3.93	3.73	3.74
I prefer ecotourism sites in which the natural attractions are interpreted or explained to me.	3.62	3.82	3.68	3.61
I try to find out as much about the natural environment of a destination as I can before I actually go there.	3.52	3.71	3.56	3.53
I like my ecotourism experiences to be mentally challenging.	3.19	3.32	3.20	3.24

Note: Underline indicates significant difference at the 95% probability level.

Case Study 2.2

Former Nazi concentration camps in Germany: Memorials or tourist attractions?

By Teresa Leopold and Brent Ritchie

As previously discussed in this chapter there has been a growth in the search for 'postmodern' tourist experiences combined with a growth in the provision of more specialised and distinctive cultural heritage product. Related to this has been the growth and development of attractions associated with death, war, disaster and tragedy (see Lennon & Foley, 2000). These attractions are categorised under the concept of 'dark tourism', which signifies the arguable change in attitudes towards these sites. Former German concentration camps can be positioned within this common trend due to their growing acceptance as visitor attractions. This trend has developed more rapidly over the last 20 years, placing increasing pressure on the managers of German concentration camps to transform their memorial sites for Holocaust families and friends into more mainstream tourist attractions catering for visitors. Some authors such as Swarbrooke (1996) question whether places such as former Nazi concentration camps should even be developed as cultural tourism products, illustrating the dilemma faced by site managers.

Although Second World War concentration camps have been perceived by visitors and indeed site managers as memorial sites, nowadays they are becoming more tourist-orientated and are facing demands from tourists for associated facilities and commercial development. As such, the changing nature of concentration camp memorials is highlighting potential conflicts between preservation and authenticity of sites versus commercial development. This pressure is made even more complicated by the reduction of government funding for many of the former German concentration camps and the need for alternative sources of funding which tourism can provide. Research was carried out in the form of a postal survey to managers of eleven concentration camp memorials in Germany during 2001 (see Leopold, 2001) asking questions concerning tourism development and changes in the management of these sites.

Figure 2.3 illustrates the phases related to the Holocaust as a disaster on a chronological basis, and the changing demand, product and marketing characteristics dominating these phases, through the use of literature and theory from Katz (1989), Kotler *et al.* (1996), Lutz (1994) and Young (1993 in Leopold, 2001). The research illustrates that the main function of Holocaust testimony has changed with the passage of time from commemorating and praying for the loss of life associated with former German concentration camps towards learning and understanding how this tragedy occurred. This transformation is interrelated with the changing target market moving away from immediate friends and families of Holocaust victims towards a broader audience interested in visiting and learning about the camps and their role in the Holocaust. Thus, the research findings identified the main market of the memorials as being German pupils, who are within the age bracket of 18 or younger. Considering that the main target market consists of pupils, the increased importance of the educational aspect becomes obvious.

Furthermore, the growing number of visitors, identified by the majority of managers of these sites, clearly supports the change in motivation of visits to the memorials. These changes in demand characteristics emphasise the change in perceptions, interpretation and representation of these memorial sites. Guided tours, information leaflets and visitor books have become regular components of the sites.

Naturally, concentration camp memorials have had to cater for the increasing numbers of visitors. Thus, new facilities have been added and new information channels have had to be developed to cater for this changing market. These new facilities often correspond to commercialisation, which plays a major role in the development of tourism at the memorial sites, including the development of visitor facilities and ancillary services.

Research undertaken illustrates a relationship between low visitor numbers at some memorials and increased self-financing initiatives such as entrance fees and visitor services and facilities. However, sites with large visitor numbers are provided with more revenue through government funding at the national or regional level and are less likely to require revenue generation through tourism, yet paradoxically they receive larger numbers of visitors. This may mean that smaller memorial sites may have to commercialise their operations in order to generate additional revenue sources and continue operating.

Furthermore, educative aspects of memorial sites are not only accompanied by elements of commodification and commercial ethics, but also include authentic features, which are the main attraction of dark tourism sites. However, some of the authenticity of these attractions may be lost due to tourism and commercial development. Nevertheless, it should be

Phase 1 (to 1960s)	Phase 2 (1960s–1970s)	Phase 3 (1980s on)
General Response Silence after the tragic event of the Holocaust Withdrawal from emotion experienced Little heard from survivors and public Inability of Germans to face their past or past of the country	*General Response* Expression of anger Attempts to understand behaviour of individuals with responsibility Emergence of concentration camps as memorials	*General Response* Emergence of more memorials Greater funding of larger memorials by government Rise in tourist use
	Demand Characteristics Small number of visitors Friends/Family/Soldiers Motivations related to commemorating and praying	*Demand Characteristics* Large number of visitors School groups and youth Motivations related to education, learning and understanding
	Product Characteristics Core product (commemoration and preservation) Facilitating product (eye-witness accounts, understanding of history, honouring friends' and relatives' 'people') Supporting product (car parking and opening times, visitor comment books re Holocaust)	*Product Characteristics* Core product (education, learning and understanding for future generations) Facilitating product (Provision of guides and interpreting 'the event') Supporting product (visitor services, souvenirs, information leaflets, visitor comment books re attraction)
	Marketing Characteristics Little in the way of traditional marketing Information provided to soldiers and friends and relatives of deceased	*Marketing Characteristics* Limited use of brochures, local tourist offices, media Price included in some attractions Visitor research and evaluation

Figure 2.3 The changing nature of concentration camps in Germany from memorials to tourist attractions

Sources: Adapted from Katz (1989)' Kotler *et al.* (1996); Lutz (1994); Young (1993). All cited in Leopold (2001)

considered that the emergence of a tourist market often facilitates the preservation of memorials and traditions, which otherwise may have perished (Cohen, 1988).

One memorial site facing increasing pressure to develop its facilities to cater for tourists is the memorial site at Dachau, north of Munich, Germany. After the Second World War the concentration camp at Dachau housed refugees and displaced persons and subsequently fell into disrepair. In 1955, on the tenth anniversary of the liberation of the camp, the first international meeting of former camp prisoners took place and the decision was made to create a dignified and worthy memorial at Dachau. In 1960 a provisional museum was opened in the former crematorium building and in 1965 the current memorial site and museum opened with the financial support of the government of Bavaria. At this time the derelict barrack buildings were demolished and two of the huts were reconstructed to cater for visitors, while a Carmelite convent was established in 1964. Further memorials were created in the following years, with a Jewish memorial temple constructed in 1965, an international memorial in 1968, and a Russian Orthodox chapel in 1995.

The museum presents the history of the Dachau concentration camp from 1933 until 1945, and illustrates how it came into being and how it was developed during the Nazi era, first as a training centre, and then as a model camp for Hitler's Secret Service and a training ground for the extermination camps of Auschwitz, Majdanek and Treblinka. Attached to the current museum are a cinema, archives and a specialist library. The museum has not undertaken any renovations or commercial development since the site opened in 1965. There is no retail or ancillary service such as a café or restaurant and technology includes the use of a cinema video. Interpretation is provided by way of captions in five languages (German, English, French, Italian and Russian) and consists of traditional static exhibits with a limited amount of sensory media and poor orientation and layout. These setting factors could very well lead to mindlessness as previously discussed in this chapter. However, the educational motives of visitors and high interest in the content may limit the amount of mindlessness at this particular heritage site; but, as time passes and visitor connections to, and knowledge of, the Holocaust decline, interest may wane. Currently half of the museum is closed (as of late 2001) for renovation and reconstruction and this may provide a substantial improvement to the setting factors (displays, interaction and orientation), which may provide more mindful experiences to a broader audience of visitors.

Only time will tell whether the redevelopment of former concentration camp memorials such as Dachau will enhance the tourist experience or whether this development will detract from the authenticity of the site through the creation of facilities and services to suit the needs of tourists.

Chapter 3

Adult and Seniors' Educational Tourism

Introduction

The adult market, and in particular the seniors' or older tourist market, is a rapidly growing component of the tourist industry that is predicted to grow in the future. The definition of 'senior' is becoming blurred due to an increasing number of early retirees coupled with increased longevity. Furthermore, there is some confusion in the industry concerning the exact age at which someone becomes a 'senior'. The tourism industry generally understands the term 'senior traveller' to be someone over the age of 55, although some travel organisations such as the Saga Group have reduced the age to 50, while others consider 'senior' travellers to be over 60 or 65 years of age (Smith & Jenner, 1997b). Ruys and Wei (2001: 409) note that the classification of someone as older or 'senior' is debatable as age is not a reliable indicator of physical health or consumer behaviour. This lack of consistency can confuse statistical collection and subsequently impair the understanding of the nature and true size and scope of this market segment.

Despite this confusion, the characteristics of the adult or 'senior' market ensure that it is not only viable, but also potentially profitable. The high travel propensity of this group coupled with their growing desire for life-long learning will continue to increase the provision of educational travel in the future. This chapter outlines the growing demand for adult educational tourism with an emphasis on adult continuing education and the 'senior'/baby boomers' market. The chapter also outlines the nature of this demand and the growing provision from the local and global tourism industry. The chapter then discusses the impacts of the adult educational tourism market and management implications associated with this specific segment.

Demand for Seniors' Educational Tourism

As discussed in Chapter 2 the growth of special interest travel combined with the self-development needs of the older population ensure the growing interest in adult educational travel. An increasing number of adults are interested in keeping active and continuing their education, while for many retirement provides an opportunity to return to study and combine this with travel. As the population demographic changes and the number of people aged over 55 increases, so too will this potential tourist market, providing significant opportunities for educational tourism providers.

The ageing population and tourism opportunities

As a result of demographic changes, including a declining birth rate and increasing life expectancy, the world population is ageing. In particular, developed countries have already begun to experience population changes, such as declining birth and mortality rates, and it is these same countries which are the largest generators and receivers of tourist arrivals (see Table 3.1). According to the United Nations (2001) 'the number of persons aged 60 years or older is estimated to be nearly 600 million in 1999, and is projected to grow to almost 2 billion by 2050, at which time the population of older persons will be larger than the population of children (0–14 years) for the first time in human history'. Other ageing population trends identified by the United Nations (2001) include:

- the majority of older persons are women;
- the older population itself is ageing with an increasing number of persons aged over 80 years as a result of lengthening life expectancy.

The tourism implications of an ageing population include a potentially lucrative market for leisure and tourism services. This market is often perceived to have a high discretionary income and time to participate in such services. As Smith and Jenner (1997b) note, in Japan and the USA workers reach their peak earnings at around the 45–54-year bracket, although some seniors' ability to finance travel will be better than others. This is conditional on their income levels, their financial dependence and whether they live with partners or dependants. Early retirement appears to be on the increase as is an improvement in income levels (see Smith & Jenner, 1997b: 54–55). However, this is dependent upon many variables, including government policy and continued economic growth and prosperity in Western countries. Other possible constraints to the market

Table 3.1 Senior (55+) population of main generating countries, 1997

Country	*Total population ('000)*	*Population 55+ ('000)*	*Senior population (% share)*
European			
Italy	57,534	16,559	28.8
Germany	84,068	23,846	28.4
Greece	10,583	2,988	28.2
Sweden	8,946	2,436	27.2
Belgium	10,204	2,725	26.7
Austria	8,054	2,101	26.1
Spain	39,244	10,257	26.1
Portugal	9,868	2,535	25.7
Denmark	5,269	1,349	25.6
UK	58,610	14,971	25.5
France	58,470	14,678	25.1
Luxembourg	422	104	24.6
Finland	5,109	1,254	24.5
Netherlands	15,653	3,603	23.0
Ireland	3,556	695	19.5
Other			
Japan	125,717	35,221	28.0
USA	267,955	55,913	20.9
Taiwan	21,656	3,288	15.2
Mexico	97,563	9,043	9.3
Saudi Arabia	20,088	1,331	6.6

Source: US Bureau of the Census, modified after Smith and Jenner (1997b: 47)

include the 'sandwich' dilemma noted by Loverseed (1997), whereby seniors may be increasingly forced to cope with a growing family and the demands of parents who may be in ill health. This could considerably reduce the amount of discretionary income and time available for travel, but on the other hand it could increase the need for ordinary or educational travel to escape from the home situation.

As Lurhman (in Dann, 2001: 236) notes, the rise in tourist arrivals combined with an ageing population will provide opportunities for the tourism industry. Smith and Jenner (1997b: 55) estimated a total of 95 million international arrivals by senior travellers in 1996, and 136 million worldwide in 2000, with 85 million in the European Union alone. Table 3.1 illustrates that Italy and Germany are large European markets for potential seniors' tourism, while Japan and the United States are also important target markets with 28% and 20.9% of their respective populations over 55 years of age. According to Smith and Jenner (1997b: 61), although people over 55 years in the USA make up one-fifth of the population, they account for almost half of the long haul trips. Lurhman (in Dann, 2001: 236) notes that Germany is the major generating market for seniors' tourism with 20% of its nationals over 60, followed by the UK (16%), France (30%) and Italy (24%); and for the over-55 market, he notes that Spain (15%), the United States (33%), Canada (28%) and Japan (27%) are the main potential markets. The differences between these statistics and Table 3.1 illustrate the confusion over the exact nature and size of the seniors' market.

As the CTC (2001: 15) note, adults and older adults are at the stage of their lives when they have the time to travel and enjoy learning. Similarly, as discussed in Chapter 1, the growth of lifelong learning as a concept and the promotion of further education in many countries will facilitate this process. In Canada tour operators and non-profit educational tourism organisers are targeting the older market and baby boomers. Table 3.2 illustrates the target markets for non-profit providers and tour operators in Canada and the differences in how they classify their target markets, with tour operators focusing on baby boomers and young adults, compared to non-profit organisations who also include adults and families.

Another factor affecting the growth of adult educational tourism concerns social tourism policies that are developed to subsidise holidays for older persons who are vulnerable and suffer from poor health or social exclusion. These people are provided with holidays as a basic human right in some European countries. As Murphy (1985: 24) comments, 'social tourism has become a recognized component and legitimate objective for modern tourism. By extending the physical and psychological benefits of

Table 3.2 Educational tourism target markets in Canada: non-profit organisations and tour operators (% respondents)

	Non-profit organisations		*Tour operators*	
Target markets	*1998*	*1999*	*1998*	*1999*
Adults	92	116	–	–
Seniors	42	47	87	100
Baby boomers	–	–	41	42
Families	17	26	–	–
Young adults	–	–	2	5
Students	7	7	3	5

Source: Adapted from Canadian Tourism Commission (2001: 15–16)

rest and travel to less fortunate people it can be looked upon as a form of preventative medicine.' Urbain Claeys (in Dann, 2001) suggests that in Belgium those participants involved in social tourism are increasingly seeking educational experiences which were postponed when they were working or raising children. Social tourism provides travel experiences for 400,000 people annually in Spain and approximately 48,000 in Portugal, with the policy of social tourism implemented in many more European countries (Dann, 2001).

These trends will undoubtedly provide many opportunities and challenges for the tourism industry as it attempts to provide products to cater for the ageing adult market segment and their educational needs. According to the British Tourist Authority (2001) the over-50 population has more discretionary income than young adults, controls 41% of discretionary income and owns 77% of all financial assets. Therefore, this is a market that has the propensity and demand to purchase tourist-related products and services. In particular, the British Tourist Authority (BTA) note that American seniors form an especially important market of travellers to Britain. In Australia, where the domestic tourism market has been slow to grow over the last few years, seniors are seen as a possible tool for growth in this market. Tourism Queensland (2001) summarise the potential of the seniors' market by way of the following:

- Australia's 2.9 million seniors (aged 60 plus) spend $986 million on domestic travel annually.
- 75% of seniors travelled in 1997.
- 80% of seniors want to travel now, or in the near future.

- The seniors market is the fastest growing population group. This will only escalate with thousands of 'baby boomers' turning 60 in a few years' time.
- Seniors spend more time travelling than younger age groups.
- Seniors' discretionary income accounts for greater percentage of their disposable income than other markets as they have significantly fewer outgoing expenses. For example, most have paid off their mortgages and have no dependants.
- Seniors spend a greater percentage of their discretionary income on travelling than any other market segment. While younger age groups have higher income levels, a larger percentage is spent on consumer goods and accumulating assets than on travel.
- Seniors are enjoying better health than previous generations, resulting in increased life expectancies and more time to travel. Nearly 70% of seniors reported feeling in good to excellent health.
- Seniors actively seek new experiences and see travel as offering this.
- Most seniors prefer to travel during off-peak periods, offering a possible solution to seasonal fluctuations.
- Businesses who adapt their products and services to meet the needs of seniors will also be more attractive to the thousands of *foreign* seniors who visit Australia each year. Australia's primary offshore tourism markets (Asia and Europe) also happen to have the largest, fastest growing over-60s populations in the world – a trend that will only escalate.
- Tomorrow's seniors will have enjoyed more regular travel throughout their lives than older generations and will undoubtedly maintain this 'lifestyle priority' in retirement.

The future demand for adult educational tourism experiences is likely to grow as the population ages, and the industry should develop suitable product to meet this demand, which increasingly includes education or learning elements. However, to date little research or attention has focused on this market and their educational travel needs.

Seniors' educational tourist characteristics

As discussed in Chapter 1 age plays a role in the tourist decision-making process and can influence travel demand and propensity. Older travellers have the ability to take holidays outside of the peak tourist season and often have no travel restrictions due to family commitments. The ability of the market to travel off-peak is of importance to the tourism industry which is often restricted due to seasonal constraints. As Smith and Jenner (1997b: 57) note, 'the senior market has long been seen as the salvation of many summer-only tourist resorts, since seniors are usually no longer constrained by school holidays and are not much interested in tanning themselves on the beach'. Research undertaken tends to suggest that older travellers participate in longer and more frequent holidays and are in favour of more geographically isolated areas (Wei & Ruys, 1998; Environmetrics, 1991), providing increased benefits for regional and rural destinations.

Educational levels of ecotourists and cultural heritage tourists have been discussed previously (see Chapter 2). Baby boomer educational levels are high with more than one in four having had a college education and 87% having finished high school (Loverseed, 1997: 47). Table 3.3 illustrates the educational level of the general population compared with participants in the Elderhostel educational travel programmes in Canada. Elderhostel is a non-profit organisation that provides holidays for over-55-year-olds (see Exhibit 3.5). The table illustrates that 90% of Elderhostel participants have post-secondary education, and, according to the CTC (2001: 30), these participants were educated at a time when access to higher education was lower than today, illustrating the potential demand of the baby boomers and future generations for educational holidays and experiences.

With regard to gender, women will outnumber men in the future and it has been suggested that a greater number of women travel today due to socio-demographic changes in the last twenty years (Ruys & Wei, 2001). Richardson (1997), in citing a PATA (Pacific Asia Travel Association) report, notes that in 1995 a total of 238 million women travelled without

Table 3.3 Canadian educational attainment versus Elderhostel participants (%)

Educational attainment	*Years*				
	25–44	*45–54*	*55–64*	*65+*	*Elderhostel 55–92*
High school or less	40	49	64	76	10
Some post-secondary	39	31	23	16	45
University degree	21	20	13	8	45

Source: Adapted from Statistics Canada (1999) and Arsenault (1998) in CTC (2001: 31)

men. The PATA report noted that women particularly travelled to places of historical, cultural or nature-based significance and preferred tours that included educational components. Gibson (1998: 1) also reported a greater propensity for females to engage in educational travel, with 25.8% of females compared with 20% of men from a sample of over 1100 respondents reporting that they took educationally orientated vacations. This increased over the course of the lifecycle with the demand for educational travel reaching its greatest popularity among women in their fifties and sixties (Gibson, 1998). Age also appeared to have an impact on demand for educational tourism, with fewer younger tourists undertaking such trips. Gibson (1998) concluded that the life-course model of Levinson (1996) was particularly important in explaining the demand for educational travel amongst adults, with many aged over 65 participating in educational tourism to provide some kind of meaning or challenge in their lives after retirement.

According to Stuart (1992 in Ruys & Wei, 2001), the older a person becomes the less interested they are in acquiring possessions and the more interested they become in simply 'experiencing' life. While a younger traveller may seek to escape from their home environment, the older traveller wishes to become actively involved in their travel experience. This involvement in a unique, novel or once-in-a-lifetime experience has also been noted by the CTC (2001: 29). Bodger (1998) also believes that a widening of people's interests and appreciation of cultural values has facilitated educational travel. According to Loverseed (1997), baby boomers will seek alternative travel experiences from mass tourism and will seek fun, adventurous, educational and individual experiences. In particular, pursuing a special interest or hobby in a different environment has been noted as important to seniors and baby boomers (Loverseed, 1997). Women in Gibson's (1998) research believed that educational tourism provided them with opportunities for self-expression, creativity and growth, while men reported similar motivations and opportunities for growth and self-discovery.

Loverseed (1997) notes that many baby boomers prefer to educate their own children, and well-travelled boomers are interested in cultural tourism experiences. Although the individual or couple market is the largest potential educational tourism market, family vacations may have promise for the future as the value of learning in travel may be passed on from one generation to the next (CTC, 2001; Dann, 2001). Evidence to suggest this was presented by Hardwick (2000), who reported that nine out of ten educational travellers agreed that international travel is an important investment in the education of their children. However, the extent to which they purchased specific educationally orientated holidays and the nature of these holidays is unknown.

Despite the growth and potential of the seniors' market and their increasing desire for educational tourism, little research has been conducted on their motivations or decision-making behaviour. Research undertaken by Arsenault and MacDonald (2000 in CTC, 2001: 30) examined the factors that influenced consumer choice of an Elderhostel programme and discovered that an intimate, safe and welcoming social environment was a key attribute. Being with like-minded people with common special interests and being able to discuss issues with expert educators were frequently cited reasons for participating in learning vacations. Understanding educational tourists is critical if the tourism industry is to provide them with interesting and satisfying experiences. It has been illustrated that, within each educational tourism segment, there are sub-segments or markets, and the adult educational market is no different.

Research undertaken by Zinell (in Dann, 2001: 236) over a 5-year period suggests that not only is the seniors' market changing, but also the socio-demographic labels are changing as the population ages and the senior market becomes larger. However, Zinell also noted a change in values over recent years from family, sacrifice, work, morals and duty to values such as individualism, enjoyment, fun, leisure and tolerance. This has translated into demand for tourism and educational tourism products and experiences. In the case of non-profit organisations, a study of North American Elderhostel participants enrolled in Canadian programmes revealed four main types of learning travellers:

- *Explorers*: who are looking for programmes, near or far, that offer the opportunity to actively explore a new part of the world. They wish to learn about the local area, history, people and customs.
- *Activity-orientated*: learning travellers who enjoy programmes that are held outdoors and who are interested in the natural environment.
- *Content-committed*: individuals who look for specific subjects (e.g. genealogy, photography, etc.).
- *Convenience-orientated*: who look for programmes close to home – destinations within a six-hour driving radius that could be reached in one day, by car, and on one tank of gas (Arsenault, 1998).

Muller and Cleaver (2000) note the potential of the baby boom generation for the development and marketing of discovery travel and adventure tourism products. According to the authors, the CANZUS

Table 3.4 Australian baby boomers' psychographic segmentation

Socially Aware	***Something Better***
• 725,000 baby boomers in cluster (18% of all boomers) form half of Australia's *Socially Aware* lifestyle segment.	• 619,000 baby boomers in this segment (15% of all boomers) form 48% of the *Something Better* population.
• Most educated segment of the population – – typically university educated and in the top jobs.	• Typically younger couples (aged 30–39), baby boomers in this group are upwardly mobile and career driven, or building up their businesses.
• Community-minded, politically and socially active, and enjoy persuading others to change their opinions.	• Both partners tend to earn good incomes, but they 'want it all now'.
• Very 'green' and progressive in their attitudes.	• They borrow heavily to finance their lifestyle and become financially stressed.
• Baby boomers in this group are avid arts goers, with no real money worries, and tend to be wealth managers.	• Over half of them have small children, but family is not central to their lives.
• They take a thoughtful and strategic approach to life, including their shopping and family affairs.	• They are confident, ambitious and progressive in their attitudes.
• They are *experiential* tourists and pursue a stimulating lifestyle – in their homes and leisure activities.	• They are also resourceful and work hard to stay ahead.
	• Many in the *Something Better* segment will eventually become members of the *Visible Achievement* lifestyle segment.

Table 3.4 (continued)

Visible Achievement	*Conventional Family Life*
• 1,041,000 baby boomers in cluster (26% of all boomers) make up nearly half (48%) of the *Visible Achievement* population.	• 961,000 baby boomers in this segment (24% of all boomers) make up 66% of the *Conventional Family Life* segment.
• Wealth creators of Australia.	• They represent middle Australia – people whose life is centred around their families.
• Literate, confident and competent, they work for financial reward and job stimulation; this group includes some 'blue-collar businessmen".	• They include the working class – skilled tradesmen and middle office workers – on average incomes, with mortgages and superannuation.
• They seek *recognition* and *status* for themselves and their families.	• They strive to give their children better opportunities in life than they themselves had.
• They have 25% of Australia's children, with traditional views about family responsibilities.	• They are not ambitious and prefer to spend their spare time with family and around the house.
• Theirs is a world of conspicuous 'good living', travel, recreation and other evidence of success.	• They are generally contented, satisfied, down to earth and practical.
• They are demanding and smart strategic shoppers and prolific consumers of visible lifestyle products.	

Source: Adapted from Cleaver and Muller (2001: 7–8)

(Canadian, Australian and New Zealand) baby boomer market comprises 13 million people, while the USA market is 75 million strong (Cleaver & Muller, 2001: 4). Wood (2001: 20) notes that 'many types of ecotourism are supported by increasing numbers of financially secure, well-educated Baby Boomers who see retirement as an opportunity for travel and exploration'. Cleaver and Muller (2001) note that 83% of the baby boomer market belongs to just four lifestyle groups in Australia (see Table 3.4). This segmentation was carried out based on Roy Morgan Value Segments research which segments the population into ten lifestyle categories based on a national survey of 60,000 consumers in Australia.

Table 3.4 and research conducted by Cleaver and Muller (2001), presented in Table 3.5, suggests that the *Socially Aware* segment has a high propensity for ecotourism-related activities, active vacations and cultural heritage tourism compared with other lifestyle segments, suggesting that target marketing would be more effective for educational holiday providers. Cleaver and Muller (2001) also note similar segmentation exercises overseas with similar results estimating a target of 14 million people. Research in Canada by the Environics Research Group formulated the *Autonomous Rebels* for the Canadian baby boomers (Adams, 1997), the Consumer Research Group (1996) identified *Educated Liberals* in New Zealand, and the *Actualizers* were named in SRI International's VALS 2 typology for the United States (Piirto, 1991). This clearly outlines the size and potential of ecotourism and educational forms of tourism based on psychographic lifestyle segmentation. Because of their characteristics, the *Socially Aware* segment may also have an interest in learning about wine and may participate in educational wine tourism as Mitchell and Mitchell note in Case Study 3.1.

Additional findings from Cleaver and Muller (2001) illustrate that the *Socially Aware* boomer:

- places more importance on travelling for discovery, illustrating the need for new and varied experiences which help this segment expand their knowledge base;
- places emphasis on warm relationships with others, self-respect and a sense of accomplishment, suggesting the need for cultural interaction and challenging or highly involved experiences, and the need for designers of study tours and educational experiences to incorporate challenge into their product;
- will not only need comfort, convenience and good value for money, but will desire learning, personal growth, nostalgia and sensory stimulation.

Table 3.5 Activities undertaken on last holiday trip by baby boomer lifestyle segment

Holiday activity	*Socially aware*	*Visible achievement*	*Something Better*	*Conventional Family Life*
Wilderness travel	208	103	65	47
National parks	156	117	95	68
Country/wildlife/scenery	152	125	79	63
Nature experiences	163	88	87	74
Bushwalking	162	123	82	63
Surfing/swimming	136	121	94	80
Snow skiing	134	151	90	27
Bike riding	133	121	94	85
Other outdoor activities	151	103	96	85
Other adventure activities	142	119	82	51
Arts festivals/cultural events	169	120	50	39
Visiting art galleries/ museums	168	118	81	61
Visiting historical places	135	118	86	67

Note: The numbers are indices against the average of 100 for all baby boomers. Therefore, read the first row, across, as follows: *Socially Aware* baby boomers are 108% (208 – 100) *more* likely, *Visible Achievement* 3% *more* likely, *Something Better* 35% (100 – 65) *less* likely, and *Conventional Family Life* 53% *less* likely to have chosen wilderness travel than the baby boomer population as a whole.
Source: Cleaver and Muller (2001: 26)

This research illustrates the need for educational tourism providers to research the characteristics of their target markets and to segment the market, noting individual needs and developing suitable products to meet these needs. If segmentation or analysis is not undertaken then market share may decline as consumers find alternative products which better meet their needs.

Supply of Educational Travel Experiences

Generated by the 'personal growth' movement (Smith & Jenner, 1997a), an increasing interest in educational travel has resulted in the provision of a diverse range of educational holidays. As Smith and Jenner (1997a: 65) note, holidays can range from 'learning to cook, to wine tasting, to painting, to off-road driving, to drystone walling' and surprisingly can consist of some elements considered traditionally as 'work', illustrating again the blurring boundaries between work and leisure. Richards (2000) notes the development of 'creative tourism' (similar to special interest tourism) which includes a range of activities from arts and crafts to gastronomy, health and healing, languages, spirituality, nature and sports. Research conducted with 1100 rural tourists in three European countries noted that 10% were interested in seeing how traditional products were made, while a higher proportion were interested in learning how to make these products themselves (Richards, 1999).

The first part of this section examines the incorporation of education and learning within many sectors of the tourism industry and highlights some key product developments in the industry to cater for the growing seniors' market and their demand for educational experiences. Many examples are provided in the section to illustrate the industry response to this demand.

Tour and resort operators

The tourism industry has increasingly become aware of this demand and is beginning to cater for these new patterns. Some tour operators, resort and accommodation providers are incorporating activities that involve some components of learning and education to target more educationally minded tourists, and this is occurring in a variety of sectors. Product development initiatives undertaken by the industry range from those of large global organisations to those of small regional and local tour operators. Large global organisations include companies such as Saga Holidays, P&O (see Exhibit 3.1), Lindblad, Odyssey and the Disney Corporation (see Exhibit 3.2), while small regional and local operators (comprising a significant proportion of the tourist industry) include wine, food and geological tour operators catering for the growing special interest and learning/education vacation market (see Case Study 3.1 and Exhibit 3.3).

However, although the tourism industry is slow to recognise that tourists are more intelligent than they appear (Crocombe, 1984), there is an increasing demand for integrity and education in tourism experiences. This point notes that the tourist industry itself has a lot to learn about educational tourism. However, there are a growing number of examples where education has been integrated into adult educational tourist experiences with a variety of settings, including tour operations, cruise ships, resorts and attractions. This section of the chapter provides some examples illustrating the growing link between education and tourism in these sectors.

Global study tour operators

A growing number of specialist tour operators and wholesalers are developing educational holidays for the adult or seniors' market. As outlined in Chapter 1, and later in this chapter, tour operators often bring together packages of educational tourism experiences for consumption by educational tourists. Saga Holidays was one of the first to specialise in the seniors' market in 1952 when it began as a hotel in Folkestone, UK, targeting retirees in an attempt to reduce seasonality and improve its occupancy rates. It later developed into the Old People's Holiday Bureau and did so well that it expanded into other UK coastal resorts such as Margate and Eastbourne. By 1958 it was using trains as well as coach travel and served a total of 12 resorts in the UK (Smith & Jenner, 1997b: 61). It expanded internationally in 1965, introducing a cruise programme in 1973 and a Far East programme in 1979, with Saga International opening in 1981 in the USA, and Australia following in 1985. The Saga Group have also diversified and sell financial services and insurance to senior travellers and publish books and magazines for the middle-aged and the elderly.

Other operators had similar beginnings, growing from small niche markets to global businesses as the demand for educational holidays increases (both Exhibit 3.1 and Case Study 3.2 provide good examples).

Cruise ships

Ocean cruising has grown in popularity since the 1960s and estimates suggest that cruise ship passengers have increased by 10% per annum on average since the 1980s (McIntosh *et al.*, 1995). A more recent WTO report on the cruise industry suggests that the number of cruise ship passengers has grown almost twice as rapidly as international tourist arrivals in the last decade (WTO, 2001). According to the study, since 1990 the cruise ship industry has grown by 7.7% to a total of 8.7 million in 1999. Although the market is small compared with the tourist industry as a whole, it is predicted that the market will grow to over 12 million by 2010 and the

Exhibit 3.1

Swan Hellenic: Education and cruising

By Brent Ritchie and Jo-Anne Lester

Ocean cruising has grown in popularity since the 1960s and this growth looks likely to continue with the planned construction of larger boats and the so-called 'super liners' to cater for even larger numbers of passengers. Destinations strategically located in the Caribbean, Mediterranean and Asia-Pacific region are becoming dependent upon cruise ships, not only for providing tourists and their direct expenditure, but also for helping to revive their derelict waterfront and port areas. For instance, since 1988 Singapore has aggressively sought to increase the amount of cruise ship traffic resulting in nearly 700,000 cruise ship passengers in 1994 and nearly one million cruise ship passengers by 1995 (a 32% increase on the previous year) (Singapore Tourist Promotion Board, 1996). Furthermore, developing countries such as Bermuda and Cuba are also becoming more reliant on cruise ship traffic as part of their strategic location in the Caribbean region.

Due to their increasing size cruise ships have been compared to hotels or floating resorts, and this is especially the case with the development of cruise ships that can cater for larger numbers of visitors. More recently hotel and resort operators such as Club Med and Raddison have entered the market because of the similarities between cruising and hotel and resort management. However, research has shown that small island destinations such as Bermuda often experience infrastructure congestion and overcrowding problems due to the seasonal nature of tourism combined with the increasing size of cruise ships (see Page, 1999). Similarly, the creation of infrastructure or docking areas for cruise ships has often lagged behind the construction of these larger cruise ships. This is certainly the case for Cuba, which has only recently completed works on a new marina due to a lack of foreign investment in tourism infrastructure.

More recently, as competition has intensified the cruise ship product has become more segmented and specialised despite market domination by global companies. The Disney Corporation has recently developed cruise ship products for families through introducing the products 'Disney Magic' and 'Disney Wonder', while cruise giant P&O has developed tours for singles and honeymooners, thus further differentiating their product options. Another example of a cruise company targeting a specialised market is Swan Hellenic, which, unlike many other cruise ship companies, specialises in small-scale educational tourism cruises for seniors.

Swan Hellenic, in operation since 1954 and a subsidiary of P&O Cruises since 1982, offers a cruise ship product that differs from traditional cruise ship operations because its product has a 'serious intent' (Smith & Jenner, 1997a). Swan Hellenic caters for only 300 passengers on board its most famous vessel the MV *Minerva* and all tours comprise an 'educational' theme accompanied by specialist guest lectures. A typical cruise, according to Smith and Jenner (1997a), includes four or five optional lectures on a range of subjects that are often well attended by passengers despite their voluntary nature and usually occur before a port arrival. Subjects can range from astronomy, archaeology, religion, politics, people, wildlife, arts and architecture. Famous specialist lecturers have included Professor Anthony Clare, a well known United Kingdom psychiatrist and an expert on the Egyptian origins of Western medicine, and Dr Patrick Moore, a well known astronomer (Smith & Jenner, 1997a: 74). In 2002 Swan Hellenic introduced a new cruise route to the Persian Gulf, including an expert guest lecturer on antiques and a lecturer with specialist knowledge of the military history of the area. Guest lecturers are scheduled to discuss the history of the region, including the history of oil and the Gulf War, and the tour will be supplemented by local museum visits. Despite many cruises visiting small and sensitive island destinations, the small size of the fleet of Swan Hellenic reduces the potential congestion and overcrowding problems that many island destinations may face. Furthermore, the small size also reduces the necessity for large-scale investment in docks and landing facilities that have so far excluded some destinations from hosting and benefiting from the cruise ship market.

The small personal scale and educational element, combined with cruise ship tours of New and Old World destinations such as the Red Sea, Arabian Gulf, India and Scandinavia, has seen the company gain many awards as testimony to its winning formula. In 2000 the *Minerva* was voted 'Best Specialist Ship' for the second time by a panel of travel industry experts in the *Daily Express*/ British Cruise Awards. Previously, Swan Hellenic was voted 'Best Cruise Company' in the *Telegraph* Travel Awards, illustrating that 'big' does not necessarily mean 'better' in the cruise ship industry despite the introduction of larger ships, and that learning and education have their place, even in the cruise ship sector.

revenues generated by the cruise ship market are substantially higher than those of other tourist markets (WTO, 2001). Driven by globalisation and the need to expand market share the cruise ship market has become increasingly integrated and consolidated, with the market dominated by four main operators: Carnival Corporation, Royal Caribbean Cruise Line (RCCL), P&O, Princess and Star Cruises. The main cruise companies rely on travel agents for selling their product, while the specialised cruise companies prefer to maintain direct contact with the consumer.

One of the issues associated with the global expansion of tourism companies is maintaining a standardised product at the same time as catering to a variety of different markets (Burns and Holden, 1995). One way of catering for these often conflicting trends is for the major cruise operators to acquire specialised medium and smaller operators who often cater to a more specialised and segmented market, as illustrated in Exhibit 3.1.

Resorts

Confusion occurs over the use of the term 'resort' and the differences in travellers' perception of what a resort means. Some authors define a resort simply as a purpose-built hotel positioned to take advantage of some form of climatic condition such as sun, snow or scenery (Pearce *et al.*, 1998). Examples include ski resorts in alpine destinations (such as Thredbo in Australia and the French Pyrenees) and sun-based resorts (such as the Whitsundays in Australia and Mahkota Melaka Resort in Malaysia). Other authors suggest that resorts often include a wide range of entertainment facilities including recreational and leisure amenities (such as sporting facilities or leisure programmes) and are therefore self-contained (Elliot & Johns, 1993 and Wall, 1996 both in Pearce *et al.*, 1998). Self-contained resorts, and in particular all-inclusive resorts such as Club Med, are becoming increasingly popular with holidaymakers.

However, resorts have become increasingly specialised in catering for specific segments of visitors, with a growing number offering educational activities and programmes as part of their suite of leisure offerings. A number of American resorts have been providing educational programmes for years, including the Mohunk Mountain House in New York, which has been in operation since the 1870s and prides itself on being a model of educational tourism. The programmes currently on offer at the Mohunk Mountain House fall into two broad categories: general learning courses such as 'classic film weekends' and skills-based programmes such as gardening (Holdnak & Holland, 1996). Other resorts offer sporting-based programmes, such as those which include tuition with a professional golfer. The Millbrook Resort in Queenstown, New Zealand is one example that has offered sporting educational programmes within its resort product. Similarly, global companies such as the Disney Corporation have attempted to integrate learning and education as part of their resort experience in an attempt to complement their theme park and attraction products and expand their client base by tapping into educational tourism (see Exhibit 3.2).

It is not only large global tourism organisations that have been incorporating education and learning in their provision. As noted earlier, a number of small and regional examples exist which incorporate special interest holidays with educational experiences, including geological, archaeological and wine tours as well as gourmet and cooking holidays in a variety of different settings throughout the world. Some products even combine food and wine tours, or wine and heritage (see Case Study 3.1), with travel experiences overlapping between cultural, educational and special interest holidays. Exhibit 3.3 discusses the provision of a cooking school holiday in Italy, and the ingredients of that particular holiday. Case Study 3.1 discusses the development of a regional wine tourism strategy in Sydney, Australia, where learning and heritage are important components of the marketing plan, and where key market segments interested in learning and education have been identified and targeted. Yet despite the obvious interest in education and learning for special interest, wine and gourmet experiences, little research has been conducted examining their educational experiences and needs.

From the previous discussion on the supply of educational tourism products and Figure 1.3 it becomes apparent that the majority of adult educational tourism is packaged in some way by tour operators or non-profit organisations. Therefore, effective packaging and promotion, often in partnership with many organisations, is critical for the success of the educational tourism experience (see Exhibit 3.5 for the approach of Elderhostel).

Packaging and promotional activities undertaken by adult educational providers differ depending on the type of provider involved and the nature of the educational tourism experience. There is a variety of learning vacations on the market and thus a diverse range of products

Exhibit 3.2

Resort educational tourism: The experiment of The Disney Orlando Institute

By Brent Ritchie

The Disney Corporation, a business often ahead of its time, has seen the potential of education and learning as a component of travel and tourism and has developed a recent product to take advantage of the changing trends. The Disney Corporation recently entered into the educational tourism market, making entertainment educational by providing 'smart fun' (Smith & Jenner, 1997a) or 'edutainment' targeted mainly at the baby boomer and retiree market.

The Disney Institute is based at the Walt Disney World resort, Florida and was opened in February 1996 by the Disney Corporation. The resort, located by Lake Buena Vista, consists of 457 bedrooms in bungalows or one/two-bedroom townhouses and has the capacity for 1300 guests per day (Smith & Jenner, 1997a: 74). The resort also has entertainment facilities which include, in addition to the 28-programme studios, a state-of-the-art cinema with seating for 400 guests; a broadcast quality performance venue which seats 225 guests; and an outdoor amphitheatre on the green with seating for over 1100. In 1995, in describing the impending new resort, Michael D. Eisner, chairman and chief executive officer, stated that,

> we live in an age where discovering new things is a lifetime priority. The Disney Institute will be a resort with a creatively charged atmosphere, where you can engage your body, excite your mind and expand your horizons. Guests can take part in activities that range from animating a cartoon, to creating a topiary, to climbing a rock wall (in Benedict, 1995).

The Disney Institute initially offered more than 80 programmes in nine different programme tracks such as entertainment arts, sports and fitness, lifestyles, story arts, culinary arts, and design arts, to list a few. Within each programme track individual programmes were offered. For example, learning to create an animation character for Disney took place under the entertainment arts track, while the 'taste of the world' individual programme was situated within the culinary arts programme track. Other programmes included designing gardens situated in the environment programme track, and antique treasure hunting positioned in the design arts programme track. Celebrity guests, including actors, sports stars, artists and authors, supplement resident instructors. Celebrity guests have included Robert A. M. Stern, the creative force behind the architecture for Disney's Yacht and Beach Club Resorts and several Disneyland Paris hotels, and comedian Bill Larkin.

Programmes were initially offered to guests staying at the resort and originally ran over several days. However, as demand waned for these programmes Disney began to offer the product to business people, with tourists then only comprising 30% of the market (Bryd, 1998). Because the demand for specialised programmes was smaller than initially anticipated, Disney has recently increased the number of mini-seminars that run from one to four hours and has aimed these seminars at theme park visitors as well as resort visitors to help boost profits. 'In the beginning, we wanted to put The Disney Institute out to the market in general,' said Mary Tomlinson, director. 'But ultimately, the people who want a Disney Institute vacation is a niche market' (in Byrd, 1998). Disney is not known for getting its marketing and product development wrong, and has begun to aim its programmes at the Disney Institute at niche markets, including photography, food and wine enthusiasts, through direct marketing: In targeting their marketing they have avoided the usual mass-marketing method that Disney has traditionally used.

As part of changing their market Disney have had to remove and modify many of their previous programmes, including antique treasure hunting and 'climbing your family tree', both of which no longer exist. According to Tomlinson, 'The guests have told us by selection what they want' (in Byrd, 1998), and Disney appear to be modifying their programmes and marketing to attract the type of tourist most likely to stay at the resort and participate in their programmes. That visitor is increasingly less likely to be the traditional mass market theme park visitor that Disney usually attracts and caters for, and instead is more individual and has specialised interests, needs and wants. Although this is a courageous initiative with respect to the blending of travel with education at a resort, Disney have many distinct challenges and opportunities ahead in the provision of an educational tourism product. One of the major challenges they face is the obvious need to provide a product that is demanded by their potential market, and the need to discard traditional marketing techniques in order to attract special interest and educational travellers.

Exhibit 3.3

The ingredients of a cooking school holiday

By Ngaire Douglas and Maree Walo

Italian Cookery Weeks Ltd is an independently owned private company specialising in its own cookery schools. The idea became reality twelve years ago when the founders and owners of the school, Susanna Gelmatti and Mihai Dragutescu, identified a gap in the Italian tourist market for those who wish to combine both travel and learning. At about this time (1988), two things were coming together; Italian food – other than pizzas and spaghetti – was becoming increasingly popular and the health values of a Mediterranean diet were being formally acknowledged. The locations chosen were then unusual Italian destinations and their schools still are located in areas which are 'off the beaten track' for the majority of tourists to Italy. We must wonder for how much longer they will be able to claim this.

The location

The Umbrian school is in Bolsena, close to Orvieto. The region is renowned for local meats, games, porcini mushrooms, olive oils of the region and sheeps' cheeses. The Amalfi Coast school is at Marina Del Cantone, between Sorrento and Positano. The specialities are fresh seafood and fruits. A third, less used location, is in Puglia at Ostuni near Brindisi, on the heel of the boot of Italy. From the Umbrian school students can visit Civita D'Bagnoregio, a famous village of ten people, Perugia, a major historical attraction, and Peinza, known for its pecorino cheese.

The participants

Participants are English speaking and 62% come from the UK. The company believes that this is attributable to the company being UK based, the easy access to Italy and the extensive UK-focused publicity in newspapers and magazines. Australians and New Zealanders account for a further 25% of clients who are reached through CIT Travel, agents who have good exposure for the Italian travel market. Another 8% are from USA. They access the information via the website or special guides to cookery schools. The 5% balance consists of independent bookings from South Africa, the United Arab Emirates and other European nations.

For most clients Italy itself is the principal 'pull' factor and to this is the added dimension of an interest in food – Italian food. They usually come from the middle to upper income bracket and their age can vary from the late twenties through to the seventies with the majority of clients in the 40–60-year bracket. Women make up the majority of students and they often enrol in small groups. When couples come to the property, the man usually does the more common tourist activities while the woman pursues her special interest. This is not to say, of course, that males do not come as students. They certainly do, although they are a small minority in the client profile.

The chefs and instructors

The chefs are always Italian, usually from the region, and have a wide range of prior experience. The company requires that they are 'presentable', have a strong understanding of the food of the region, have worked in a reputable restaurant and have a comprehensive approach to the preparation of dishes, which should include both modern and traditional ideas. Many appointments are made through recommendation from other chefs and notable 'foodies' in Italy. Locals are brought in for specialty demonstrations. For example, the students learn how to throw pizza bases from the local pizza shop owner. The support staff comprises mainly young Australians on working holidays.

The programmes

The programmes are set by Italian Cookery Weeks Ltd. In 2001 they offered five one-week programmes in two locations – Amalfi Coast and Umbria. Approximately 20 people make the maximum number for each school. Italian Cookery Weeks ensures that the right mix of cookery lessons, excursions, relaxation and, of course, eating and drinking is achieved. Their marketing claims that

> Italian Cookery weeks are a recipe for a fabulous gastronomic holiday. They combine a relaxing Mediterranean holiday with first-class instruction in Italian Cuisine. Each program incorporates,

where possible, daily excursions to surrounding villages, markets and specialty food shops of the region.

Schools are offered during the Northern Hemisphere Spring (May/June) and Autumn (August/September).

Good tour planners realise that leisure activities must be a part of the total experience. Souvenir shopping, sightseeing, swimming, lying around the pool and something labelled 'free time' are timetabled into the programme. Thus the presence of a cooking school can bring financial benefits to other local and regional businesses, not only through the purchase of materials needed to run the school and employment of local staff, but by encouraging the students to experience other features of the locality.

The cuisine

All dishes revolve around local fresh produce with regional specialities a feature: fresh figs, blackberries and porcini mushrooms in Umbria and baby wild artichokes and wild fennel on the Amalfi Coast for example. Recipes must be able to be reproduced at home (i.e. the UK primarily), so alternative ingredients are incorporated where necessary.

The concessions

Certain dishes, which may be delicacies in Italy, are not suited to an 'English' palate. High salt content, extensive use of lard, and the consumption of certain game and meats which is not considered politically correct in some countries are avoided as much as possible. The chilli, a common ingredient in many Italian dishes, is used with considerable caution. So, while cooking school tourists may well be seeking a REAL tourism experience, providers are erring on the side of caution when menu planning.

The language of instruction

As unfortunate as many people may think this to be, English has become the lingua franca of tourism. It is an interesting experience, for example, to be the only English native speaker on a domestic tourist bus in the heart of India, only to find that English is the language which the guide uses because of the numerous Indian dialects spoken by the other 56 people on the bus! The authors suggest, from their experience at other cooking schools in Indonesia and Australia, that attendance at cooking schools is Eurocentric behaviour. At the Italian school, even those who come from the United Arab Emirates are Europeans who live there on contracts.

The shopping

Participants can join the shopping expeditions if they choose. Sometimes local produce is picked up while on afternoon excursions, so participation is by default. Food shopping behaviour in Italy is decidedly different to that practised in the everyday lives of the majority of participants. In Italy it is a daily exercise for several reasons:

- the importance of very fresh food;
- the general absence of, and associated cultural indifference to, or lack of access to, refrigeration; and
- the historical cultural behaviour whereby the daily market shopping trip is an essential part of social life.

It is the participation in such a fundamental activity that the Italians have transformed into an important social and sensory experience which lingers as one of the fondest memories for many cooking school students.

The cost

The Italian cooking school costs approximately 1249 GBP (2001 price). Included in this are return flights from London to Rome, minibus transfer to Umbria, seven nights twin share accommodation,full board with 'excellent food and wine', tuition on cookery and excursions to nearby historic and interesting towns. For students from the US the cost is US$1791 ex London. A transatlantic fare would have to be added. The Italian Umbrian accommodations have been described as rustic by past participants.

and services on offer. However, generally these vacations involve travel to the destination, some form of accommodation, meals, food and educational or learning activity at a site or number of sites. As discussed in Chapter 1, they include those offered by primary educational tourism providers and secondary support service providers (see Figure 3.1). Organisations that can be involved in developing and packaging their own educational holidays include:

- individual sites or attractions such as museums and art galleries;
- individual travel planners or agencies;
- tour operators such as Odyssey Travel, and Lindblad;
- universities and colleges offering continuing education programmes; and
- non-profit organisations.

In many cases these organisations work together to combine a suite of products and experiences that will create the educational tourism experience. As Bodger (1998: 2) notes, a successful educational tourism experience depends upon a good relationship between three main groups of stakeholders:

- *The programmer*: who prepares the programme with the tour or travel leader, and helps with setting up suitable accommodation and planning. They may undertake this themselves or work with professional travel companies.
- *The leader*: who are experts in the particular field and may have academic qualifications. They communicate knowledge to participants and need to be motivated and resourceful.
- *The participants*: who need time to reflect on material presented and may have different agendas such as shopping or exploring destinations.

As noted in Figure 3.1 and the previous discussion, the resource specialists are central to the educational tourism experience and can be employed at attractions as curators, subject matter specialists, interpreters, lecturers, storytellers or researchers and academics. They may be employed by client organisations such as alumni and non-profit organisations to develop suitable programmes for educational tourists and can complete this with the help of tour and receptive operators or organise the programme and support services such as accommodation and social activities individually. Furthermore, they may be employed by tour and receptive operators to deliver an educational programme or workshop

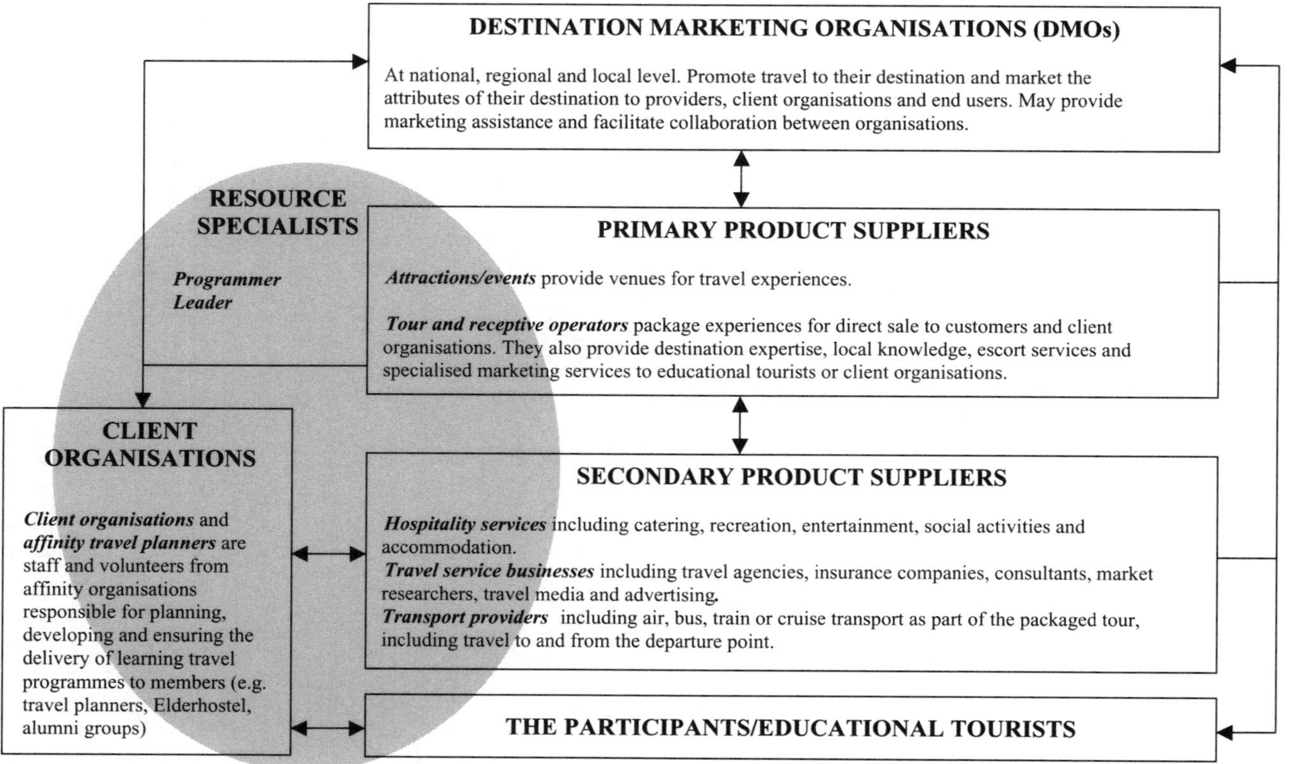

Figure 3.1 Relationships between adult educational tourism providers and clients

Source: After Bodger (1998) and CTC (2001)

directly to educational tourists. Whatever role they play, it is central to the educational tourism experience (Bodger, 1998).

As noted in Exhibit 3.5 Elderhostel have developed many relationships with local museums or sites as well as partner institutions. Universities and colleges may work with travel planners or tour operators on behalf of their alumni or continuing education programmes, while individual attractions and national parks may work with universities and colleges in order to stimulate learning trips, improve visitation levels and promote their educational charters. Table 3.6 provides some indication of the type and cost of these programmes for the seniors' market as well as identifying the variety of organisations involved. The table illustrates the mixed involvement of alumni and universities alongside commercial tour operators and non-profit organisations such as Elderhostel. Prices per day can vary from US$83 for a five-day Elderhostel vacation to US$779 for a high arctic adventure from Adventure Canada.

As the CTC (2001) note, the challenge in packaging educational travel is building partnerships between different organisations to provide educational tourism products that are respectful, appreciative, sustainable and enhance mutual understanding. The task is to ensure that the public sector and educational organisations and attractions (such as museums and other sites) work together in partnership with the private sector (such as the tourism industry) to provide educational opportunities for the adult and seniors' tourism market. As one Canadian educational institution commented, the 'challenge for learning vacations is that educational institutions operate on a budget and are not used to looking at things from a commercial, tourism perspective. Putting this type of program together is like merging four cultures (NGOs, government, academic institutions and the private sector), each with their own politics and ways of operating' (in CTC, 2001: 44).

This quote illustrates the fragmented and diverse nature of the educational tourism industry and the need for the development of partnerships, packaging and promotional campaigns between providers of educational tourism. However, as noted above, the different ways of operating, including the commercial versus educational agenda, are important issues to consider as there are obvious economic and intangible benefits related to educational tourism (such as personal development and self-fulfilment), which may be outcomes favoured by some stakeholders. There is a need for providers to form alliances and networks to expand their marketing budgets, improve the diversity and quality of product offered, and undertake research into adult and seniors' educational tourism. Chapter 6 examines issues concerning fragmentation, collaboration and networking in more detail and discusses the importance of partnerships in educational tourism for maximising both the marketing and regional development benefits of educational tourism.

Table 3.6 Cost of learning vacations in Canada (US$ in 2000)

Provider Programme	*Nights*	*Total cost in US$*	*Per day cost in US$*
Adventure Canada High Arctic – Greenland and Canada	14	5,890 to 10,990	420 to 779
Bear Treks (California Alumni Association) Newfoundland	16	3,795	237
Canadian Cultural Landscapes Historic Montreal and Quebec City in the summer	6	1,369	228
Elderhostel Camp Arnes/Lake Winnipeg	5	413	83
McGill University Oh Canada 'Wings over the Rockies'	5	1,337	267
National Audubon Society New Brunswick Discover: Featuring the Bay of Fundy	7	1,069	153
Smithsonian Odyssey Tours Western Canada and National Parks (includes air)	9	1,899 to 2,249	211 to 250
Study Abroad Canada English Adventure for the Young at Heart in PEI	6	737	123
University of Michigan Stratford Festival and Shaw Festival	5	1,350	270

Source: Modified from CTC (2001: 40)

Exhibit 3.5

Elderhostel: A pioneer in adult educational tourism

By Heather Hardwick

History of Elderhostel

Elderhostel is a not-for-profit organisation that was founded in 1975 by Marty Knowlton, a social activist and former educator, and David Bianco, a university administrator. Inspired by the youth hostel concept in Europe, which provides safe, inexpensive accommodation and opportunities to meet other travellers, and the folk schools of Scandinavia, where older adults hand down age-old traditions to younger generations, Marty and David sought to create and offer similar educational and cultural opportunities for older adults in the United States. The first Elderhostel residential learning programmes were offered in 1975 at five colleges and universities in New Hampshire in the north-eastern United States; 220 adults participated in the programmes.

Market profile and demand

Elderhostel participants are, by definition, mature travellers – the organisation specifically targets adults aged 55 and over (although they have widened their target as the age minimum was previously 60 years and over). Elderhostel participants also tend to be experienced travellers. Although education correlates with the travellers' interest in Elderhostel, no formal educational training or prior experience is required to participate in an Elderhostel programme, just a desire to learn.

Part of the appeal of Elderhostel programmes is the opportunity to share an educational experience with people who share similar interests. Elderhostel's programmes work to provide a welcoming and inclusive social atmosphere that encourages learning and participation. As a result, Elderhostel attracts a lot of single or solo travellers, who are drawn by the opportunity to share a unique experience with like-minded travellers and the opportunity to make new friends. Further, Elderhostel offers participants a room-mate matching service for those interested in sharing a room, which also eliminates the need for single supplements that sometimes deter single travellers from travelling as part of a group. There is also a high incidence of repeat travel with Elderhostel, attesting to participants' satisfaction with the programmes and the experience.

According to Hardwick (2000), based on Menlo Consulting Group's research with American international travellers, 21.6% of travellers over age 55 were found to be extremely or very likely to take an Elderhostel vacation. Not surprisingly, this likelihood correlated strongly with the educational levels of travellers. Travellers who show a general preference for being as part of an escorted group also have an above-average interest in Elderhostel. The demand for Elderhostel programmes is growing and several trends in the US market contribute to this, such as ageing – the population group known in the United States as the baby boom generation is entering its prime travel years. Further, speciality travel is increasing in popularity in the US right now. Elderhostel programmes are by definition special interest in nature, given their educational and cultural focus. However, because of the breadth of its programme, Elderhostel is able to offer a wide variety of themed trips as well as activity-based programmes such as hiking and cycling tours. Popular theme programmes are focused on art, events, gardens, food, family, theatre, walking, museums and politics.

Key product characteristics

Education

Providing older adults with lifetime learning opportunities is the core of the Elderhostel mission; as such, education plays a central role in Elderhostel programming. Programmes include lectures, classes (although no exams or grades are involved), discussions, field trips, and extracurricular activities. Programmes are often based in a location that is significant to the topic, or are hosted by an educational or cultural institution. Elderhostel partners with a network of 1900 educational and cultural sites, many of which serve as host sites for programmes. These partners include colleges and universities, state and national parks, museums, theatres and environmental education centres.

Location

Elderhostel programmes take participants to literally every corner of the globe. Although the first programmes started in the northeastern United States, by word-of-mouth promotion alone the Elderhostel programme grew to serve more than 20,000 participants all over the United States and Canada in its first five years. In 1981, Elderhostel offered its first international programmes, which more directly incorporated travel with education to foster experiential learning. The international programmes have a strong cultural focus, often studying local history, traditions, literature, arts, cuisine and language. The popularity of Elderhostel's international programming has fuelled tremendous growth; international programmes now comprise nearly one-fifth of all Elderhostel programmes and the organisation offers programmes on all seven continents.

Elderhostel programmes, particularly the domestic ones, typically revolve around a base location or host institution, with participants learning about an area or topic in depth and exploring the region around the base. However, in 1998, Elderhostel introduced the new Adventures Afloat programmes, using ships and barges as floating classrooms and setting participants in motion on some of the world's most magnificent waterways. Similarly, it is possible to take an Elderhostel programme where the classroom is a train, moving from one study location to another.

Duration

Most programmes in the United States and Canada are five or six nights in length, with some programmes lasting only a weekend and others extending to two or more weeks. International programmes tend to be longer, typically lasting one to four weeks.

Cost

One of the core components of Elderhostel programmes is value. As a non-for-profit organisation and a travel provider, the costs to the consumer for participating in an Elderhostel programme are based on covering the basic programme costs. Programme tuition is all-inclusive, including all classes and field trips, activities, meals and lodgings at about US$100 per day, well below the average cost of tours offered by most commercial suppliers. Elderhostel helps to keep costs down by sometimes using alternative accommodation such as university housing. There are also a limited number of scholarships available for participants who desire to take part in the domestic programmes, but do not have the financial means to do so.

Innovation

Elderhostel has been changing with the times; as the programmes expand, they also branch off in new directions, to meet consumer demands and trends in the market. In 1985, Elderhostel launched its intergenerational programmes, pairing Elderhostel participants with their grandchildren or other young family members as a means of bringing generations together for shared learning experiences. The intergenerational programmes tend to be more hands-on in nature and are often activity oriented. In 1999 the intergenerational programmes expanded to include international destinations such as Ireland, Greece and Norway. Building on the increasing trend towards family travel in the United States, these programmes have become immensely popular; one Elderhostel representative reported that participants in the intergenerational programmes often remark that these trips are life-changing experiences, providing a unique educational setting for interaction with loved ones.

Elderhostel has also launched its Service Programmes, pairing participants with public-service organisations around the world, adding the element of service and hands-on experience to the educational travel experience. Volunteer work can range from conducting environmental research, to teaching English, to helping to build affordable housing. A portion of the cost of these programmes goes to the charitable organisations involved.

In 1988, Elderhostel formed a voluntary association with established Institutes for Learning in Retirement (ILRs), known as the Elderhostel Institute Network. ILRs are self-governing community-based organisations that pursue lifelong learning through campus-based workshops and semester-long courses. The network extends Elderhostel's commitment to education beyond the travel sphere, as 52,000 Institute Network members take more than 3000 courses each year.

Summary

Elderhostel is leading the way in providing experiential learning and educational travel opportunities for older adults. A pioneer in its field, Elderhostel continues to expand and innovate and succeed in the process. Over the course of 25 years in business, Elderhostel has grown from its initial programmes in New Hampshire that served 200 participants, to become the largest supplier of adult educational travel experiences for adults in the United States, with more than 200,000 adults taking more than 10,000 programmes in more than 100 countries.

Impacts of Seniors' Educational Tourism

As discussed in Chapter 2, the impacts of cultural and nature-based tourism upon the economic, environmental and social environment can be both positive or negative. Few studies have been undertaken concerning the economic impact of the adult educational tourism market. Those that have been undertaken are limited in size and scope. For instance, Conter (1994) estimated the impact of the Elderhostel programme in Arizona to be US$35,000–45,000 per week to the income of an area based on 50 participants. Ross (1998) estimated that US$402.3 million was spent by over 143,000 participants on over 6000 tours, but excluded the largest provider, Elderhostel, from the analysis. Research is needed to accurately quantify the impact and potential of adult educational tourism; however this is unlikely to happen until the industry realises the potential of this market segment and the research base improves substantially.

According to Morrison *et al.* (1994) the desire for seeking intellectual refreshment and spiritual fulfilment increases with age, making the adult tourism market more susceptible to learning and educational tourism experiences. Bodger (1998) notes that educational travel can provide certain personal benefits, as it:

- provides an immediate and personal experience of an event, place or issue that cannot be duplicated;
- offers opportunities for individuals within the group to explore specific and individual issues and interests with other participants and the leader in a way that is usually impossible in the more usual educational environments;
- provides the opportunity to combine leisure with a learning experience that is directed and meaningful; and
- is an immersion situation, in which the daily exposure to a different set of cultural values can lead to dramatic changes in a participant's perceptions and attitudes.

However, not all impacts are advantageous. In the case of Antarctic visitors (see Exhibit 3.4 and Case Study 3.2), although Antarctic tourists may be well educated and well travelled this does not ensure that all their behaviour is responsible. As Hughes notes in Exhibit 3.4, there is evidence to suggest that some visitors are souveniring from heritage sites in Antarctica and suggests that more measures are required to limit this behaviour.

Exhibit 3.4

Management of Antarctic historic sites as a tourism resource

By Janet Hughes

Some 72 historic sites are recognised by the Antarctic Treaty (Headland, 2001). Although not all of them are of interest to tourists, at least 30 of these sites on the Antarctic Treaty list are visited each year by thousands of cruise ship passengers or by hundreds of national expeditioners on 'jollies' (see Plate 3.1).

Plate 3.1 Tourists often visit historic sites during Antarctic educational excursions

Source: J. Hughes

Perhaps the best known sites are those of the early era of Antarctic exploration including the huts on Ross Island used by the Scott and Shackleton expeditions in the early twentieth century. More remote sites are those of Borchegrevink at Cape Adare (1895), Australian scientist Mawson (Cape Denison) and Swedish explorer Nordenskjold (Snow Hill Island, Antarctic Peninsula). These are typically 'rustic' wooden buildings close to the sea with varying quantities of food, clothing, furniture and other supplies typical of the era. Unusual items include snowshoes for ponies, exotic canned foods, a leg of ham over 80 years old, sledges, a stuffed penguin and the occasional nude picture.

More recently abandoned bases, such as those of the International Geophysical Year (1957–58), are often not considered to be historic and some sites (such as the US Wilkes base) have been stripped by souvenir hunters. The sites typically consist of small buildings clustered around logistics facilities such as radio transmitters and meteorological equipment. Buildings are typically of plywood or are metal-clad prefabricated structures. Later sites also may contain considerable quantities of hazardous materials, such as asbestos, chemicals, oils and putrescible items, and thus there is considerable potential for conflicts with the environmental values of the area. Shackleton's hut at Cape Royds is next to a penguin rookery that is also a 'Specially Protected Area'. The 1991 Madrid Protocol requires an abandoned base or building either to be declared historic or to be removed. There are many vagaries of the Antarctic Treaty and Madrid Protocol since no framework is provided for assessing the heritage values nor standards for preservation and management of the sites.

Many tourist itineraries in Antarctica include visits to historic sites as these provide a unique insight into the lives of early explorers and poignantly show the isolation and risks they suffered. Visitor numbers are generally increasing, particularly to some sites such as Whalers Bay at Deception Island in the South Shetland Islands. Few studies of Antarctic tourists have specifically considered issues of historic sites. However, research at Mawson's Huts at Cape Denison has shown divergent views: most accept strict prohibition on touching and removal of historic material, but others do not like the wind-blown and messy nature of the building debris and 'rubbish' considered historically valuable by archaeologists. Visitors to the sites are often keen photographers and crowding inside buildings and tripping hazards from tripods in poor light conditions present clear risks. Artefacts outside buildings seem to be considered less important and some have been trampled by visitors who are usually only supervised inside the buildings.

Ongoing research on managing visitors at Antarctic historic sites is focusing on:

- monitoring impacts such as temperature and humidity variations during visits to assess appropriate numbers of visitors;
- assessing patterns of visitor behaviour to improve the visitor experience;
- improving the quality of 'interpretation' (information provided about the site); and
- providing visitor education to reinforce appropriate behaviour and minimise risks and thereby ensure this tourist resource is available for future generations.

In the field of wine tourism many studies have identified wine education and learning as key components of the wine tourism experience (Ali-Knight & Charters, 1999; Mitchell *et al.*, 2000). Studies undertaken by Charters and Ali-Knight (2002), concerning the motivations and behaviour of wine tourists, found that many respondents viewed wine education as an important factor in their overall tourist experience. The researchers noted that 'integration' between their purpose (from learning to buying) and their interest (from no interest to high interest) may help understand their experiences. For instance, those wine tourists with a high level of learning as the purpose of the trip combined with a high interest in wine ('wine lovers' segment) would enjoy a highly integrated educational experience. Yet, despite the importance of satisfying segments of tourists through education and learning, little research has been undertaken concerning educational or learning needs of special interest travellers. In the case of the Sydney Wine Region the educational elements of wine tourism are critical for its success and the differentiation of this wine region from competing regions (see Case Study 3.1), yet little is known about the educational needs of this tourist segment.

Conclusion

This chapter has discussed the ageing population and the growing interest in travel for learning which has seen increased demand for educational holidays from seniors and baby boomers. The chapter has identified that key market segments have a greater propensity and motivation to choose educational holidays, and that, in particular, senior females are a major target market, while countries such as Germany and the USA have large numbers of baby boomers and seniors as part of their populations. The chapter has also outlined some developments in the tourism industry to cater to this market, which involve tour operators, resorts and attractions. Product development is occurring through large global organisations but also through smaller individually owned operators. Although positive economic and personal development benefits exist, educational tourists can impact negatively upon fragile destinations and sites and so adequate management and interpretation is critical.

This chapter has also outlined that the relationship between providers is complicated, fragmented and potentially diverse. However, all educational tourism experiences are dependent upon partnerships between the education or learning providers (such as universities, colleges, museums and sites) and the tourism industry (such as accommodation, transport and tour operators). Strategies need to be put into place to ensure that these two groups work together to develop mutually beneficial products and experiences to meet their needs as well as the needs of educational tourists. A lack of research and understanding of the demand, supply and impacts of the seniors' educational tourism market is hampering future planning and management, and an increase in research activity is required.

Case Study 3.1

Learning and discovery: Cornerstones of the marketing of the Sydney Wine Region

By Richard Mitchell and Carleen Mitchell

Wine tourism and education

In 2000 Australia had 1197 (Winetitles, 2000) wineries spread throughout all of its States and Territories. In this increasingly competitive market, Australia's wineries and wine regions are striving to gain an advantage. Nowhere is this more true than in the Sydney Wine Region, a relatively new entrant and minor player in the wine tourism market place. The Sydney Wine Region faces strong competition from the well-established Hunter Valley region and the new and emerging wine regions of Mudgee, Young and ACT. These regions have established and growing reputations for both wine and tourism and are within a relatively small radius of Sydney (no more than three-and-a-half hours).

The Nepean Hawkesbury Wine and Grape Growers Association (NHWGGA) currently has 46 members including nine commercial wineries, seven of which have cellar door operations. The cellar door operations are located throughout the western reaches of the Sydney Basin and existing cellar door experiences range from bulk retail to heritage properties and a 5-star bed and breakfast.

Key strengths and opportunities

In order to establish itself in the wine tourism market place the Sydney Wine Region is attempting to brand itself by taking advantage of its key strengths and opportunities. At first glance, it appears that the region's key advantage over its main competitors is that it is the closest wine region to the Sydney metropolitan area: home to some 3.5 million people. However, this close proximity to Sydney also presents some problems for Sydney wineries. In particular, the region may be too close for many Sydney-siders to consider it as a destination (i.e. it may not represent enough of an 'escape' from the city). As a result the Sydney Wine Region Regional Marketing Strategy (2000) gives careful consideration to how the region is positioned and the type of image that is to be projected to the Sydney market (i.e. it must sell the benefits of closeness).

Of particular significance is the region's rich history as Australia's first major agricultural area. Much of the region is still active in primary production and the recent development of business networks such as the Hawkesbury Harvest is evidence of the value primary producers have to the tourism industry. Many of the cellar door operations have roots that are grounded in this early period of agricultural production and several have connections to events and people of major significance to agriculture and winemaking in Australia. In fact, the Sydney Wine Region is the birthplace of the Australian wine industry (first in Parramatta and then in Camden in the early 1800s). This is the Sydney Wine Region's point of difference – no other region can claim to be the birthplace of the Australian wine industry!

All cellar doors within the region have significant heritage values and stories to be told. The region's rich settler and convict history and, in particular, the location of the five Macquarie Towns (Castlereagh, Pitt Town, Richmond, Wilberforce and Windsor) make an important contribution to local tourism. As such, much of the tourism in the region is based on its central importance in Australian history. A number of cellar door operators are already taking advantage of this but the Regional Marketing Strategy attempts to further develop the theme to include, at its core, heritage interpretation and wine education.

Key market characteristics

An analysis of the general winery visitor market, the business environment of the Sydney Wine Region, the Roy Morgan Value Segments (1997) and work carried out by Macionis and Cambourne (1998) identified a range of markets with potential for the Sydney Wine Region. Table 3.7 provides a summary of the three main Roy Morgan Value Segments of winery visitors to different wine regions throughout Australia. Canberra, as an emerging wine region, has the most similar characteristics to those of the Sydney Wine Region and the *Socially Aware* segment is the most likely to visit such regions.

The primary target market for the Sydney Wine Region, then, is *Socially Aware Sydney-siders*. This market, as the market most likely to seek new and innovative products and services, are most likely to visit this emerging region (Macionis & Cambourne, 1998). They are more likely to be risk takers and, if satisfied are likely to provide an important source of 'word-of-mouth' promotion to other sectors of the market. *Socially Aware* consumers also have similar demographics to that of the 'typical winery visitor'. The market also represents a relatively large proportion of the NSW market place (around 850,000 people), second only to *Visible Achievers* (Table 3.8).

More significantly for the development of the Sydney Wine Region's tourism product and core branding, however, is the fact that *Socially Aware* individuals are:

> Information vacuum cleaners, this segment are always searching for something new and different and new things to learn. They believe strongly in the concept of learning a living rather than earning a living, always seeking new opportunities for training, education and knowledge. (Roy Morgan, 1997)

Targeting *Socially Aware* individuals has a number of implications for branding and image and product development. Implications include the need for the development of interpretation on wine and winemaking to meet the thirst for knowledge of this market and the development of products and packages that meet the experiential nature of their needs. Branding and imaging also have to appeal to this focus on learning and experiences (e.g. the use of words, concepts and images such as exploration, discovery, learning and experience).

Discovery and learning at the core of the brand

According to the Sydney Wine Region Regional Marketing Strategy (2000) the catch phrase for the regional wine tourism brand (The Sydney

Table 3.7 Percentage of Roy Morgan Value Segments that visit wineries

Value Segment/ Characteristics	*Australia*	*Hunter Valley*	*Barossa Valley*	*Canberra District*
Socially Aware Tertiary educated people in top jobs, the most educated segment	20.5	18.5	15	28
Traditional Family Life Over 50, empty nesters and mostly retired version of Middle Australia	18	12.5	7	24.5
Visible Achievers Around 40 years old, the wealth creators of Australia	26	19	28	18

Source: Adapted from Macionis and Cambourne (1998: 46–47 after Roy Morgan, 1996)

Wine Region: Australia's newest wine region is also its oldest) is *'What's Old is New'*: *'Discover Australia's newest wine region while learning about its oldest'*.

This will be used to develop promotional material and new products that tie the old with new, taking advantage of both the historical significance of the region and the relatively recent resurgence of the region. In particular, concepts such as 'discover', 'new' and 'learning' provide important cues to the *Socially Aware* segment that the region offers an experience that is educational, informative and innovative – values that are core to this target market.

The core concept of the brand image of the Sydney Wine Region is the marriage between the old and the new, while the core experience to be promoted is that of learning, discovery and exploration. To this end, there are two sets of core concepts that act as both contrasting and complementary values, each of which is based on a learning experience. This dialectic is as follows:

Table 3.8 Primary target markets

Target	***Demographics***	***Values***
Typical winery visitor	• Mature (30–50 years old) • Professional/managerial • Moderate to high income • Well educated • Intra-state or regional area • Regular consumers of wine • Intermediate to advanced wine knowledge	• Various, but in Australia mainly: • *Visible Achievers* (26%) • *Socially Aware* (20.5%) • *Traditional Family Life* (18%)
Primary target		
Socially Aware, Sydney*	• Tertiary education • Professional/managerial • Public servants, politicians and researchers • Well educated • 13.4% of NSW (*c*. 857,000) • 20.5% of winery visitors • 28.0% of emerging wine region visitors	• Attracted to things new and innovative • Learning a living rather than earning a living • Seek education and knowledge
Greater Western Sydney	• Local region • Rapid population growth • 1.5 million residents • 70% post-secondary educated • *c*. 30% professional/managerial	• Various • Target *Socially Aware, Visible Achievers and Traditional Family Life*

Note: * See www.roymorgan.com.au/products/values/sa.html for detailed description of the *Socially Aware* segment.
Sources: Greater Western Sydney Economic Development Board (2000); Macionis and Cambourne (1998); Mitchell (1999); Mitchell and Hall (2001); Roy Morgan (1997)

The Old:

- Australia's wine and agricultural heritage.
- Heritage interpretation.
- The traditions of wine making.
- The stories of pioneer winemakers.

The New:

- Sydney's modern wine industry.
- Wine education and interpretation.
- New winemaking techniques.
- The hard work of the modern winemaker.

A critical component of the marketing strategy, therefore, is the development of heritage and wine interpretive material that can be used by all cellar door operators to enhance their products and services. The strategy recommends that, along with training staff to interpret the wine and the wine-making process, educational material should be developed on the histories and stories from the individual wineries, the history of agricultural and viticultural production in the Western Sydney region, and histories and stories on prominent historical personalities associated with wine in the region.

Other product developments recommended include the introduction of a wine trail and brochure that allows the visitor to learn about the history of wine in the region and the story of the agricultural/horticultural heritage of the area. Similarly, the strategy suggests that there are a number of opportunities for the Sydney wineries to develop a range of tour packages that could meet the needs of their market. In particular, there is the possibility to develop strong partnerships between the wineries and a range of food producers, B&Bs, heritage properties and tour operators. The strategy recommends that packages be developed that have a similar educational theme that is likely to be attractive to their target market. Suggested themes for package tours include:

- gourmet education and experiences (e.g. cooking schools, wine and food matching and wild foods and wine);
- heritage experiences (e.g. learning about Sydney's agricultural heritage and heritage foods); and
- wine, art and music (e.g. tours of galleries and wineries and winery concerts)

Implementing the Strategy

At the time of this case study the Sydney Wine Region Regional Marketing Strategy is in its early phases of implementation. In this formative stage the NHWGGA will itself be undertaking an educational programme to ensure the success of the educational and learning experiences at the core of its branding. The NHWGGA will be gathering the necessary interpretive material and developing staff training packages that will form the cornerstone of the tourism product that the strategy envisages.

Case Study 3.2

Antarctic tourism: A unique educational experience

By Thomas G. Bauer

Antarctica is the least visited of all the continents. It covers 13.9 million square kilometres (nearly twice the size of Australia) and has the distinction of being the highest, driest, coldest and windiest of all the continents (Bauer, 2001). Because of its remoteness and lack of transport infrastructure the only way to get to the place is by joining a commercial cruise. A voyage to Antarctica is a unique experience for those privileged to undertake it (see Plate 3.2).

The first recorded commercial cruise to Antarctica took place in 1957/58 when 194 passengers went south. The first regular series of cruises was started by Lars Eric Lindblad in 1966/67 when 94 passengers reached Antarctic waters, and cruises have been conducted ever since. During the decade of the 1970s an estimated 14,328 went south. This figure increased only slightly for the 1980s when 15,209 paying tourists arrived. During the 1990s the situation change substantially and, by the end of the decade, 84,173 ship-based passengers had visited the Antarctic. The end of the twentieth century made the 1999/2000 season (which lasts from November to March) the most popular ever with 14,623 passenger arrivals recorded.

During the seven Antarctic seasons between 1994 and 2001 a total of 71,379 ship-borne visitors sailed to Antarctica and an analysis of the countries of origins of travellers reveals that the United States of America (45.3%), Germany (11.6%), United Kingdom (9 %), Australia (7.4%), Japan (4.3%) and Canada (2.2%) accounted for a total of nearly 80% of all tourists

Plate 3.2 Zodiac with passengers and staff from the MS Bremen in the Ross Sea

Source: T. Bauer

to Antarctica (NSF, 2002). The 'typical' Antarctic tourist is a mature-age person of either gender who has extensive travel experience. During one of the author's recent voyages to the Antarctic Peninsula, nearly 50% of the 100 passengers aboard raised their hands when the question was asked for whom this was the seventh continent they had visited. Antarctic tourists are typically professional people such as doctors, lawyers, teachers and engineers. They have undergone a lengthy education process and this no doubt has also contributed to their eagerness to learn more about Antarctica.

Antarctica is unlike any other place that tourists visit because no dedicated tourism infrastructure exists there. There are no markets or shopping malls, no pubs or restaurants and, unlike in the Arctic, there is no local population that can put on traditional dances or sell locally produced handicrafts. What the traveller does find, however, is the world's last great wilderness – a world of ice and snow, of mountains, glaciers and unique fauna. It is the grandeur of Antarctica that is most often mentioned by those who return from their voyage south.

The Lindblad Model

In 1966, when Lars-Eric Lindblad, a Swedish-American travel entrepreneur, organised the first cruises south he wanted to make them not just holiday trips but also learning experiences. Thus, what is now known as the 'Lindblad Model of Antarctic Tourism' was born. This means that cruises are accompanied by several Antarctic specialists/naturalists who share their knowledge of the continent with their guests.

On-board learning takes place in formal and informal ways and, depending on the type of vessel, the presentations take place in a dedicated lecture theatre (mainly on the larger ships) or in the ship's dining room. During a typical cruise to the Antarctic Peninsula two or three presentations are scheduled each day while the ship is traversing the 1000 kilometres of often rough ocean that separate the Peninsula from the South American mainland. Because there is so much to see and do during the time the ships are in Antarctic waters there are usually no formal lectures scheduled. There are however daily briefings on planned landings and the lecture programme resumes on the way back across the Drake Passage.

With few exceptions presentations rely heavily on the presenters' own photographs, usually slides. Presentations last from 40 to 60 minutes and are fairly informal affairs. Questions from the audience are always welcome and at the end of most talks there is often much discussion. Since travellers have all-day access to the Antarctic specialists, informal Antarctic-related education takes place in settings such as the ship's bridge, the bar or even the sauna. Learning does however also happen during Zodiac excursions and during shore visits. On these occasions the lecturers become guides whose main role is to interpret and explain the sites that are being visited. Antarctic travellers, unlike tourists at most other destinations, are very knowledgeable about the destination and many have read several books on the region prior to travelling there. Sometimes these readings, particularly in the context of the 'Heroic Era' of Antarctic exploration commonly associated with names like Mawson, Shackleton and Scott, can provide the reason why people select Antarctica as a travel destination in the first place. Ships also have polar libraries on board and passengers make good use of them to deepen their understanding of Antarctic matters.

The lecturers come have diverse backgrounds but have one thing in common – they love Antarctica. Some of them are former Antarctic expeditioners who may have worked at an Antarctic scientific station in the past. They are able to share with their audience their experiences with living in Antarctica – quite different from visiting the place as a tourist. They also provide an insight into what it is like to be isolated from the rest of the world through the long Antarctic winter, during which the sun does not rise for many months and they speak of the problems that can arise when one is isolated in Antarctica with only a handful of other people. Another group of lecturers comprises professionals and researchers in the various topics covered during the voyages. The most popular topics are Antarctic history, exploration, geography, geology, glaciology and ice, wildlife (in particular marine mammals and seabirds, including, of course, penguins), wildlife adaptation, regulations/codes of behaviour, shipping and environmental protection.

The International Association of Antarctica Tour Operators (IAATO) has compiled a set of slides that introduce the various issues, rules and regulations concerning environmental protection in Antarctica. Members of IAATO (nearly all Antarctic tour operators are members) are obliged to present these slides to their clients prior to their arrival in Antarctica and attendance at these lectures is compulsory. Passenger names are checked prior to them being admitted to the lecture room. The various aspects of Antarctic tourism, in particular a discussion of its potential environmental impacts, are also covered on some of the cruises. Taking education in the south one step further, some cruises are sub-chartered by an organisation called 'Students on Ice' to introduce young people to a diversity of Antarctic issues.

In conclusion, a voyage to Antarctica is much more than a holiday. It is a unique experience that takes place in an almost pristine and very beautiful setting, an experience that is greatly enhanced by the knowledge transmitted to the participants by the Antarctic experts on board. One of the aims of the educational programmes is to turn Antarctic travellers into ambassadors who speak up for the preservation of this unique environment.

Chapter 4

Schools' Educational Tourism

WITH NEIL CARR AND CHRIS COOPER

Introduction

For the purpose of this chapter schools' educational tourism is defined as incorporating all school/field trips organised by primary and secondary schools for children between 5 and 18 years of age, as well as language schools, where people travel abroad to a school to learn a foreign language. However, language schools are not restricted to children, rather the majority of language school participants appear to be adults. Both form a growing and potentially important segment of the tourism industry, yet little research has been conducted on either. This chapter will focus on secondary and primary schools as there is more in the literature on this form of educational tourism, although some discussion of language schools does occur.

School trips encompass domestic and international trips, and student exchanges. Broadly speaking, school trips (for both types of schools) can be divided into two categories: first there are curriculum-based ones that are directly linked to the lessons taught in the classroom and represent either an integral part or extension of the formal learning experience; and, second, there is the type of field trip that may be defined as extra-curricular excursions. These are designed outside the constraints of curriculum demands and are not linked directly to a particular class or discipline. Language schools range from private and public organisations providing courses seasonally or on a year-round basis to providers ranging from small in-house businesses to multinational organisations. Provision can comprise general English learning or providing training for Teachers of English as a Foreign Language (TEFL). However, as Batchelor (2000) notes, the majority of students attend general English or vacation courses, underlining the importance of destination and tourism activities alongside language learning and education.

Overall, schools' tourism is a poorly researched and understood segment of the tourism industry, particularly with regard to its scale and specific nature. The educational value of field trips is the most researched area of schools' tourism, but the majority of studies have only dealt with the perspective of teachers and educational experts. The views of the school participants have only rarely been directly studied and the parents, often the people funding the trips, do not seem to have been asked about their perception of the value of field trips or why they often help to pay for them. School trips provide a variety of benefits to both children and those in adult education. Curriculum-based trips, structured around lessons taught in the classroom, can offer an effective experiential learning opportunity that allows individuals to see how theories and concepts work in reality (Lai, 1999).

International curriculum-based field trips have been specifically linked with the ability to motivate children to learn foreign languages in a manner that is not possible in the classroom (Pasquier, 1994). The recognition of the value of curriculum-based field trips as experiential learning tools, is not a modern phenomenon; rather, the field trip has a long history in children's education (Tal, 2001; Nespor, 2000) that, according to Hurd (1997), can be traced back to at least the 1500s. School trips are also utilised to stimulate interest amongst children in specific disciplines and lead to higher quality learning experiences back in the classroom (Hurd, 1997; Robertson, 2001). See Exhibit 4.1 for a discussion of a secondary school educational programme in Zanzibar. Attempts to measure the benefits of curriculum-based field trip participation on children's education have indicated that these trips provide students with cognitive gains and increase learning if they are well structured and planned (Tal, 2001; Hurd, 1997). For example, in a study of geography-based field trips, MacKenzie and White (1982) found that children who went on a course-related trip performed better in a test of knowledge than those who did not go on this type of trip.

Field trips can also be used to help develop traits in children, that while of value as part of the maturation process and general education of the child, are not specific to a course taught in the classroom. Indeed, Lai (1999: 239) states:

> apart from helping students consolidate and apply classroom learning and acquire practical skills, it [the field trip] also contributes to affective goals such as development of environmental attitudes and personal and social development.

Exhibit 4.1

Ecotourism and secondary school students: The Chumbe Island Coral Park, Zanzibar

By Eleanor Cater

Chumbe Island Coral Park (CHICOP) in Zanzibar was established in 1991 as the first fully functioning Marine Protected Area (MPA) in Tanzania, and the only privately created and managed MPA in the world. The project was developed along the lines of a commercial enterprise, using ecotourism as the revenue-generating component of the project with all profits from the tourism operations going into conservation management and education programmes for local schoolchildren.

All employment on the island is targeted at the neighbouring fishing communities, which promotes awareness raising at all levels and empowers the local Zanzibari community to feel committed towards the preservation of their natural heritage. The island is managed by rangers who were former fishermen from neighbouring communities. These rangers play a key role in teaching fellow fishermen of the importance of Chumbe as a protected area. With the pristine Chumbe reef based upstream from the major fisheries areas of the West Zanzibar coast, Chumbe is a vital fish nursery that continues to replenish the exploited resources of the fisheries ecosystem around Zanzibar. In this way anti-poaching tactics rely on education and awareness raising in the local communities and have proved immensely successful as a unique approach to MPA management in the region.

In an area where the economy is now heavily dependent on the income from tourism, Chumbe is a blueprint for environmentally friendly tourism management and is a leading case study exemplifying that it is possible to have conservation, education and ecotourism working in harmony. Schoolchildren have themselves become key members of the Chumbe Community, through the Chumbe Education Programmes operating in the park that sponsor local school visits to the island. As elsewhere in the region, school education in Zanzibar is based on rote learning of extremely academic syllabi that have little relationship with the surrounding world. Though Zanzibar is a coral island, coral reef ecology is insufficiently covered in school syllabi. Formal education also does not yet provide environmental information on marine issues, as revealed by an analysis of the syllabi of primary and secondary education (Riedmiller, 1991; Riedmiller & Cooksey, 1995). Also extra-curricular activities, such as field excursions, are rarely organized, and very few children ever have a chance to visit coral reefs and coral-rag forests. This is also partly due to the fact that schoolchildren, and particularly girls, do not normally learn how to swim and snorkel.

To help improve this situation, CHICOP has over the years conducted school excursions for secondary students and their teachers to Chumbe Island. Guided by park rangers along the nature trails in the reef and the forest, the participating children benefit greatly from the insight they gain into marine biology, forest ecology and environmental protection. The excursions are in cooperation with secondary schools in Zanzibar, and consist of one-day school excursions to Chumbe Island that provide informal hands-on environmental education for schoolchildren, and at the same time give accompanying teachers a first insight into how to teach practical field-based environmental education. Teachers have not been trained for linking classroom teaching to field excursions and so this is a novel and innovative approach for all concerned. In 2001 the Education Programmes developed to the extent that a module on 'The Coral Reef', produced by CHICOP, was officially recognised by the Ministry of Education and was expanded to encompass teacher training workshops and evaluation seminars to link the learning experiences particularly with the science syllabi. The Chumbe Education Programmes are now a leading force within the Chumbe Project and CHICOP enables funds to be directed towards assisting the schools from around the coast of Unguja to be transported to Chumbe, and providing all training, equipment, use of facilities, etc. for free. Additionally, funds are being put towards providing literature for teachers manuals, classroom aids and educational tools for use both on and off the island.

Similarly, Robertson (2001: 78) claims that 'field-trips challenge children's perceptions, building their confidence and changing their attitudes towards themselves, their environment and others'. In addition, international field trips have been attributed with helping to expand students' understanding of their home country and its position in a global context (Anonymous, 2002). While curriculum-based trips may offer children these opportunities, extra-curricular trips tend to be designed specifically to provide this type of educational experience.

Demand for Schools' Tourism

Demand for primary and secondary schools' tourism

The number of children taking domestic, and especially international, school trips is currently expanding. Indeed, Baker (2001) states that, in the UK, school trips are growing in popularity, and although 'local museum visits are still staple fare ... even primary schools seem to be opting for residential trips these days'. Although there has been a lack of research into the scale of schools tourism, Cooper and Latham (1989) estimated that, in England, this market undertook approximately 12 million domestic visits, which is equivalent to 5% of the entire sightseeing market, and generated £8 million annually in the late 1980s. In addition, Revell (2002) stated that, on average, schoolchildren in the UK spend two days on field trips each year. Within Australia the number of children visiting the national capital, Canberra, on school trips was estimated at 108,000 in 1998, contributing AUS$10.2 million to the ACT economy (Coughlan *et al.*, 1999). Further research was carried out in 2001 to assess changes in demand as a result of marketing of the this segment of schools' tourism and is discussed in Exhibit 4.2.

Another example of the growth in schools tourism in developed countries is provided by Japan. In 1984 Ogura Commercial High School was the first school in Japan to take its students on an international, curriculum-based field trip. Since this time, as Figure 4.3 demonstrates, there has been a huge growth in the number of Japanese high school students taking international curriculum-based field trips, known as 'shugaku ryoko'. By 1998 a total of 936 high schools in Japan provided overseas field trips to 148,703 students. The annual increases noted in Figure 4.3 are in contrast to declines in other Japanese international tourism segments that have been adversely affected by the relatively poor performance of the national economy. Shugaku ryoko is still in its infancy with a number of prefectures in Japan – such as Tokyo, which

Exhibit 4.2

Making the most of your assets: School excursions and tourism to Canberra, Australia's National Capital

By Brock Cambourne and Pam Faulks

Introduction and background

Canberra, as Australia's National Capital, has a plethora of national institutions that are relevant to a range of curriculum areas (such as history, science and technology, civics and government, art and culture and the environment). Therefore, Canberra can be considered a pre-eminent educational destination for the schools' market in Australia. Tourism activity as a result of overnight school excursions can also result in significant economic and promotional opportunities for a destination. A previous study of the [schools] educational tourism market to the Australian Capital Territory (Coughlan *et al.*, 1999) showed that:

- approximately 108,000 students visit the National Capital each year as part of an educational tour; and
- these educational tourists injected approximately AUS$10.2 million into the ACT economy annually.

This study also contended that destination marketing to schools is as important as any other major market segment for several reasons, including:

- the potential to stimulate repeat [individual] visitation to the destination following a positive school excursion experience;
- the potential of the schools' market to bolster off-peak attendances at attractions and increase supplementary revenue from shops and catering outlets; and
- that there is considerable latent demand for school excursions to the ACT and that coordinated and targeted marketing could significantly increase the size of the market (Coughlan et al., 1999).

In the light of these findings the National Capital Education Tourism Project (NCETP) was established in 2000 as a marketing and product development programme designed to facilitate a significant increase in the number of schoolchildren visiting the Australian Capital Territory for educational purposes. Its stated aim is to 'provide the opportunity for students to engage in Australia's democracy, excellence in art, culture, heritage and sport in the National Capital and encourage them to appreciate the significance of the National Capital as the symbol of Australian unity, culture and achievement' (NCETP, 2001).

The NCETP coordinates a range of activities including:

- development and distribution of a range of marketing collateral targeted specifically for the schools' tourism market;
- the promotion and administration of a federally funded rebate scheme for remote and regional schools visiting Australia's National Capital; and
- the conduct of marketing activities such as a travelling 'road show' promoting educational tourism to Australia's National Capital.

The Project is funded and managed by a consortium of the Australian Capital Territory Government, the National Capital Authority and the National Capital Attractions Association (representing over 40 major Canberra tourist attractions). To monitor the success of the Project and provide strategic direction for the further development and marketing of educational tourism to the ACT a research programme was established to:

- develop a methodology to accurately monitor monthly and annual visitation to the ACT by school groups;
- profile the nature of the school excursion market to the ACT; and
- examine the impact of a visit to the National Capital upon visiting students' sense of nationhood and their development of citizenry concepts and ideals.

Methodology

Data for calculating the size and effect of school excursions to Canberra in 2001 was obtained in three ways:

- face-to-face interviews with coach drivers at a selection of Canberra attractions;
- self-completion surveys with teachers visiting the ACT; and
- monthly visitation data provided by ACT attractions.

The interview and survey instruments examined among other things:

- characteristics of school excursion groups (such as origins, numbers of children and accompanying adults on the excursion, frequency of visit/s and grade composition);
- behavioural aspects of the visit (including length of stay, type of accommodation used, mode of travel, and attractions visited);
- impact of the visit on teachers and students;
- teachers' school excursion needs and curriculum priorities and Canberra's performance as a school excursion destination in comparison to these needs/requirements; and
- destination information sources and planning tools.

To monitor the volume of the interstate school excursion market to the Australian Capital Territory in 2001, data derived from interviews with coach drivers was used to determine on a monthly basis:

- the total number of interstate schoolchildren on each excursion; and
- the attractions that schools visited.

These data were then 'triangulated' with actual attendance figures supplied by attractions to calculate the current volume of school visitation to the ACT. This permitted the calculation of the total number of interstate schoolchildren accounted for in each monthly survey period, and the subsequent determination of the percentage of schoolchildren visiting each attraction. Simply knowing that 75% of excursions go to the Australian War Memorial, for example, does not necessarily provide an accurate estimate of schools' visitation to the ACT because the excursion groups are of differing sizes. By utilising both the total number of schoolchildren on each excursion and the itinerary details it is possible to calculate the total volume of the interstate schools' market. Table 4.1 provides an example of this calculation for three participating attractions in August 2001.

How many schoolchildren visited Australia's National Capital in 2001?

In 2001 it is estimated that 127,956 interstate schoolchildren visited the National Capital. This represents an increase of 11.4% in the total volume of the market. These data are detailed in Table 4.2. Given that the Australian Capital Territory suffered a decrease in overall

Table 4.1 Example of calculation of total interstate school visitation to Canberra, August 2001

Attraction	*A*	*B*	*C*	*D*
Parliament House	91.7	92.9	20,456	22,019
Australian War Memorial	85.1	84.4	19,289	22,854
Questacon (National Science and Technology Centre)	73.6	72.3	21,095	29,177
Total = average of total volume figures				24,683

Note: A = % excursions visiting attraction, B = % interstate schoolchildren visiting attraction, C = No. of interstate schoolchildren reported by attraction, D = Total volume of interstate schools market, August 2001 = (C/B) × 100

overnight visitation of approximately 11% in 2001, these figures highlight the success of the NCETP in focusing on and developing the school excursion market. Approximately 10% of schools visiting the ACT in 2001 were visiting Australia's National Capital for the first time. Significantly, the largest proportion of schools that were visiting the ACT for the first time were from Queensland (6% of the total market, but 18% of schools visiting for the first time) and Victoria (16% of the total market, but 33% of schools visiting the ACT for the first time). This has been attributed to increased and extra activity in these States by the NCETP via increased marketing, and attendance and presentation at teachers' conferences.

Table 4.2 Number of interstate student visitors to the National Capital in 2001

Year[a]	*1997*	*1998*	*1999*	*2000*	*2001*
Total number of schoolchildren	101,042	112,989	115,238	114,845	127,956
% change		+11.8	+1.9	–0.3	+11.4

Note: [a] Figures for 1997–2000 are derived from a previous study of schools' visitation to the ACT, which used multipliers based upon the proportion of schools visiting several key attractions.

Why did they visit?

A visit to Australia's National Capital is increasingly being seen by Australian teachers as vital in supporting enhanced learning outcomes of important Australian curriculum areas such as 'Civics and Government, 'Australian History' and 'Art and Culture'. In order to examine the impact of visiting the National Capital on educational outcomes, teachers were presented with a list of statements referring to the value of visiting Canberra, and, using a scale of 1 (strongly agree) to 5 (strongly disagree), were asked to rate the extent to which they agreed or disagreed with the statements. These statements and the mean scores are presented in Figure 4.1.

These curriculum concepts, which are represented in Canberra by national institutions such as Parliament House, the Australian War Memorial, Questacon (the National Science and Technology Centre) and the National Gallery of Australia are seen as important drivers in stimulating schools' tourism activity to the ACT. Figure 4.2 shows the mean scores for the relative importance of a range of curriculum areas in planning a trip to Australia's National Capital. Interestingly,

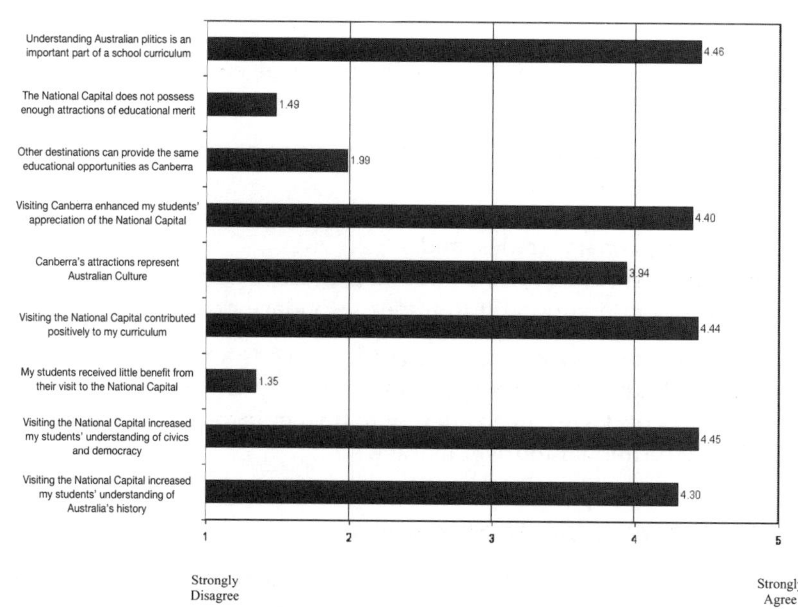

Figure 4.1 Value of visiting the National Capital

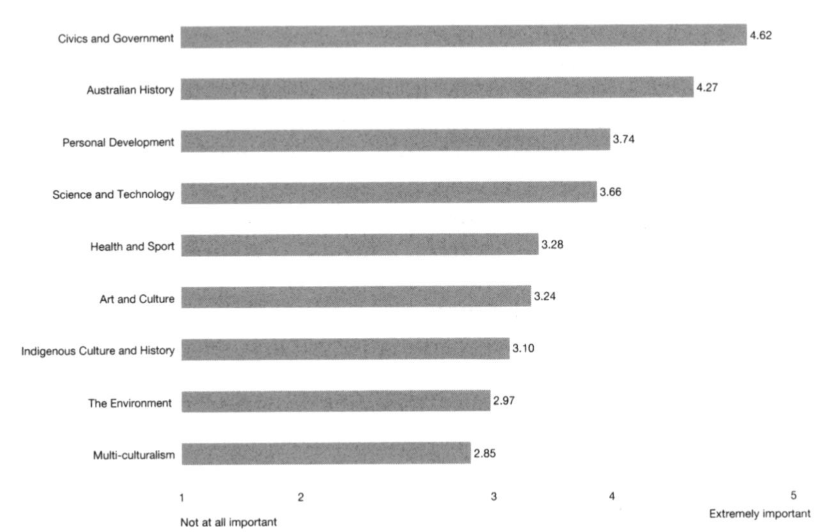

Figure 4.2 Importance of curriculum areas in planning a visit to the National Capital

there is a relative shift in the importance of curriculum areas to various grades, with:

- Science and Technology being more important to lower and middle primary grades;
- Civics and Government being more important to middle and upper primary grades; and
- Australian History, and Art and Culture as curriculum concepts being more important to upper secondary grades.

An understanding of these curriculum needs and expectations is being used by the regional tourism industry to develop relevant 'curriculum packages' in an attempt to further increase the size of the schools' educational tourism market.

Product development considerations

The outcomes of this study are also being used by industry stakeholders to facilitate the development and delivery of enhanced schools' tourism products. For example:

- knowing that more than 25% of visiting schools consist of groups of more than 70 students has significant implications for how attractions manage their individual capacity considerations;
- similarly, with 44% of visiting schools comprising multiple grades, attractions involved in the schools' market are now developing experiences that meet the multiple curriculum needs and outcomes required by such visiting school groups;
- knowing that 92% of visiting schools travel to Canberra via hired coaches has refocused marketing activities onto these important suppliers of schoolchildren; and
- understanding the expected educational outcomes desired by teachers is facilitating the identification and development of new relationships amongst stakeholders to implement curriculum-based destination packages.

encompasses a high proportion of the country's schools and students – yet to loosen their restrictions on international school trips. Furthermore, the numbers shown in Figure 4.3 do not account for the extra-curricular overseas field trips undertaken by Japanese schoolchildren (Anonymous, 2002).

One reason behind the growth in the numbers of children going on school-organised field trips relates to the desire of parents to provide their offspring with the best possible educational opportunities. In Japan it has been claimed that this desire is so strong that in times of economic recession parents will alter the household budget but not the funds available for their children's education, including curriculum-based field trips (Anonymous, 2002). In addition, based on research in Hong Kong, Lai (1999: 239) states that:

> despite some students' negative experiences of previous field trips, there was a universally strong desire to escape from their perceived boredom and constraints of the classroom. Field trips were cherished for their rarity and freedom, and the field sites were sought for their novelty.

This desire helps to sustain the increase in the quantity of school trips being offered by schools. Another factor driving the growth in the number of schools offering increasingly exotic, and as a result expensive, field trips may be the decline in the numbers of school-age children in the

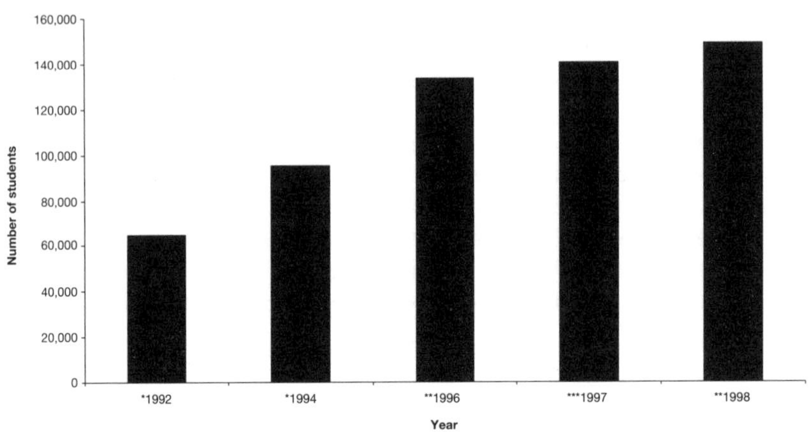

Figure 4.3 Number of high school pupils in Japan taking an international field trip

Source: *Ministry of Education, Culture, Sports, Science and Technology (1996); **Anonymous (1998); ***Anonymous (2002)

developed countries of the world. This downturn has increased competition amongst schools, particularly private ones, forcing them to find new ways to market themselves and entice students to them. One method of doing this is to offer field trips that are appealing to both children and their parents (Admin, 2001; Anonymous, 2002). Cheaper and easier travel options have also been flagged as potential reasons for the growing numbers of children going on school-based field trips (Baker, 2001). As the number of field trips offered increases, pressure rises on parents who cannot easily afford to send their children on these excursions. They are forced by peer pressure from other children and parents to find ways to subsidise trips so as to avoid themselves and their children being stigmatised. Indeed, Nespor (2000: 30) notes how 'the stakes can seem quite high to parents and children [because] field trips are signs of status'. As part of this process it has been claimed that some students in Australia are now working and saving money to pay for field trips (Admin, 2001). If students spend too much time working to pay for their school excursions the benefits of the trips to their education of the trips may be negated by the impact of their employment on the time they can spend on other aspects of their education, such as their homework.

At the global level, the school tourism market appears to have the potential to expand for the foreseeable future. This prediction is based on the fact that, as Figure 4.4 illustrates, the numbers of children in primary and secondary education consistently increased, at the global level, between 1970 and 1997, to a total of 1,066,566,000. However, the growth in school populations has not been uniform across the globe. Rather, since 1970 it has been most marked in Africa and Asia, which have witnessed increases of 249% and 93% in the numbers of pupils in primary and secondary education, respectively. In contrast, Europe recorded only a 13% growth in the numbers of children in educational institutions between 1970 and 1997 (Cooper, 1999). The geographical nature of the increases in primary and secondary school populations is reflected by the fact that least-developed, developing and developed countries' increases in the numbers of schoolchildren over the same time period were 218%, 117%, and 12%, respectively. By studying the primary school population data in isolation it is possible to predict how many children will be attending school in the future. While there was a 51% growth in the size of the primary school population at the global level, least-developed countries and developing nations witnessed 203% and 85% increases, respectively. In contrast, the numbers of children in developed countries attending primary school shrank by 10% between 1970 and 1997, with Europe recording a 16% drop (UNESCO, 2002).

The decline in the numbers of primary schoolchildren in European and other developed nations indicates that the overall school population is likely to continue to decline in these countries for the foreseeable future.

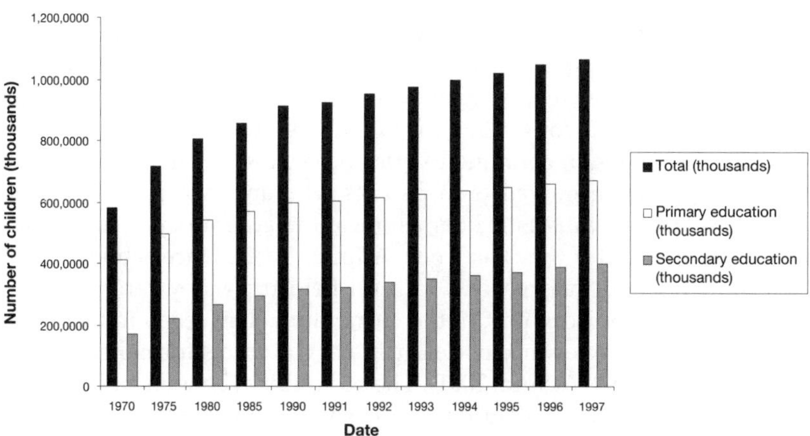

Figure 4.4 Number of children attending school at the global level

Source: UNESCO (2002)

This situation is confirmed by declining birth rates in most of the developed countries of the world. For example, the current birth rate in the European Union of 1.45 is as low as it has been since the Second World War. Furthermore, the low birth rate in the European Union has been a persistent trait for the last 20 years, with childlessness steadily increasing throughout the 1990s (Dietl, 2002; BBC News, 1999). As a result of the decline in the school-age population in developed countries the demand for school tourism in these nations is likely to decrease, which will have adverse consequences for the operators who cater to this segment of the tourist population. However, the rising overall and primary school populations in developing countries, combined with the increasing economic wealth of these countries, indicate that there is a potential for growth in demand for school tourism in these nations. But, while the size of the school population in the world's least-developed countries rose rapidly between 1970 and 1997, there is little reason to suggest that these children will be a major source of customers for the school tourism industry. This is because the relatively poor state of these countries' economies militates against the educational authorities and/or parents being able to afford to provide children with school tourism experiences.

As well as the decline in the numbers of children attending school in the developed nations of the world, there are several other issues that threaten the future demand for schools' tourism. One of these issues is that education systems are coming under increasing economic pressure, leading to a desire to focus spending on core educational requirements rather than optional extras such as field trips. Indeed, in a study of Australian schools, Coughlan and Wells (1999) found the primary barrier to schools undertaking field trips was financial, while the ability to link the trip to curriculum requirements was also a major constraint. Exhibit 4.3 discusses demand constraints for the school excursion market.

In order to be able to continue to offer field trips, the financial burden is increasingly being moved onto parents who are then forced to 'find ways to say no to enthusiastic kids who want to accompany their friends and feel stigmatised if they can't go' (Admin, 2001). Once schools begin to ask students and their parents to fund field trips they can no longer make them a compulsory part of the curriculum. This leads to increased concerns about the relevance of field trips to children's formal education (Coughlan *et al.*, 1999; Admin, 2001). The educational benefits of field trips are also coming under pressure in an era when educational authorities appear to be increasingly concerned with standardised teaching and examination practices that field trips do not easily conform to (BBC News, 1998). The potential for field trips to cause divisions in schools between

Exhibit 4.3

Barriers and constraints in the schools' market: The case of Australia

By Duane Coughlan, Josette Wells and Brent Ritchie

Introduction

From a tourism marketing perspective, those people who take part in an activity represent existing demand while those individuals who express an interest but do not participate because of particular constraints represent potential or latent demand. The value of understanding those factors that act as a barrier or impediment between the 'preference for an activity' and participation in it (Crawford & Godbey, 1987) lies in awareness, which allows the marketer to convert that latent demand into existing demand. Constraints on the demand for travel are well documented in the tourism economic (Bull, 1995) and leisure literature (Godbey, 1990; Goodale, 1992; Jackson & Scott, 1999). Two major themes have emerged in research: activity-specific participation and the impediments or constraints facing particular segments of the population. In the case of the former, studies have centred on the barriers causing – non-participation in specific activities such as sport and recreation (Backman & Crompton, 1989), while research into specific population groups such as females and disabled groups is more recent (Williams & Basford, 1992 in Coughlan & Wells, 1999a). Further empirical research has focused on more conceptual approaches, highlighting common dimensions, such as time commitments, costs, facilities and opportunities, skills and abilities and transportation and access, and various models describing the interaction of individuals and groups in order to explain constraints (Jackson & Scott, 1999; Hinch *et al.*, 1998).

The role of the marketer in converting the aforementioned latent demand is to overcome those barriers which market research will uncover. In this situation, both economic and leisure constraint theory can be useful in grouping variables which are, broadly, economic (costs), spatial (time commitments), personal/psychological (lack of motivation/interest, attitude), institutional in the generating region (timetable, curriculum) and institutional in the destination region (appropriate accommodation, the variety of attractions, access to medical facilities).

Research on the latent demand of schools' tourism in Australia

Research carried out on the schools' market in Canberra, Australia involved a latent demand component as well as examination of actual school excursion visits to Canberra. The latent market analysis was conducted in the form of a self-completion mail questionnaire to 4000 schools throughout Australia in November 1998, excluding schools in Canberra. Schools were selected randomly from a complete list of Australian schools, randomly generated from a list supplied by List Bank, a commercial mailing list supplier in Australia. Of the initial distribution, 807 surveys were returned completed and useable, providing a response rate of 20.2%. Although this response rate was low, Ryan (1995) believes that a response rate of between 15% and 20% percent is normal for this type of survey methodology. Although a wide range of data was collected, for the purpose of this exhibit perceived barriers to school visits will be outlined.

Overall the latent market survey was relatively representative. Most significantly there was an over-representation of schools from New South Wales and an under-representation of schools from Victoria. However, the sample was representative from the perspective of whether the school was a primary or secondary school and, additionally, whether the school was a government or non-government school.

Schools within the latent market study were asked if they were able to make as many excursions as they would like; only 23% answered in the affirmative. The majority (77%) felt that they were restricted in some way by various constraints. The constraints listed were ranked based on their mean scores on a four-point Likert scale ranging from 'not important' to 'very important'. The primary barrier or constraint to the undertaking of school excursions was financial (see Table 4.3). Almost all respondents felt that this was of concern. Secondly, distance to travel was seen as a major concern for those schools that did not undertake as many activities as they would like. From a positive angle the constraints that appear in the second half of Table 4.3 deal with issues that marketers are concerned about. That is, information and knowledge about school excursions, range of attractions, access for the disabled and medical facilities.

It would appear that the primary constraint from a schools perspective is financial. However, given that a large number of the schools

Table 4.3 Barriers to school excursions in Australia

Constraint	*Mean score*	*Constraint*	*Mean score*
Financial	3.9	Availability of transport	2.4
Distance to travel	3.4		
Relevance to school curriculum	3.0	Staff willingness	2.2
		Access to medical facilities	2.1
Timetabling	2.7		
Lack of time	2.6	Limited attractions	1.9
Logistical organisation	2.5	Facilities for the disabled	1.8
Staff shortages	2.5		
Appropriate accommodation	2.5	Lack of knowledge/ information	1.7

Source: Coughlan and Wells (1999b)

surveyed in this study were unaware of financial subsidies, such as the Citizenship Visit Program (CVP) operated by the Commonwealth Government, some of the effects of this constraint can be mitigated through marketing of such programmes to schools. As mentioned earlier, these constraints can be sorted into broad variable groupings: economic, spatial, personal/psychological, institutional in the generating region and institutional in the destination region. Although the rank order does not naturally put these constraints into these groupings further examination via factor or cluster analysis would be a useful exercise.

those who can and cannot afford to go on them, and a lack of trust by teachers in schoolchildren's behaviour have also been noted as reasons why schools have ceased to provide field trips (Nespor, 2000).

Despite the variety of sources of pressure being exerted on the educational system to stop field trips, probably the largest issue is related to the deaths, accidents and other incidents that occur on school trips and how they are portrayed in the media (Anonymous, 1994). For example, in the UK it has been estimated that seven children died while on school trips in 2001 and 47 between 1985 and 2001 (Revell, 2002). Seeing these deaths examined in detail by the media it is not surprising that Robertson

(2001: 78) has claimed that 'parents are increasingly nervous about allowing their children to participate in out-of-school activities'.

With teachers and other organisers of school trips increasingly facing criminal charges and the process of public inquiries when a child is injured or killed while on a field trip, it is not only parents who are having second thoughts about field trips. In addition to death or injury, the recent revelation that over one-third of British schoolchildren aged 16 or under have had sexual experiences while on holiday, 60% of which involved penetrative sex, shows how schools and teachers may face litigation linked to field trips (Lacey, 2001). Speaking after the publication of the sexual behaviour of children on school trips Nigel de Gruchy, general secretary of the National Association of Schoolmasters and Union of Women Teachers (NAS/UWT), which is the UK's second largest teachers' union, said:

> teachers are taking enormous risks by taking children on residential trips, especially abroad. The irony is that it could happen at home and the parents would turn a blind eye but if it happens on a school trip they sue the teacher for lack of supervision. (Lightfoot, 2001)

Faced with the threat of legal action as a result of incidents that occur during field trips the NAS/UWT now advises its members not to organise or go on school trips (BBC News, 2002). While not participating in field trips removes the risk of litigation and/or criminal charges from teachers and schools it also robs students of the opportunity to take part in school trips and experience the educational benefits associated with them. In effect, the blame culture and litigation mentality increasingly being cultivated around the world could lead to the end of school trips (Robertson, 2001; Smithers, 2001). The British government has attempted to reduce the risk associated with school trips by providing teachers with highly detailed field trip preparation guidelines. While these are, in theory, a sensible approach to risk management, as Baker (2001) states, 'just reading them [the guidelines] could frighten you off organising a trip'.

Demand for language schools' tourism

The demand for language schools, and in particular English language schools, has given rise to a growing sector that has many tourism implications. The rise in demand for international skills is reflected in the impact that education has had on tourism through international travel to participate in language schools. According to Smith and Jenner (1997a) travelling abroad to learn a language is perceived to be one of the most important segments of educational tourism worldwide. The range of courses provided illustrates the diverse range of market segments within language schools' tourism. According to Batchelor (2000), the market can include:

- general English;
- adult vacation;
- junior vacation;
- executive English;
- English Plus (where English is studied along with other subjects);
- one-to-one tuition, in school or in the teacher's home;
- English for Academic Purposes (EAP), including foundation and pre-sessional courses;
- English for Specific Purposes (ESP); and
- English for Teachers of English as a Foreign Language (TEFL).

McCallen (2000) notes that, due to the proliferation of courses, by the year 2000 a total of 1.2 million English as a Foreign Language (EFL) students will be taking courses abroad with expenditure on travel, course fees, accommodation and related expenses approaching £2 billion. Data collection on this market is 'patchy', although this is improving as the size and scale of the market is increasingly being recognised by the public and private sectors (Batchelor, 1998). There are four main data collection outlets in the UK that collect information on language school students. They provide useful information on the size and nature of the demand side of this type of educational tourism. They are:

- *MINE (Marketing Intelligence Network)*: A co-operative of 40 accredited course organisers who analyse student length of stay, origins and course demand. Data are only available to subscribers and allow providers to benchmark their individual performance with other providers.
- *ARELS (the Association of Recognised English Language Services)*: Publishes data from its members on numbers of students and length of stay and distinguishes between junior and adult courses, student weeks and origins.
- *ELT Course Monitor*: This is a sample survey of quality ELT course providers who are members of accredited organisations, and it measures student weeks, country/area of residence and course duration.
- *International Passenger Survey*: This survey is undertaken by the Office of National Statistics and asks ELT-related questions every

six years. Data have been collected in 1984, 1990 and 1996 and examine students' motivations and main purpose of visit, visitor numbers, expenditure, country of residence and length of stay (in Batchelor, 1998).

Results from the data sources collected by these organisations suggest that, although ELT students represent 2.6% of visitors to Britain, they spend more, contributing 6.25% (£773 million) to Britain's tourism foreign currency earnings (Batchelor, 1998) and have the potential to help regenerate declining seaside resorts (see Case Study 4.2). McCallen (2000) notes the top three student source markets by destination, illustrating the origin of demand for various language school destinations (see Table 4.4). The table illustrates the importance of Asian countries such as Japan and South Korea, as well as European countries such as Germany, Italy, France and Spain. Furthermore, proximity appears to be a factor in attracting language school students, with source markets located close to destinations being particularly important. For instance, both New Zealand and Australia are heavily reliant on short-haul Asian markets from Japan, South Korea, Thailand and Indonesia. The UK is reliant on a large number of source markets, compared with Canada and Malta who are dependent upon three markets for over 80% of their total market share. This could be potentially dangerous for these two countries in the case of economic hardship, as evidenced in the 1997/98 Asian economic crisis, which caused a downturn in demand from some Asian source countries (Batchelor, 2000).

According to a study commissioned by the British Council in 1997, language school students' decisions to study in Britain were due to a variety of reasons, some of which were related to recreation and cultural heritage. A total of:

- 72% stated that they wanted to learn English and 62% mentioned the reputation of Britain for teaching English;
- 48% mentioned that they wanted to study in a safe country;
- 46% mentioned value for money;
- 37% wanted to experience British culture;
- 31% wanted to continue studies at a British College;
- 29% wanted to combine holidays with study; and
- 29% wanted to learn more about Britain and its heritage. (in Batchelor, 2000)

Grant *et al.* (1998) also note the motivational aspects of culture and heritage for language school students, and note that these issues need to

Table 4.4 Top three student source markets by destination

Destination	*Source markets*						*Total share*
	Largest (%)		*Second largest (%)*		*Third largest (%)*		
Canada	Japan	39	S. Korea	31	Taiwan	13	83
Malta	Germany	44	Italy	26	France	12	82
New Zealand	Japan	48	S. Korea	21	Thailand	7	76
Ireland	Italy	27	France	25	Spain	23	75
Australia	Japan	32	S. Korea	24	Indonesia	9	65
USA	S. Korea	22	Japan	22	Taiwan	7	51
UK	Italy	17	Japan	12	Germany	8	37

Source: McCallen (2000)

be considered in the planning, marketing and management of the language school experience. The authors believe that students are often looking for leisure activities to escape from classes, and Batchelor (2000) also notes that a good social programme and immersion in British culture is important to students, especially as many travel alone. Students stay on average for between 29 and 32 days during their trip (Grant *et al.*, 1998; Batchelor, 1998), with students on public sector courses (often university foundation or pre-sessional courses) having a longer length of stay. A total of 85% of ELT students are classified as adults and 15% are juniors, but, as Grant *et al.* (1998) comment, these figures mask the range of ages, from children as young as ten to people over 50. However, they believe that the majority of language school students are comparatively young and between the ages of 16 and 30.

Although the market is still heavily seasonal, there has been an increase in visits during the first few months of the year in Britain, reflecting a growth in the ESP market. In 1996, according to Batchelor (1998), a total of 32% of language school visitors arrived in the third quarter (July–September), 27% in the second quarter (April–June), 22% in the last quarter (October–December) and 19% in the first quarter from January to March (up from 4% in 1984). This provides opportunities, especially for destinations to offset the seasonal nature of tourism. Students may also complement the existing tourism market as they are often placed with host families and do not require accommodation infrastructure and are therefore less likely to displace other visitors. Students are influenced heavily by word of mouth from previous students, friends and family, although specialist travel agents/language school agents, the British Council and the British Embassy are important information sources as well.

Supply of Schools' Tourism

Supply of primary and secondary schools' tourism

From the point of view of the tourism industry, the schools' market remains something of a 'Cinderella', with those who provide for schools demonstrating clear competitive advantages. For example, for many commercial tourism attractions, the primary and secondary schools' market can represent at least 10% of their total visitor numbers, and for some this figure can exceed 15% (Cooper, 1999). Nonetheless, much of the rest of the tourist industry dismisses the market as low yield and too much effort to provide for, failing to see the benefits of the market and actively discouraging school visits, especially in peak periods. However, for those who seek to attract the primary and secondary schools' market there are clear advantages:

- schools can be encouraged to visit in the off-peak and quiet times of the day;
- schools are an excellent source of positive word-of-mouth marketing and children often return with their families;
- children's exhibits are newsworthy;
- there is an opportunity to promote the non-financial benefits of the visit, including an understanding of, for example, sustainability, environmental concerns, social and cultural issues, and issues of race and conflict;
- children are the adult market of the future;
- the schools' market is remarkably loyal and, once they have undertaken a successful visit, will return regularly; and
- while schoolchildren typically gain entry to commercial attractions at a substantially discounted price, they do spend on retailing and catering.

In addition, many publicly funded destinations and attractions – such as museums and art galleries – have an educational mission which demands that they provide for this market.

As noted above, education authorities in most countries support the concept of school pupils visiting destinations and attractions outside of the school environment; not only does this encourage 'learning outside school', but also the visit can be integrated into subjects such as geography, environmental studies and biology and into cross-curricular approaches (Lai, 1999). Of course, this does imply that tourist destinations have to provide a genuine educational experience if they are to cater successfully for schools: indeed, the majority of schools can only justify a visit on educational or curriculum grounds.

Estimates suggest that around 50% of the volume of school visits are day visits (Keeley, 1993), with the remainder comprised of overnight stays on field visits. For day trips, the focus of the visit is usually an attraction such as a theme park, museum, art gallery, science centre, garden, zoo or wildlife park. Here, the tourist sector is involved in providing transportation and the focus of the visit itself. However, for overnight stays, the accommodation sector also becomes involved (Roberts, 1986; Holdbak & Holland, 1996). Typically, these trips last up to a week, utilise budget accommodation such as youth hostels or guesthouses and use coach or minibus transport (Bywater, 1993a; Smith & Jenner, 1997a).

Despite differences across the various market segments of the education market, there are three key principles that characterise the supply environment of the schools' market (which are also highlighted in Exhibit 4.4). These are:

(1) understanding the needs of children;
(2) understanding the school curriculum; and
(3) understanding how schools are managed and make visit decisions.

Understanding the needs of children

The issues involved in supplying the schools' market vary according to the ages of the children. In most countries, the majority of visits are from children aged from 9 to 13 years. This is due to the constraints of formal examinations for older children and the logistical difficulties of organising visits for very young children. Children of different ages have differing attention spans, curriculum needs, energy, interests and backgrounds and this has to be built into any successful product for schools and the learning experiences created (see Table 4.5). For example, younger children require more support for the visit, such as pupil packs, specialist staff and teachers' support materials. Younger pupils also relate better to more tactile and physical products than do older children, for whom audio-visual or print materials are more successful. Older children are more self-sufficient and the visit, as it is specialised, tends to be more dependent upon the teacher's own resources. Older children too, respond well to the provision of follow-up materials on CD-ROMs or on web sites.

There is a range of special needs that destinations and attractions supplying the schools' market have to provide (Cooper and Latham, 1988):

- coach or bus access and parking – a hired coach or bus is the most common means of travel for these groups;
- catering facilities that are geared to children, or the provision of lunch rooms or picnic areas where children can eat packed lunches;
- ensuring that the visit can be managed in around 2–4 hours to allow the group to fit the visit into the school day when travelling time is included;
- logistical support for the visit – pre-visit information sheets, maps, good signposting, a web site and timing estimates;
- for serious providers, dedicated areas for pupils with teaching space, technology, workrooms and places to hang up coats, etc.; and
- facilities for differing types of disability – wheelchair access, resources for the sight and hearing impaired, and so on.

Exhibit 4.4

An attractions perspective: The Wimbledon Lawn Tennis Museum and school visits.

By Brent Ritchie

The Wimbledon Museum is set within Centre Court at The All England Lawn Tennis and Croquet Club, home to The Wimbledon Championships which hosted 476,711 visitors (60,000 overseas visitors) in 2001. Although the Championships have been played at Wimbledon since 1877, the museum has been a more recent addition, opening in 1977 as part of the Wimbledon Centenary Celebrations. The museum was expanding in 1985 to provide 20% additional exhibition space, and in 2001 the museum was again extended to include a new audio-visual theatre, art gallery and museum offices. A full-time education officer was also appointed in 2001 to develop a schools and outreach programme.

Highlights of the museum include:

- a view of the world-famous Centre Court;
- the original Championships' trophies which are presented each year;
- film and video footage of players in action from the 1920s to the present day;
- a rich collection of tennis memorabilia, equipment, trophies, costume and pictures which explain the evolution of lawn tennis;
- re-creations of a racket maker's workshop, an original gentlemen's dressing room, a Victorian parlour with an extraordinary collection of tennis objects, and a tennis garden party;
- action clips from previous Championships that can be called up on videos;
- an interactive quiz which tests visitor knowledge of Wimbledon; and
- the Ladies' Costume Gallery which explains the radical changes that have occurred in women's tennis fashions in little over a century; examples range from the 1880s to the present day.

Ancillary services at the museum include the Café Centre Court, with seating for up to 70 people and a further 40 seats beyond the conservatory area in an outdoor courtyard, and a museum shop which has a wide range of souvenirs catering for all budgets. School trips are of particular importance to the museum as illustrated by the recent appointment of an education officer and expansion of the museum. The museum has a specialist education team who provide a full educational programme for school visits. School teachers can select from a range of museum workshops, children's guided tours and educational room workshops, which are available for pre-booked groups. All workshops and tours help to deliver the national curriculum and complement curriculum schemes of work in a range of subjects. The museum offers children the opportunity to have fun, to learn through a range of subjects and to explore the game of lawn tennis in a safe and stimulating environment. The museum has provided a wide range of facilities and resources to cater for the school group market including:

- free classroom facilities;
- free indoor packed lunch room/outdoor eating area;
- free familiarisation visit to the museum for one adult;
- free coach parking/car parking;
- free admission for coach drivers plus a £5 refreshment voucher;
- free adult for every five children (primary);
- access to a specialist education team;
- access for special needs; and
- secure storage for belongings.

The museum provides education workshops that are additional to the museum visit and that are interactive, including practical activities for school students involving drama and role-play, practical involvement and a unique handling collection. Examples of workshops and their descriptions from the museum website (2002) include:

- **History Tellers KS1 & 2**

  Why do we remember Maud Watson?

  Take a journey back to Victorian times and meet Maud Watson, the very first Wimbledon Ladies' Lawn Tennis Champion of 1884. Be inspired as she relives her triumphs with you. Discover the pleasures and perils of playing in petticoats and corsets!

  History QCA Unit 4

- **Victorian Wimbledon KS1 & 2**

  How did life change for the people of Victorian Wimbledon when Lawn Tennis became a hit?

  Explore the impact of Lawn Tennis on the lives of local Victorian inhabitants. Take on their voices as they debate the future of The Championships.

  History QCA Unit 12/Geography QCA Unit 6

- **Fit for Play KS1 & 2**

  How did Victorian Tennis Champions stay healthy?

  What do you think it takes to become a Tennis Champion and stay in shape? Leeches? Smelling salts? Blood mixture? Physical drill? Come and accept the Champions' Challenge!

  Science QCA Unit 2A/3A/4A/5A

To complement the education workshops the museum provides guided educational tours for school students, including the following curriculum tours:

- **Can Buildings Speak? KS1**

  Explore size, shape and structure, and question the purpose of the buildings. What shape is the Millennium building? Why does the Broadcast Centre have darkened windows?

  Art QCA Unit 2C

- **Take a Seat on Court KS1 & 2**

  Consider aspects of chair designs, the materials used to make them and their purpose. This is a unique opportunity for children to make thoughtful observations and to share their views.

  Art QCA Unit 4B

- **Keeping Healthy KS1 & 2**

  How do the players prepare for their game? Imagine what the Dressing Rooms are like and how the players warm up. What is the best diet for a tennis player and how do Champions keep healthy?

  Science QCA Unit 2A/3A/4A/5A

The museum is well aware of the importance of the school market and has put human resources and time into developing and providing educational programmes, workshops and guided tours for school students. Understanding the needs of students and teachers makes it easier to attract school visits, with teachers able to justify the trip on educational grounds. By focusing on providing students with an opportunity to learn outside of the classroom in a safe, fun and enjoyable way, the museum promotes the game of lawn tennis to an important audience and places it within its wider historical and scientific context.

Sources: The All England Lawn Tennis and Croquet Club (2002); Little (2001)

Planning in this type of provision for schools from an early stage in the development of attractions and destinations – will ensure that they can:

(1) build and maintain market share in the schools' market;
(2) minimise pupil management problems; and
(3) provide a valuable service to the educational community in the region.

Understanding the school curriculum

A clear understanding of the nature of the school curriculum is also important in supplying the schools' market. In the UK for example, the National Curriculum is quite prescriptive in encouraging schools to move out of the classroom and experience the world outside. Destinations and attractions that understand these opportunities and provide for them do well in this market.

Understanding the curriculum is critical when designing support materials for the visit, including teachers' and pupils' packs, interpretive materials and follow-up exercises. Schools must be able to demonstrate clear educational objectives for the visit, objectives that are linked to the curriculum (Hurd, 1997; Tal, 2001). Nonetheless, destinations must also ensure that the visit is enjoyable as well as educational – schools look for fun and a social element to their visit.

It is therefore vital to provide lively, exciting and memorable material for teachers and pupils and to plan these into the development of an attraction or destination from the start (Newberry, 1996). These materials should be both age- and subject-specific. Educational materials and displays should:

- encourage pupils to interact with others;
- allow pupils to relate to the material;

- reward pupils wherever possible;
- not preach or over-teach;
- make the teacher's job easier and less stressful;
- provide especially for the 9–13-year age group; and
- keep it simple.

Table 4.5 Providing for the schools' market: the needs of different age groups

Age group	*Needs*
General	In order to make the most of learning outside of the normal classroom situation, it is important to provide for the distinctive developmental phases that children go through.
Up to the age of 8 years	Children of this age need direct contact with exhibits at the destination (taste, smell, touch, look) as they move around. Experience rather than learning is important. Visits tend to be short – half a day maximum.
	In school, follow-up work will include drawing, models, drama, writing about the visit and creative writing about the exhibits/destination.
8–12 years	Children of this age can begin to understand simple relationships and cope with some project work. In particular, children at the older end of this range are often free from examination restrictions and will be responsive to learning by discovery at first hand and be able to record and observe. Interactive exhibits and games, which draw out relationships, are more effective than just talking about them.
13–18 years	Work at this level tends to be more academic and subject-oriented. Students can think inductively and cope with more complex issues and concepts and be better able to analyse and respond to problem solving as a learning method. It is essential at this stage to have an understanding of the various curriculum needs and provide a range of resources to meet these needs.

At attractions and destinations that successfully provide for the schools' market, the following types of provision are typical:

(1) free familiarisation visits for teachers;
(2) pre-visit information sheets, normally free, giving maps and details of locations, what there is to see and the logistics of the visit (timings, etc.) for all parties;
(3) for young children, a range of games, crosswords, quizzes, puzzles, fact-sheets, comics, etc. targeted at the relevant curriculum;
(4) for older children, study packs on particular issues with photographs, documents, web links, CD-ROMs, etc. which support teaching for the relevant curriculum;
(5) teachers' packs with ideas for pre-visit, post-visit and on-site activities; and
(6) a web site providing details of the opportunities available from the visits, often including downloads of educational materials (sometimes password-protected and accessible once a booking is confirmed).

Clearly, provision for the schools' market depends upon the exact nature and size of the destination or attraction. Generally speaking, at very small attractions all that is needed is a well-organised visit and sympathetic, helpful staff. However, schools see teacher and pupil education packs as important everywhere and, where they are employed, specialist education staff are much appreciated. They are to be found in many of the larger attractions in the developed world. However, for older children, admission prices become a more important factor and provision of education packs and specialist staff less so, because teachers are more self-sufficient in terms of their needs from the visit.

Innovative provision for the schools' market is evident in a number of sectors of the tourism industry, from theme parks, through nature reserves and national parks to science centres and museums. In museums, this approach has a long pedigree (see, for example, Harrison, 1970). Bloch (1998) details the development of children's museums and also specialist children's galleries. In such galleries attention is paid to the height and legibility of exhibits, but in particular they are designed to be 'hands-on' and 'interactive'. Bloch (1998) classifies provision into four types:

- children's museum;
- children's gallery within a museum;
- child-friendly exhibits; and
- special programmes for children.

Museum exhibits for schools are distinctive in their design in that they are age-appropriate; they encourage interaction between children and with adults, and the spaces are often staff-intensive. Interpretation for children has become a specialist arm of the interpretation profession (see the special issue of *The Interpreter*, Summer 1985, for early developments in this field). Gardom (1996) highlights the more recent development of the blurring of education and fun in such museums and galleries, where the public sector has tended to lead the way, particularly in the USA with the concept of 'edu-tainment', or 'info-tainment', partly responding to the increased sophistication of children and their exposure to high quality productions in the media.

Understanding how schools are managed and make visit decisions

An understanding of the changing management of schools is critical in supplying and marketing to them. In many countries, schools are being given increased autonomy to organise their own management and budgets; in effect they act as small tour operators. This does, however, bring with it increased responsibility in terms of insurance, liability and the funding of visits. An example here is the uncertainty in the schools' market created in the late 1980s/early 1990s by the UK's Education Reform Act. The Act stated that education was free, that parental contributions for visits must be voluntary and that schools cannot charge for activities that take place within school hours. This severely reduced the numbers of school visits until the early 1990s when legislative confusion was removed (Cooper & Latham, 1989; NFER, 1991).

The changing management environment of schools also impacts upon the financial management of school trips, although this is country-specific. In Australia, for example:

> Forty-six percent of schools disclosed that they receive funding to subsidize their school excursions and this funding derives primarily from sources such as Pupil Contributions (65%), Parent Funds (54%), the CVP [Citizen Visits Program – a school trip subsidy scheme] (17%), and Sponsorship (3%). (Coughlan *et al.*, 1999: 13)

Marketing to schools requires a distinctive approach. The education market is loyal and once attracted and satisfied with the services of a destination, they will become regular, repeat visitors. From a marketing point of view, it is important to recognise the differences in types of school and ages of children. This is for three key reasons.

First, when mapping the catchment areas of a destination or attraction for potential school visits, research shows that schools are reluctant to take younger children on lengthy distances and will confine journey time to around an hour (Cooper & Latham, 1985). This severely limits the potential catchment for destinations and attractions. For older children, distances travelled can be greater, but schools still like to complete the visit within the school day.

Second, the timing of marketing to schools is crucial and will depend upon the age of the children involved (West Country Tourist Board, n.d.). Dependent upon climate, many countries concentrate their visits into spring and early summer. Decisions on such visits are generally taken early in the school year – September/October in the northern hemisphere; February/March in the southern hemisphere. Keeley (1993) notes that, for younger children, decisions on visits are made approximately one semester ahead of the trip, whereas senior schools tend to operate on an annual cycle. This variation in visit decision taking is important from a marketing point of view as schools will be more receptive to promotion at certain key times of the year.

Finally, the person in the school who makes the visit decision also varies depending on the age of the children. For younger groups, the head teacher, or deputy head, makes the decision; while for older children, the subject teacher makes the decision – this is also the case for tertiary education groups where the lecturer makes the decision.

Because of the very personal nature of contact with schools and individual teachers, marketing to schools tends to use relationship-marketing approaches such as direct mail. However, other approaches and incentives, such as free familiarisation visits and price discounts, are essential if the promotion is to convert to a visit. Other techniques include:

- contact with educational authorities;
- advertising in the educational press; and
- attendance at school visits fairs. (Keeley, 1993)

Remarkably few destinations or attractions research the schools' market or monitor satisfaction levels. At best, managers keep a database of schools and teachers for direct mail purposes.

Supply of language schools' tourism

Strong provision of language courses exists in the UK, USA, Canada, Australia, New Zealand, Ireland and Malta (see Table 4.6). Britain attracts

Table 4.6 Estimated number of ELT students by country of study, 1997/98

Destination	*Students*	%
UK	640,000	51.7
USA	216,000	17.4
Ireland	185,000	14.9
Canada	78,000	6.3
Australia	69,400	5.6
Malta	31,000	2.5
New Zealand	18,500	1.5
Total	1,237,900	100.0

Source: Brian McCallen Research (in Batchelor, 2000: 24)

over half of the market, as the UK is perceived to be a unique destination for language schools. As McCallen (2000: 19) notes, the UK 'is recognised internationally for the high value of its general education system. This helps the universities and colleges attract English as a Foreign Language students and also provides benefits for the private language schools sector.' However, its market share is declining (from a 60% share in 1984) as competition intensifies from other countries. Since 1984 visitor traffic to the UK has increased by 85%, yet the ELT traffic has increased by only 40%, suggesting that the UK could do better (Batchelor, 1998). Batchelor (1998) believes the decline is due to:

- a changing product demand;
- increased competition from course organisers abroad;
- better provision of English tuition in source markets;
- static or negative growth in established markets; and
- high cost of entry to new markets.

A total of 380 accredited suppliers account for over half of the ELT students visiting Britain (Batchelor, 2000), with 38% of providers located in London and the South-East of England (Grant *et al.*, 1998). The top preferred locations for ELT establishments in Britain include historic towns (26%), capital cities (23%) and heritage seaside resorts (14%). Grant *et al.* (1998) note seven main management considerations related to the development of language schools, which are important considerations for destination managers and language school organisations:

(1) *Development pressure*: Most year-round schools operate from purpose-built facilities or converted buildings (especially larger houses). This may alter the character of the area, or lead to a loss of residential housing stock and a decline in property values, which could undermine community acceptance of this visitor market.
(2) *Accommodation*: Although some accommodation is provided in universities or colleges and most students stay with host families, some stay in hostels and hotels, adding to the total demand for housing. In some destinations local students and young people are priced out of the market.
(3) *Leisure activities*: As discussed earlier, ELT students are young and often single and looking for leisure activities. If such activities are not provided by ELT organisations, who may not see it as their role, then this may lead to people congregating in the streets and open spaces, possibly creating conflict with local people. This is confirmed by crime figures in Eastbourne leading to 'Operation Columbus', whose aim is to monitor and protect international students from crime and criminal activity. A total of 17% of robbery victims in Sussex, England are international students and police have developed a set of actions to deal with the increase in crime. Reports from local police suggest that crimes against international students are pre-planned by groups who are targeting students specifically.
(4) *Congestion*: As discussed earlier, language schools' tourism is still heavily concentrated in the summer season. This and the fact that provision is also heavily concentrated in parts of Britain and in certain cities and towns, adds to congestion already being felt in the destinations which provide language schools. This impact occurs at attractions and transport hubs such as train stations.
(5) *Safety*: Issues may arise with children under 16 years and students who are over 16 but away from families for the first time. These students may be keen to enjoy a new city but could place themselves at risk or in jeopardy due to unfamiliarity with cultural differences and behaviour. As already noted, the importance of destination safety and positive word of mouth is paramount. If students are assaulted this could have major impacts upon positive recommendations and future business for language school providers.
(6) *Economy*: This group are high spenders and leakage is low because they use host family accommodation, local premises, local tour operators and local teachers. Grant *et al.* (1998) believe that this local value should be maximised.

(7) *Reputation*: Grant *et al.* (1998) note that ELT students can act as ambassadors and generate repeat leisure visitors in the future, but reputation can be damaged due to poor teaching and social programmes, poor accommodation, crime, congestion and overcrowding throughout the student experience. They note that quality provision of the whole language school experience is critical.

Quality is essential within the language schools' market, yet there is no central regulation of the ELT sector in Britain' which makes quality and consistency difficult. Exhibit 4.5 discusses the issue of accreditation in this market for Britain.

Exhibit 4.5

Quality and accreditation in the British ELT market

By Sara Muñoz Gonzalez

English Language Teaching is an important sector of the British tourism economy, attracting over 50% of the global market share (McCallen, 2000). Over the 12-year period covered by the International Passenger Survey, starting in 1984, it is apparent that English Language Teaching has experienced rapid growth. Visitors attending English language courses in the UK rose from 477,000 in 1984 to 669,000 in 1996, according to the Survey (Office of National Statistics, 1996). Moreover, ELT providers in Britain are estimated to number approximately 1200 organisations, although the exact number is not known since there is no mandatory need to register and, thus, no governmental regulation (Batchelor, 1998, 2000). Therefore, the issue of quality has gained increased recognition in both the private and public sectors, especially after a reported decrease in visitor figures since 1996 (McCallen, 2000).

The British government insists there is no need for governmental regulation. However, it recognises that it is in the public interest to have a quality assurance scheme. As a consequence, the 'English In Britain Accreditation Scheme' (EIBAS) was established by agreement between the British Council, the Association of Recognised English Language Services (ARELS) and the British Association of State English Language Teaching (BASELT). The EIBAS is a widely recognised indicator of quality, although not the only one. The Association of British Language Schools (ABLS) and the British Association of Lecturers in English for Academic Purposes (BALEAP) also include an accreditation scheme for their members, who do not necessarily participate in the scheme administered by the British Council.

Nonetheless, it is the EIBAS which is mostly accredited for setting quality standards within the industry. On one hand, it aims to protect international visitors studying English in the UK and provides students with the assurance that the standards of service in the areas inspected by the Scheme will be met (British Council, 2000). It also has a system for processing complaints concerning the Scheme members. On the other hand, it aims to offer a series of services to accredited organisations, such as promotion, advice, accreditation and inspection. It grants these institutions the right to use the British Council logo and to access promotional services through the extensive network of overseas British Council offices and through the British Council's web pages (British Council, 2000).

In order to qualify for accreditation, language centres need to have been operating for at least two years and have to provide high standards of tuition in the areas inspected: management and administration, academic resources, staff profile, academic management, premises, teaching and welfare (Batchelor, 2000). The scheme is fully financed through membership and inspection fees that cover the administration costs (British Council, 2000).

The British Council also runs various joint ventures with the British Tourist Authority in order to provide assistance for ELT institutions and to respond to the acknowledged need of customers for quality assurance in ELT services. However, these efforts are mainly restricted to accredited organisations, which currently include over 97 from the public sector (BASELT, 2002) and approximately 280 members from the private sector (British Council, 2002). Although accredited institutions are in the minority, they are believed to provide half the instruction to language visitors (Grant *et al.*, 1998). The unregulated sector, on the other hand, is mainly composed of temporary organisations.

In the light of the success of the EIBAS, it becomes evident that customer assurance has achieved growing importance among ELT visitors and that accreditation schemes within this particular sector are becoming as vital as any quality assurance scheme in other industry sectors.

Conclusion: The Future of Schools' Tourism

The future of schools' tourism is inextricably linked to both global demographics and to the changing nature of the educational system. The demographics clearly show that the primary and secondary market is shrinking in most parts of the developed world, but that there is huge potential for growth in the developing world. A key issue here, however, is the fact that supplying the primary and secondary schools' market is a very specialised activity, demanding careful product development and a sound knowledge of the needs of schools. As this chapter demonstrates, that expertise is now available, but for many sectors of the tourism industry, the effort needed to attract this market is not deemed to be worthwhile. In part this is not helped by the fact that the market is almost 'invisible' in the tourism statistics – it is not researched and children are not separated out in the statistical profiles of the tourism sector. At the same time, the market is undergoing a number of threats, not only from the increased centralisation of the curriculum in many parts of the world, but also particularly from technology and safety issues.

From the technology point of view, the Internet appears to have the potential to offer an alternative to school field trips. In the case of learning a foreign language, email, computer-generated sound clips, video cameras attached to computers and desktop video conferencing offer students the chance to talk to children in different countries without having to travel on exchange visits. This has the potential to overcome the discomfort some students and families feel in going to stay with and hosting other children. It is also cheaper, once the technology has been purchased, and offers the chance to interact with other nationalities that children from low-income families may not have been previously able to afford. In an era of increasingly tight and prescriptive national standardised curricula, there is also often not the time to take students on exchanges or field trips during term time, something the Internet has the potential to overcome. Despite these benefits, the Internet fails to really allow students to experience living in another country and the lack of immersion leads to a poorer quality learning experience. As Leman (2002) states, 'I maintain that one week abroad is worth one term of teaching back at school.'

The other key concern for the future of the schools' market is the safety issue, as parents rightly become more litigious. The following quotes paint a clear picture:

> Accepting that accidents do happen, we should learn from them and try to help teachers, parents and children better understand the nature

> of risk. We need to set standards which achieve the required level of safety while avoiding a culture of over-regulation and bureaucracy. (Robertson, 2001: 78)

> British schoolchildren are growing into a generation of 'softies' because risk assessment, blame culture, and cautious licensing authorities are preventing schools and youth organisations from arranging field trips and expeditions. (Uhlig, 1999)

In the case of language schools' tourism similar issues are evident. Little data collection occurs concerning the market and therefore the industry has little understanding of the variety of different market segments and the nature of source markets. Competition has intensified in the provision of ELT and Britain has lost its market share as a result of a slow response to competition and issues of quality and accreditation (Batchelor, 1998). Although language school students can provide economic and tourism benefits to communities, they can also cause congestion and potential problems due to the nature of the location and seasonality of popular summer language programmes. However, reducing seasonality for both types of school trips is difficult due to curriculum and school constraints. Ensuring the benefits are maximised and spread over all parts of the year is a challenge, as is protecting language school students from crime while allowing them to immerse themselves in culture and nightlife. Better management mechanisms and research are required if the language schools' sector is going to grow in a more sustainable manner.

Case Study 4.1

Schools' educational tourism in Europe

By Chris Cooper

Introduction

As detailed throughout this book, educational tourism is a distinct segment of the tourism market, demanding a particular approach in terms of products and promotion, and with its own very different market characteristics and influences (see Cooper and Latham, 1990). For the consumer, demand arises at the level of schools and individual purchasers, with only a small number of specialist tour operators.

In Europe, this gives rise to a market segment that is:

- perceived as difficult to reach;
- fragmented;
- suffering from a lack of industry coordination;
- suffering from a lack of real understanding of the needs and demands of the sector;
- dominated by word-of-mouth communication; and
- suffering from a lack of market information and real statistics.

In Europe, educational tourism is ignored in official surveys and tourism reports. Apart from some in-depth research in the UK, and a European Commission report on youth travel, the market is almost totally ignored in official statistics and consultants' reports. It is also difficult to draw together the picture in terms of provision for educational tourism in the various destinations across Europe. In part this is due to the fact that children tend not to be interviewed in most border surveys. It is also the case that there is a deep-rooted view in the industry that the educational travel sector generally is both unprofitable and difficult to reach in marketing terms and this has held back the calibration of the market (Seekings, 1998).

Demand for educational visits

The educational tourism market in Europe is a significant one – within the European Union (EU) alone there are almost 70 million pupils and students who are potential travellers (Cooper, 1999). This market comprises both day visits and visits involving an overnight stay.

Day visits

The day visit market is significantly larger than the market for overnight stays. Authors' estimates suggest that the market approaches 100 million visits in the EU and European Free Trade Agreement (EFTA) countries. There are clear geographical differences in the market, caused by both the number of children resident in a region (Tables 4.7 and 4.8) and the educational system in different countries. The countries dominating the market are Germany, Spain, the UK, France and Italy.

Day visits are dominantly made by children aged between 9 and 13 years in primary and junior schools. The dominance of this age group is due to the fact that the curriculum encourages them to *learn outside school*, and also the fact, that for older children, demands of formal examinations reduce the available time for visits. As would be expected, the market

Table 4.7 Numbers of children by age band in selected European countries ('000s)

Country	*0–4 years*	*5–9 years*	*10–14 years*	*15–19 years*
Belgium	604.2	612.2	600.6	618.5
Denmark	343.2	303.5	273.0	316.1
Germany	4038.2	4699.9	4500.4	4390.2
Greece	513.2	558.0	666.0	761.9
Spain	1933.4	2026.5	2468.2	3091.0
France	3593.0	3833.0	3885.2	3836.8
Ireland	255.0	285.5	328.3	343.1
Italy	2740.0	2782.3	2994.8	3514.0
Luxembourg	27.6	25.6	23.1	22.5
Netherlands	980.9	963.8	903.1	923.8
Austria	468.0	464.0	477.6	458.7
Portugal	555.7	543.7	645.2	778.5
Finland	324.9	316.6	330.3	327.1
Sweden	582.3	581.2	501.9	506.8
UK	3802.4	3861.4	3678.8	3499.2
Iceland	22.4	21.8	20.8	21.2
Norway	303.3	289.5	261.1	266.9

Sources: Euromonitor (1998); Cooper (1999)

differs in each European country, but it is possible to make a number of generalisations:

- Schools are reluctant to travel long distances for day visits – typically younger children will travel up to about 70 kilometres to visit a destination, while older children will travel up to 100 kilometres. There is a clear pressure here as, the further the visit, the more expensive it is and schools may therefore make one long visit annually but confine other visits in the year to smaller, local attractions.
- Equally, in order to approximate the visit to the school day, a maximum journey time of 90 minutes is the norm and pupils tend to be present at the destination between 10 a.m. and 3.30 p.m.
- Most schools use either their own, or hired, coaches/minibuses.

Table 4.8 Numbers of pupils in selected European countries

Country	*Number of primary pupils ('000s)*	*Number of secondary pupils ('000s)*
Belgium	711.5	765.7
Denmark	326.6	443.8
Germany	3524.2	7796.3
Greece	723.7	851.3
Spain	2477.9	4734.4
France	4011.0	5737.4
Ireland	398.7	362.2
Italy	2863.0	4715.6
Netherlands	1056.8	1352.5
Austria	381.6	778.0
Portugal	910.7	778.5
Finland	390.9	459.1
Sweden	600.4	607.2
UK	5143.2	4537.0
Iceland	24.7	30.9
Norway	309.9	380.3

Sources: Euromonitor (1998); Cooper (1999)

- Visits occur throughout the year, particularly in southern Europe. However, most visits are concentrated in the late spring and throughout the summer terms (i.e. April through to July) as this fits well into the school year.

Overnight stays

The market for overnight stays by unaccompanied children is significantly smaller than the day visit market (Bywater, 1993a). For EU and EFTA countries it is estimated at between 15 and 20 million trips annually. Most visits are organised independently of the travel trade, partly because this is dominantly a domestic market, although there are significant movements of school trips across European borders. For example, it is estimated that the schools' market in the UK generates 300,000 overseas visits annually, while the market for schools travel' from France to the UK is at least 200,000 trips a year. The market for overnight stays differs from the day visit market in the following ways:

- school exchanges and language learning are the key motivations;
- the market is dominated by older children aged 12–18 years;
- residential school trips are an important element for private schools in attracting pupils;
- trips tend to use surface transport – coaches, minibuses, ferries and train travel (Eurostar is popular) – although the use of budget airlines is increasing;
- most trips tend to be in the long summer holiday; and
- trips tend to use either domestic accommodation (for exchanges) or budget accommodation.

There are three key factors that have an important influence in shaping the demand for educational tourism across Europe (European Commission, 2001):

(1) *Demographics*: Almost one-fifth (67 million) of the population of the EU is in school or university education, although the number of students has declined because of the falling birth rate. Forecasts suggest that the falling birth rate is a long-term trend and is a real cause for concern for the educational tourism market. There are however exceptions to the picture of an ageing Europe proportional to their populations. Europe's youngest regions are Ireland, Iceland, northeastern France, Portugal and southern Spain (Tables 4.7 and 4.8).
(2) *Educational structures*: Demand for schools' educational tourism is heavily determined by educational structures. For example, the period of compulsory schooling varies by country – it lasts for 11 years in the Netherlands but only eight in Italy. There are also variations in both the entry age and the completion age of compulsory education. The actual numbers of official teaching days also vary (from 160 in Iceland, to 214 in Austria for primary education, for example), and there is a large variation in class hours. Holidays also vary – summer holidays are not programmed in the Netherlands, but last for 12/13 weeks in Spain and six weeks in England. These factors affect the time available for educational tours.
(3) *Educational administration and initiatives*: Here, a number of key educational trends will shape the future development of schools' educational tourism in Europe (European Commission, 2001):
    - Decentralisation of administration and financial arrangements is leading to greater autonomy for schools. This means that

schools treat themselves as *businesses* and effectively act as small tour operators when organising educational visits.

- Efforts by many European countries to extend the period of compulsory schooling by lowering the entry age, raising the leaving age or providing incentives to continue schooling will expand the market.
- There is a trend for minimum core national curricula, which are then defined at greater depth in the school. This allows locations to tailor their educational provision to local needs. The exceptions here are England, Wales and Northern Ireland with a centrally-imposed National Curriculum.
- The emphasis on certain subjects is increasing across Europe – foreign languages, information technology, cross-curricular themes, civil and social behaviour, and Europe itself. Destinations will need to focus on these areas to attract visits from schools in the medium term.
- 'Learning through discovery' is increasingly being adopted as an educational approach, and will stimulate educational tourism.
- There is an increasing number of Europe-wide initiatives to encourage the mobility of children and students. These are meeting with considerable success and the number of students taking part in EU exchange programmes is increasing, thus benefiting the educational tourism market.

Trends in supplying schools' educational tourism in Europe

Supplying the educational tourism market in Europe demonstrates a clear schism between the traditional approaches of some destinations, and the more innovative and technolog-driven approaches of others. The more exciting initiatives are based in Europe's leading museums and tourist attractions.

Many of Europe's museums have re-invented themselves with regard to educational provision, not only in terms of utilising technology, but also in the quality and imagination of exhibits (see Bloch, 1998). Here the trend is clearly towards partnerships in provision – with schools, other educational institutions and industry. While school travel has to be justified on the basis of the educational motive and content, many museums and attractions combine education and entertainment to deliver *edutainment.* This puts the fun into 'learning out of school' and allows the more fun-based attractions to enter the education market, while the more serious, education-oriented attractions, such as museums, are adopting the principles and technology of the entertainment industry.

The rapid progress in the use of technology and communication to deliver education for destinations has the potential to transform education provision, but in reality its penetration has been slow, partly due to the costs involved. Nonetheless, we are now seeing the replacement of the traditional school worksheets by technology, with the use of multimedia computers, CD-ROMs and the Internet.

Conclusion

The European educational tourism market is facing a number of important issues (Smith & Jenner, 1997a). The market itself is very poorly documented – there is no serious research to underpin commercial judgements and evaluation of consumer satisfaction is not widely implemented. The image of the sector is poor and often educational tourism is discounted as low yield. Here there is a real 'Catch 22', as without the research base it is difficult to disprove such perceptions. This is exacerbated by the declining market base as birth rates fall across many countries in Europe.

On the supply side, issues include real concerns about the quality of the product in some parts of the industry, particularly the language school sector. However, elsewhere, and particularly in Europe's larger museums and commercial tourism attractions, provision is both innovative and of high quality. Quality concerns have led to calls for stronger consumer protection, a trend also driven by the need to protect children as consumers. Here the issues are ones of safety standards on transport, in accommodation and on field courses involving physical risk. Concerns are such that some companies have purchased and operate parts of the product – such as accommodation and study centres – in order to control and guarantee health and safety.

Educational tourism in Europe remains the 'Cinderella' of the tourism sector, but despite falling birth rates, trends in education and travel are set to see the market grow rather than contract.

Case Study 4.2

Language students and the economy of Eastbourne, England

By Sara Muñoz Gonzalez and Brent Ritchie

Travel abroad in order to learn a language has been cited as one of the most important purposes of educational travel (Smith & Jenner, 1997a), but it is only recently that students have been suggested as a powerful, long-term investment for destinations due to their economic and promotional potential (Roppolo, 1996). For many destinations, as is the case Eastbourne, English Language Teaching has provided a viable alternative to many of the problems faced by the continuous shift in travel patterns.

Coastal resorts in Britain have had to adapt to continuously changing market trends since the decline of the domestic seaside holiday (Yale, 1992). During the 20-year period from the 1970s to the early 1990s, seaside holidays decreased from 75% to 25% in the UK (Yale, 1992). Although an estimated 85% of British holidays take place in England, relatively few overseas visitors choose British seaside resorts, and figures clearly suggest that the traditional one- or two-week family holiday has given way to a much shorter pattern in length of stay, as well as changes in elderly population concentrations (Yale, 1992). In Eastbourne, a traditional seaside resort at the foot of the East Sussex South Downs in England, the tourism industry has increasingly had to rely upon different segments. The so-called 'sunny pearl of the south', which was once among the UK's first real tourist destinations, has seen the difficulty in preventing a further decline in domestic tourism. A study carried out by the Tourism Board and the Eastbourne Borough Council in 1998 highlighted that tourism in Eastbourne is mainly reliant on the domestic market, which accounts for 58% of total visitor spending, but that it is increasingly reliant on conference tourism, English language tourism and day trips (Eastbourne Borough Council, 1998).

Since 1990, the town has seen an increase in the 55+ tourism segment, accounting for 66% of total staying visitors. The key holiday patterns show a clear seasonality problem, with over 61% of holidays taking place during the peak season and a substantial decrease in repeat business (from 72% to 66%). Further, Eastbourne appears to be becoming a secondary destination, with only 8% of visitors citing Eastbourne as their main holiday destination (Eastbourne Borough Council, 1998). In addition, the visitor length of stay has also declined, with over 52% of overnight visitors staying less than five nights. Eastbourne has recognised the need to attract new visitors to replace those no longer able to travel and thereby reduce their reliance on older markets. The study also stressed the importance of the overseas market and, given the results of the Language School and Student Survey included in the study, identified English Language Schools as a key component of the town's foreign market and one from which it could largely benefit. The importance of this foreign market was recognised by the English Tourist Board when David Quambry, Chairman stated:

> Eastbourne's main stake in overseas tourism is in the English language study market. This market has become very competitive internationally. It is vital that all involved achieve value for money and high standards of tuition, accommodation, and student care. Equally, developing trends in the market, for instance learning English for specialist purposes, should be exploited.

Although Eastbourne is estimated to be only slightly behind some of the most important English Language Teaching towns, it is only recently that the English language schools' contribution to the town's economy has started to be recognised (Glyn-Jones, 2001). The 1998 Language School and Visitor Survey estimated that 41,000 students had visited Eastbourne for an average of 20 days and had spent approximately £126.66 per week on accommodation, food, entertainment and shopping and an additional £97.11 on tuition fees. Nonetheless, the visitor estimate may not be entirely reliable since the East Sussex Police recorded student numbers of only 27,987 (Overseas Students' Advisory Committee, 1999).

In 2001, a study was carried among Eastbourne's English language schools seeking to investigate their role within the town's tourism industry and economy (Muñoz Gonzalez, 2001). Both qualitative and quantitative methods were used for this purpose. From a sample frame based on the 26,837 English language students recorded in 1999, a total of 370 questionnaires were distributed among the students of eight different schools, out of which 231 were returned. In addition, seven semi-structured interviews were carried among a number of ELT organisers. Since the study was undertaken during the winter months of 2001, findings provide a basis for comparison with the Borough's study, which took place during the summer of 1998. From both studies it can be drawn that some findings differ greatly. Although in 1998 students were predominantly West European, following the pattern identified by McCallen (2000) for the UK, results from the survey show that the main source market was the Far East. Regarding the age group, findings showed that the majority were adult students, with the early twenties' category being

Table 4.9 Eastbourne study sample length of stay and course length

Length of stay	*Frequency*	%
1 week	1	0.43
2 weeks	21	9.09
3 weeks	6	2.60
1 to 3 months	63	27.27
4 to 6 months	70	30.30
7 months or over	70	30.30
Total (base rate)	231	100.00
Course length		
1 week	1	0.43
2 weeks	23	9.96
3 weeks	10	4.33
1 to 3 months	74	32.03
4 to 6 months	75	32.47
7 months or over	48	20.78
Total (base rate)	231	100.00

only 4% behind and the 25 to 28 age group category accounting for 25% of the sample.

Although both studies show that the further the country of residence, the longer the stay, the length of stay is considerably higher for the 2001 survey, with the vast majority of students staying one month or over (see Table 4.9). In fact, the calculated average stay equals 18 weeks (128 days). This sizeable difference could be attributable to the time of the year in which the research was carried out. Thus, it could be argued that summer visitors tend to stay for shorter periods. Another important factor is that respondents slightly extended their stay beyond the length of the course, which represents a significant change in travel patterns compared to the Eastbourne study of 1998 and could mean higher economic gains for the local community.

Beside expenditure on course fees, which was not quantified in the 2001 research, interview results explicitly emphasised the direct contribution of language visitors to the local economy. Survey results confirmed the significant contribution: students were found to spend a weekly average of £172, which represents an increase of 36% since 1998, on items including accommodation, food and drink, entertainment and transport

Table 4.10 Calculation of Eastbourne language student spending, tuition excluded

Item	*Frequency*	%	*Weekly spend (£)*	*Daily spend (£)*
Accommodation	224	41.06	70.62	10.09
Other	16	15.80	27.17	3.88
Food and drink	196	13.28	22.84	3.26
Shopping	152	12.21	21.00	3.00
Entertainment	154	9.52	16.37	2.34
Transport	96	8.14	14.00	2.00
Total		100	172.00	24.57

(Table 4.10). Thus, the 2001 survey estimated that, excluding summer visitors, which according to McCallen (2000) account for approximately 54% of total ELT visits, the economic contribution made by English language schools in Eastbourne to the local economy was equivalent to £39,306,816. Moreover, results showed that the benefit to the local economy goes beyond direct spend since it generates visits in the form of friends and relatives, who, in turn, will be spending money in the local community. More than a third of questionnaire respondents were found to receive visits from friends and relatives from outside the UK. In addition, a further 82% of respondents agreed that they would recommend Eastbourne to a friend.

In relation to the type and nature of the language schools in Eastbourne, findings identified that, according to the numbers recorded by the East Sussex Police, Eastbourne accounts for approximately 29 ELT organisations (Muñoz Gonzalez, 2001). These institutions, from the accredited and unregulated sector, provide both seasonal and year-round tuition and vary greatly in size and scope. Following a general pattern organisations provide the visitor, in addition to a wide range of courses, with accommodation, mainly in host families, and general leisure offerings (Batchelor, 2000). However, in spite of the clear tourism elements identified by all respondents, it was apparent from results that the experience was seen as mainly educational. This helps explain the fact that only half of the respondents held that the tourism industry appreciates the contribution of language schools to the industry.

Nonetheless, some of the respondents stressed that language students provide an all-year-round market for the tourism industry as opposed to the senior market and that they help balance the demographics of the town. In addition, some corroborated quantitative findings by stating that language students were seen as a valuable means of promotion that attracts and generates new visits in the form of relatives and friends and repeat visits if the student is satisfied with the experience. These results corroborate previous research by Roppolo (1996) and also by Grant *et al.* (1998), which stressed that 'English language teaching is economically important as a sector for the tourism industry. It is also of a great indirect value as a gateway to Britain, a showcase for Britain and a projection of Britain abroad.'

In addition, findings identified that language schools rely heavily on both tourism and educational agents for promotional ends. However, and despite the clear contribution of language schools and students to the local economy and tourism industry, a mere 3.5% of the students saw themselves as tourists and they clearly identified the purpose of their journey as educational, more specifically to study English (see Figure 4.5). The study on the role of English language schools in Eastbourne's tourism industry and economy identified that language schools contribute significantly to the local economy, not only through direct spending in the community, but also through less obvious means. It is evident that students bring money from outside the community, which is providing additional income for host families, keeping merchants employed and providing business for local service companies.

Although the educational nature of the courses undeniably stands out as the main objective, schools attract visitors, contribute to the promotion of the town and include tourism-related activities as part of the final offer. Therefore, the tourism nature of schools extends beyond attracting foreign individuals, for tourism activities and education seem to go hand in hand. Moreover, language schools provide Eastbourne with an all-year-round market that combines lengthy periods of stay with high spending patterns from which the town can greatly benefit. Results identified that, directly or indirectly, language visitors are often encouraged by schools to participate in external or in-house social events. However, survey findings identified that, even though language visitors are frequently involved in tourism-related activities, their general perception is that, first of all, they are students.

It should be emphasised that a survey exploring language students' motivations and travel patterns could provide Eastbourne with the basis for obtaining considerable competitive advantages as an ELT destination and therefore benefiting from alternatives to further prevent visitor number recession, seasonality problems and a decrease in tourism

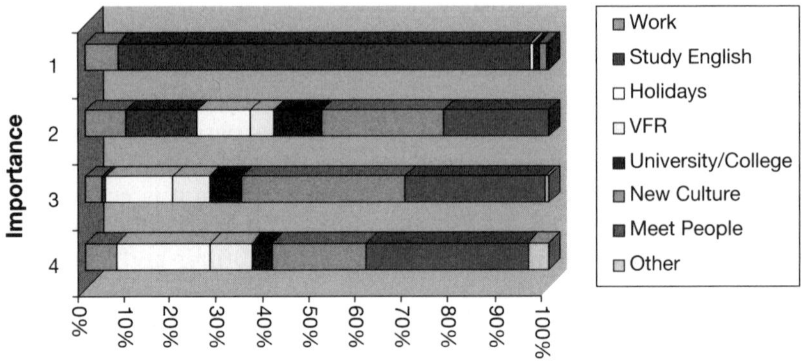

Base Rank 1	Base Rank 2	Base Rank 3	Base Rank 4
230	137	116	142

Figure 4.5 Eastbourne language students' purpose of stay (ranked)

revenues. A first step towards this end could come from an agreement in a common code of practice ensuring high quality standards. To achieve that goal, greater cooperation between the Council, the Tourism Board and the different organisations from both the self-regulated and the unregulated sector could prove a sound advantage. Future studies could also benefit from making continuous observations of the language student population. Thus, if language visitors were to be surveyed in summer as well as in winter throughout the same year, the gap between the two markets could be analysed and generalisations could be made of the language student population at large.

In conclusion, the significant contribution of English language schools to both the economy and the tourism industry in Eastbourne should be strongly emphasised in terms of the income and the promotion of the town. Furthermore, the role of language schools as tourism providers should be fully acknowledged by the industry in order to maximise their potential: as an alternative to the present elderly market, as a means to reduce dependency on summer visitors, and as a valuable promotion tool for the town.

Chapter 5

University and College Students' Tourism

NEIL CARR

Introduction

Despite the fact that the majority of university students may be chronologically defined as belonging to the youth population (18 to 30 years old) they are actually a distinct population with different age, socio-cultural, educational and economic characteristics (Davies & Lea, 1995). As such, it is not possible to directly compare the holiday experiences of the youth and student populations, despite the attempts of some previous studies (e.g. Josiam *et al.*, 1994; Kale *et al.*, 1987). Indeed, Pritchard and Morgan (1996) have claimed that there is a clear distinction between the holiday patterns of students and those of young people in full-time employment. Consequently, while recognising the existence of overlaps with the youth population this chapter focuses exclusively on university and college students.

The development of universities in a modern context may be traced back to mainly the twelfth and thirteenth centuries (Encyclopaedia.com, 2002). However, the growth of mass tertiary education has been a more recent phenomenon and has its roots in the economic growth and social liberalisation that has taken place since the end of the Second World War. For example, as Figure 5.1 demonstrates, in the UK the student population increased from approximately 400,000 in 1965/6 to almost two million in 2000/1. The UK has also witnessed an expansion in the percentage of the general population entering university, from approximately 10% in the 1960s to over 30% by the end of the twentieth century (Scott *et al.*, 2001). The expansion of the university student population is set to continue in the UK with the British government announcing its intention to see 50% of 18- to 30-year-olds entering tertiary education by the year 2010 (Major, 2002a). The pattern of growth in the UK has been mirrored in numerous countries, including Japan, where the university student population increased by 67% between 1984 and 2001 (Lifelong Learning Policy Bureau, 2002). The growth in the student population has been the result of increasing numbers of young (under 25 years of age) and mature (25 years of age or older) people entering higher education. For example, in Australia the number of mature students at university increased from 182,100 in 1990 to 272,900 in 2000. Over the same period the proportion of university students who were defined as mature increased from 37.5% to 39% (Australian Bureau of Statistics, 2002). The result is that the university student population increasingly cannot be regarded as the same as the youth population. Overall, the rising number of university students means this population should be recognised as a significant segment of the global population.

At the same time as the size of the university student population is expanding the amount of money available to students appears to be declining. Reductions in the funding of universities by national governments, the abolition of student grants and creation of student loans/tax schemes, and the increase in the number of students from poorer economic backgrounds have contributed to a situation where students find themselves burdened with ever increasing debts. The university system in England and Wales provides an example of the degenerating state of student finances. In 1990 the British government abolished a means-tested grant system for students going to university in England

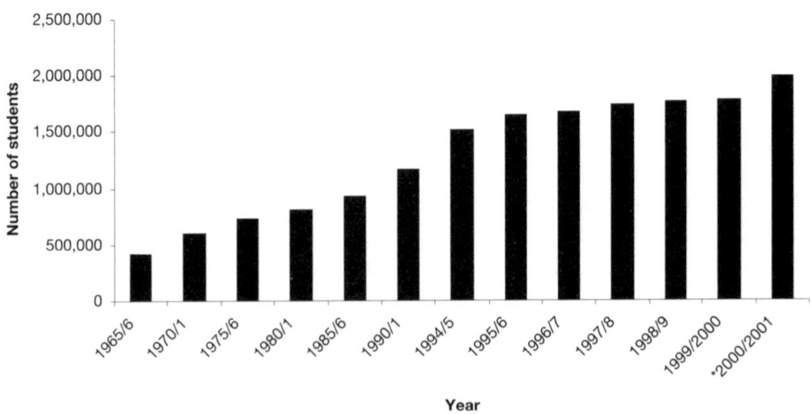

Figure 5.1 Number of university students in the UK (1965–2000)

Source: Adapted from *Times Higher Education Supplement* (2002); *Major (2002b)

and Wales and launched a student loan system. Without a student grant most people who go to university are now forced to take out a student loan during their time at university that they must begin to repay once they have graduated and found full-time employment with earnings above a specified level (Christie & Munro, 2001). In addition, universities in the UK now impose tuition fees of approximately £1000 on all but the poorest students. As a result of the changes in the funding of students and universities, and the increase in students from lower economic classes, student debt has been rising since the early 1990s to a point where 73% of all undergraduates and 76% of postgraduates in England and Wales in the year 1999 were in debt. Indeed, in 2002 it was estimated that the average student will owe £10,000 when he/she graduates (Anonymous, 2002a), compared to an average debt of £2745 in 1997 (Jones & Copley, 1997). As a result it has been claimed that 'abject poverty appears to be an inevitable consequence of student living' (Watt, 2000; Callender & Kemp, 2000). To help combat their rising debt students are spending an increasing amount of time working during their university careers. It has been estimated that 70% of students in the UK now work throughout the summer vacation and 50% continue doing so throughout term-time (Knight, 2000). The increasing reliance amongst students on loans and overdrafts is not restricted to the UK; rather it is a widespread phenomenon in the developed world (Scott *et al.*, 2001).

University Students' Tourism

Despite the size of the university student population relatively little research has been undertaken to understand the travel needs and desires of students or how they behave while on vacation (Sirakaya & McLellan, 1997; Babin & Kim, 2001). Most of the studies of this population have focused on specific issues or segments of the overall student population. For example, although Hsu and Sung (1997) and Field (1999) examined some aspects of the holiday behaviour of university students, neither provided anything about the holiday motivations of their samples and both ignored sexual, drug and alcohol-related aspects of behaviour. Similarly, although they noted the holiday motivations of the New Zealand students they studied, Chadee and Cutler (1996) failed to discuss how these people behaved on vacation. Meanwhile, Mewhinney *et al.*'s (1995) and Hobson and Josiam's (1992, 1995) work has focused on the American Spring Break vacations, while work by Clark and Clift (1994), Ryan *et al.* (1996), and Smeaton *et al.* (1998) has focused on the sex, drugs and alcohol-related holiday behaviour of students. Although these studies are important in their own right they may contribute to a distorted image of the holiday experiences of university students. This is because these papers do not discuss the potential for students to take different types of vacation and engage in different activities to those researched.

As has already been noted, full-time employment is rare amongst students and income tends to be correspondingly low (Davies & Lea, 1995). However, they generally have few external commitments and have over 20 weeks of free time outside of the university term-time each year. The university environment also encourages students to travel and take holidays (Smeaton *et al.*, 1998). This situation is developed through the presence of travel agencies catering specifically to university students, by society's view of the student lifestyle, peer pressure to conform to the travel-oriented image of students, and parental expectations of student travel behaviour (Christie & Munro, 2001). As a result it has been estimated that 20% of all international travellers may be identified as students, making the university student tourism market a multibillion-dollar industry (Bywater, 1993a). Work conducted in the United States (Kale *et al.*, 1987; Sirakaya & McLellan, 1997), New Zealand (Carr, forthcoming, b), and the UK (Carr, forthcoming, a) supports this view by indicating the relatively high travel propensity of university students. Sirakaya and McLellan's sample took 3.8 holidays each per year while Carr's British and New Zealand samples took 1.9 and 2.4 holidays each in a 12-month period, respectively.

The increasingly poor state of university students' financial circumstances may be having an adverse impact on their ability to engage in tourism. For example, Josiam *et al.*'s (1994) study of American students found that the two main reasons given by their sample for not going on a holiday during Spring Break were work commitments and a lack of money. Josiam *et al.* (1994: 325) stated that these results may 'reflect a change in the way college education is financed in the USA [where] a growing number of students are required to work to support themselves through college'. However, Carr's (forthcoming, a) study of British students found that, although they were frequently living in a state of debt, students were often unwilling to let this prevent them taking holidays and engaging in international travel. This provides support for the suggestion that students are becoming increasingly accustomed to borrowing money (Davies & Lea, 1995). There is even evidence to suggest that these students do not generally view the use of interest-free loans, such as the student loan and bank overdrafts, as a form of debt (Christie & Munro, 2001). Overall, students tend to pay for their holidays via a combination of personal savings, which tend to be the dominant financial source, bank/student loans and assistance from relatives (Carr, forthcoming, a; Chadee & Cutler, 1996; Hobson & Josiam, 1995).

Despite the apparent dearth of studies of university students' holiday experiences it is clear that this population has a preference for independently organised travel and vacation arrangements. They also tend to use informal sources of holiday information (e.g. friends, relatives and personal experience) more than formal sources (e.g. travel agents, travel brochures, newspapers, magazines and television) (Sung & Hsu, 1996; Chadee & Cutler, 1996; Field, 1999; Carr, 2001b). For further analysis of university students' use of and trust in different sources of holiday information readers should refer to Case Study 5.1. The main holiday destinations of university students seem to be strongly related to the geographical position of their home country. For example, the favourite international destination of the New Zealand students surveyed by Carr (forthcoming, b) and Ryan and Robertson (1997) was Australia. Similarly, Europe, and in particular the Mediterranean region, was the most popular international destination of the British students surveyed by Carr (forthcoming, a). However, Chadee and Cutler (1996) found that Australia was the least popular international destination for the New Zealand students they studied. Student tourism follows a clearly defined temporal pattern that is related to the university calendar. The peak times students engage in travel correspond with the university vacation periods, with the summer vacation being the time when the majority of holidays are undertaken (Carr, forthcoming, b).

University students' holiday motivations encompass a desire to engage in a combination of passive, social and hedonistic activities. The passive desire is associated with relaxing, the hedonistic motivation is related to a wish to 'party and dance/drink', and the social activities include meeting/being with friends/relatives (Josiam *et al.*, 1994). Sirakaya and McLellan (1997) also identified the importance to students of entertainment and drinking opportunities in their holiday destinations. In addition, students appear to be motivated by a desire to get away, or escape from their normal lives (Josiam *et al.*, 1994). In contrast, students do not seem to be strongly motivated by educational, anthropological or employment-related issues (Carr, forthcoming, b; Chadee & Cutler, 1996). The behaviour of students on holiday tends to reflect their motivations, with passive, hedonistic and social activities predominating. This is reflected in Carr's (forthcoming, b) study of New Zealand students that found relaxing/resting, drinking alcohol, sunbathing, having sex and visiting nightclubs were some of the holiday activities most frequently engaged in by this population. The hedonistic nature of university students' holiday behaviour is heightened in the case of the North American Spring Break phenomenon, where the focus is on the pursuit of hedonistic pleasure including sexual activity (Mewhinney *et al.*, 1995) and binge drinking (Smeaton *et al.*, 1998).

The propensity for students to consume alcohol while on holiday has been noted by Ryan and Robertson (1997) and Clark and Clift (1994), who found that 80% of the New Zealand students and 83% of the British students they surveyed, respectively, stated they had drunk alcohol while on holiday. These two surveys also reported that 13% of the New Zealand sample and 16% of the British sample used illegal drugs while on holiday. Sports/physical activity are also engaged in by university students while they are on holiday, albeit not as frequently as they demonstrate hedonistic/passive/social behaviour (Carr, forthcoming, b). In common with their desire to take independent holidays, students generally prefer to spend their holiday time engaged in unstructured and unconstrained activities (Kale *et al.*, 1987). For example, Carr's (forthcoming, b) sample of New Zealand students engaged in 'unguided tours' more frequently than guided ones while on holiday.

Although it may be tempting to regard the university student population as a homogeneous group, it is important to recognise the potential for differences within the population's holiday experiences. For example, Field (1999) identified a variety of differences between the domestic and international students he studied at an American university, including the fact that international students had a lower travel propensity (54%) than domestic ones (71%). Similarly, Ritchie and Priddle (2000) found that more domestic than international students in Australia took day or overnight domestic trips while studying at Canberra. The higher proportion of international students who took international trips in Ritchie and Priddle's sample may be attributed to travel to the homes of these students rather than tourism-oriented travel. In terms of their holiday behaviour, the international students surveyed by Field (1999) engaged in sightseeing more frequently than the domestic students, whose most frequent activity was 'going to the beach'. The international students surveyed in Australia and the USA by Ritchie and Priddle (2000) and Hsu and Sung (1997), respectively, also demonstrated a strong desire to visit attractions and engage in sightseeing. A study of differences in the holiday experiences between domestic and international students at the University of Canberra and the Australian National University is provided in Case Study 5.2. Field (1999) also reported the existence of differences in the holiday behaviour of international students based on their nationality. This supports the results of work by Carr (2001a) that found differences in the holiday behaviour of domestic students that were related to their nationality. Similarly, Chadee and Cutler (1996) reported finding significant cultural differences in the international travel behaviour of university students. The existence of differences in student holiday behaviour based on nationality means that it is difficult to compare the results of studies of university students where the nationalities of the samples are not the same. Gender (Sirakaya & McLellan, 1997), age (Hsu & Sung, 1997), marital status (Field, 1999; Sung & Hsu, 1996) and whether a student is an undergraduate or postgraduate (Field, 1999; Hsu & Sung, 1997) also appear to have an influence on the nature of the student's holiday experiences.

Promoting and Facilitating University and College Tourism

To promote the benefits of travel to university students and facilitate their engagement in this activity a number of organisations have been developed that have their origins in the student movement, academic institutions and/or government. The largest one is the International Student Travel Confederation (ISTC) (see Exhibit 5.1). While other organisations, such as the Federation for Youth Travel Organisations (FIYTO), deal with student travel requirements, their core business tends to be the youth population rather than the university student one.

ISTC was established in 1949 by university student unions to make travel affordable for students. One of its primary objectives was, and still is, to increase international understanding through the promotion of travel and exchange opportunities among students and the academic community. UNESCO officially endorsed the aims of the ISTC in 1993. The ISTC provides full-time university students with the International Student Identity Card (ISIC) that was created in 1954 and incorporated with the International Union of Students Card in 1989. This provides holders with access to a range of discounts, including tickets issued by the Student Air Travel Association, which offers relatively cheap and flexible air travel. Seven years after its creation, ISIC sales reached 750,000, in 1973 over one million cards were sold, and by 2001 ISIC sales exceeded 4.5 million worldwide. ISTC now acts as an umbrella organisation with over 70 specialist student travel companies working through the not-for-profit member associations of the ISTC. The International Student Travel Confederation now has over 5000 offices in more than 100 countries. In the year 2000 ISTC's member organisations and companies serviced the travel needs of approximately ten million students generating a turnover

Exhibit 5.1

The evolution of ISTC

The ISTC was founded as a loosely-knit federation to allow members a forum for exchanging ideas and to examine the needs of the expanding worldwide network of student travel agencies. Organisations that initially joined were often the non-profit travel departments of national unions of students and were concerned with the well-being of students who travelled internationally, the development of student products and international trading agreements. In the early years, members collaborated primarily on joint ventures – chartering planes, trains and ships. Efforts were also made to protect the welfare of the student traveller and the ISTC introduced codes of conduct for trading among member organisations. As member needs became more specific, the membership organised into specialised commissions so that individual interests in air transportation, tours, finance and surface transportation could be addressed.

At the 1990 ISTC Annual General Meeting, members agreed to restructure the ISTC and changed it from a 'Conference' to a 'Confederation'. Five independent associations were formed to represent specific interests. Associations work collectively to negotiate with airlines, governments and providers of goods and services for the benefit of the worldwide student, youth and academic community. They include:

- *ISIC: International Student Identity Card Association.* The ISIC Association is an international not-for-profit membership association of the International Student Travel Confederation (ISTC). Member organisations are the world's leaders in developing specialised student and youth travel products and services. The International Student Identity Card (ISIC) is the primary product offered by the Association. The ISIC is the only internationally recognised proof of full-time student status and provides cardholders access to worldwide benefits and services. There are more than 4.5 million cardholders annually. For those who are no longer students but are under 26, or who are full-time teachers or professors, the ISIC Association also administers the International Youth Travel Card (IYTC) and the International Teacher Identity Card (ITIC). Both cards offer similar benefits, services and savings to those of the ISIC.

- *SATA: Student Air Travel Association.* The Student Air Travel Association (SATA) is an international membership association of student travel agencies that share a commitment to providing affordable and accessible travel to young people. Recognising that student travellers are a unique customer niche, SATA began 30 years ago to provide specialised air travel products that meet young people's unique needs. SATA is best known for the 'SATA type ticket' – a uniform flight ticket providing special fares to full-time students and those under 26. SATA tickets are negotiated via Ticket Acceptance Agreements between air carriers and individual SATA members. SATA members and agents of the SATA ticket have established a distribution network of 2500 retail outlets worldwide. As student and youth travellers have a specific need for flexibility and often change plans or make new ones on the road, this network ensures that they can find a SATA ticket agent almost anywhere they go. This distribution network and level of customer service are unique and are what makes the SATA ticket attractive to students.
- *ISSA: International Student Surface Travel Association.* Established in 1992, the International Student Surface Travel Association (ISSA) is one of the newest ISTC Associations. It works to facilitate special surface travel products for students and young people. Through ISSA, student travel agencies and organisations from around the world cooperate to research and develop new rail, bus, coach and urban transport travel opportunities. ISSA works closely with its sister association, the International Student Identity Card Association, to give discount providers a means to identify eligibility for special concessions through the ISIC – the International Student Identity Card.
- *IAEWEP: International Association for Educational Work Exchange Programmes.* The International Association for Educational Work Exchange Programmes (IAEWEP) is an international association of the ISTC whose members specialise in arranging work-abroad programmes for students and young people. More than 20,000 students and young people participate annually in IAEWEP member-sponsored work-abroad programmes.
- *IASIS: International Association for Student Insurance Services.* Protecting students and young travellers with an insurance policy specifically tailored to their unique needs was one of the earliest collective efforts of ISTC members. In 1951, members of

the International Association for Student Insurance Services (IASIS) developed the International Student Insurance Scheme (ISIS). Over the years the ISIS product has become more sophisticated and refined to meet the needs of travelling students and young people. Through IASIS, ISTC members have a forum to refine the ISIS product, to develop new forms of student insurance coverage, to assess market demand and to represent the needs of the community to the insurance industry.

Source: ISTC (2002)

of over US$3 billion. In addition, tickets issued by the Student Air Travel Association are now accepted by over 100 airlines and serve six million travellers annually (ISTC, 2002).

As a result of the numbers of students engaging in travel, a section of the tourism industry has developed to cater specifically for the holiday requirements of university students; one of the largest of these companies is STA Travel. While the student population remains a prime market for these companies, they have increasingly diversified into the youth market, in the process helping to blur the difference between the youth and student populations. STA Travel was created in 1983 and has joint origins as Student Travel Australia and STA Travel in the UK, both of which have been operating since the 1970s (Bywater, 1993a; STA Travel, 2002). The company was initially created to meet the travel needs of university students and their offices were located on university campuses. Today, like the ISTC, STA Travel (2002) recognises the potential for education through travel. It is the stated belief of the company that:

> There is nothing like it [travel] to open the eyes, mind and heart. And we believe that travel is a powerful agent of social change. Getting people to meet face-to-face is the most effective way of ending racism, intolerance and prejudice.

By 2001, STA Travel employed over 2000 people, operating in numerous countries throughout the world. They helped more than five million travellers organise their vacations and generated a turnover in excess of AUS$5 billion (STA Travel, 2002). A more detailed discussion of the nature and origin of companies catering for the travel and holiday needs of young people and university students was published by Bywater in 1993 (Bywater, 1993a). Readers should note that USIT International (renamed USIT Campus) ceased trading early in 2002 (Anonymous,

2002b). In addition, the Council on International Educational Exchange sold its travel company in 2001 and focused on the study abroad and international exchange aspects of the organisation (CIEE, 2002). While companies and organisations such as STA Travel and ISTC help to facilitate student travel, they are by no means the only ones students seek help from when planning their vacations. Rather, students are free to take advantage of holiday opportunities offered by holiday companies that cater to the general population and/or the youth market. Therefore, the scale and economic significance of university student tourism may be far larger than appears to be the case based on information provided by student travel organisations and companies.

Tourism as an Educational Component of the University Experience

In addition to engaging in tourism outside of university term-time, students have the opportunity to take part in international travel as part of their degrees. Students who take advantage of these opportunities can be divided into two groups: those engaged in 'spontaneous mobility', where an individual undertakes international travel between universities without any prior inter-institutional agreement or financial support, and 'organised mobility', where an individual student's international movement is facilitated through inter-institutional and/or intergovernmental agreements and/or governmental programmes. Although student mobility can be traced back to medieval times, it has only become a mass phenomenon in more recent times. By the end of the 1980s it was estimated by UNESCO that approximately one million university students engaged in international mobility at the global level each year (Teichler, 1996). The receiving universities make considerable economic gains from internationally mobile students. For example, by the mid 1990s British universities' income from international student fees was over £700 million (Bown, 2000), while Australian universities gained AUS$1544 million in international student fees in 1997/8 (Australian Tourist Commission, 1998 in Ritchie & Priddle, 2000). These figures do not include money spent by this population on living expenses, books, insurance, travel or special equipment, all of which contributed approximately US$4 trillion in 1994/5 to the USA economy (Hsu & Sung, 1997).

Students also gain from engaging in international mobility as it offers them access to new learning experiences and, potentially, higher quality education than in their home country (see Exhibit 5.2). In addition, studying abroad can be cheaper than studying in a student's home

Exhibit 5.2

Study abroad and personal development benefits for university and college students

By Brent Ritchie

According to some authors the goals of foreign study are consistent with the traditional goals of higher education, including intellectual and professional development, general education, personal growth and the furthering of international understanding (Carlson & Widaman, 1988: 1). Other authors have noted that study abroad (through either spontaneous or organised mobility) will bring about enhanced levels of international understanding and concern (see Coelho, 1962; Deutsch, 1970). Var *et al.* (1989) examined the perceptions of Argentinian university students with a focus on whether participants viewed tourism positively and were aware of its potential for fostering international understanding and world peace. However, despite this work little research has been conducted to examine the personal development associated with study abroad. This exhibit highlights key research in this field that suggests that travel during study-abroad programmes provides personal development benefits that may last longer than knowledge from study programmes themselves.

Gmelch (1997) examined the educational and personal development impacts of a group of American students studying in Austria. Data was collected through the journals and 'travel logs' of 51 students involved in the programme which explained their activities and movements, who they travelled with and what they did throughout their long weekends. At the end of term an open-ended questionnaire was administered to gather data about their experiences and informal discussions were undertaken concerning these trips. The research indicated that students visited an average of 1.72 countries and 2.4 cities per weekend, with 5.5 countries visited in a six-week term (Gmelch, 1997: 478). According to the students, seeing as much of Europe before they went home was the most important factor, while getting to know the places mattered far less. A large amount of time was spent waiting for trains or travelling; in fact Gmelch (1997) notes that nearly a third of their time was spent in transit. One student suggested that 'Americans approach their leisure time like work . . . they exhaust themselves running about trying to get in as much as they can. I am guilty of this too, but now I try to spend some time pondering where I am' (in Gmelch, 1997: 479). Other students noted that just visiting a place and taking a photo was an important motivation for many of their peers.

Group sizes declined over the period of the six-week term as students became more confident and aware of the problems in visiting tourist destinations in larger group sizes (Gmelch, 1997). According to Carlson *et al.* (1990) the most important medium for personal experience in the host country is conversation with host nationals, which Gmelch (1997) notes is limited when students travel in large groups. However, despite the lack of contact with host nationals and a tendency to eat in fast food franchises and visit major tourist attractions, students did develop personally, although they did not develop cognitively or acquire knowledge as such (i.e. they learnt little about European culture). As Gmelch (1997) notes, students felt that they had:

- gained self-confidence due to travelling without parents or other adults and felt they could deal with many situations because of this; and
- become more adaptable and able to cope with surprises and to deal with unfamiliar situations and minor adversity.

This is similar to other studies that have explored the impacts of international study programmes. Hansel (1988: 87) discovered that AFS students appeared to become 'less materialistic, more adaptable, more independent in their thinking, more aware of their home country and culture, and better able to communicate with others and to think critically'. Other studies such as that undertaken by Stitsworth (1988) have shown similar findings. Carlson and Widaman (1988) noted from their research that those who studied abroad had higher levels of international political concern, cross-cultural interest, and cultural cosmopolitanism than those who did not. Those that studied abroad were more positive, but also critical of their own country. Carlson and Widaman (1988) concluded that travel abroad appears to 'result in more mature and objective perceptions of the students' home country as well as changes in attitudes on a number of dimensions related to international awareness' (Carlson & Widaman, 1988: 14).

Gmelch (1997) found that travel required organisational ability, the ability to deal with unpredictability and cultural and language barriers and good communication skills. Personal growth and development from travelling abroad during study occurs when students have to cope with change and solve problems (Chickering, 1969; Brueggemann, 1987). As Gmelch (1997: 487) states, 'individuals acquire new understanding about life, culture, and self when they deal with changes in their environment and circumstances . . . whereas little change occurs when students are in situations of equilibrium'. Experiential learning through cross-cultural travel appears to directly facilitate personal growth, and Gmelch (1997) suggests that enabling students to travel on their own or in small groups would increase their likelihood of learning experientially and meeting host nationals. Both of these situations would improve the personal development benefits of study-abroad programmes and add value to the formally organised component of educational programmes.

The results of the above studies suggest that organised mobility (through exchange programmes and internships) have obvious personal development and cross-cultural impacts for students, but perhaps more surprising, that travel and tourism experiences during study abroad may be more significant from a personal development perspective. Further research is required into the links between educational tourism and personal development resulting from both organised and spontaneous mobility.

country. Indeed, American students can attend one of the UK's top universities for approximately £7,000 per year compared to attending Harvard at an annual cost of about US$25,000. These savings helped to increase the number of US students studying in the UK by 84% in the 1990s (Van Miert, 1998). However, increasing numbers of international students in universities may not be all good news. Indeed, Sir Clive Saville, chief executive of UKCOSA, has claimed that British universities 'are becoming dependent on international students' fees not just for general income but for the viability of entire departments'. He suggested, 'if you consider that in some subject areas more than 50 per cent of postgraduate students are international, then an enormous proportion of universities' research effort depends on them. A large number of research departments would close without them' (Baty, 2000). The potential pitfalls of over-dependency on international students' fees were illustrated during the Southeast Asian economic crisis in the mid 1990's that led to a sharp decline in the number of international students from this region attending British universities (Van Miert, 1998).

Spontaneous mobility

A growing number of students are engaging in spontaneous mobility, travelling to foreign universities either for a part or the whole of their degree. Indeed, at the global level there was a rise of 55% between 1990 and 1996 in student mobility (Bown, 2000). Much of this increase was within Europe, where there was a 33% increase in the number of international students studying at institutions within the European Union between 1990/91 and 1993/94. During this time France, Belgium, and the UK recorded some of the highest growth rates, while Italy and Germany posted much slower rates. By 1993/94 the European Union calculated that there were almost 123,000 foreign spontaneously mobile students registered in the higher education institutes of the 15 member states. This figure deliberately did not include students registered at a university outside of their country of origin who had lived in the foreign country before entering higher education. France was the top host country, followed by Germany and the UK, with these three countries accounting for 72% of all the foreign tertiary education students in the EU. Approximately 35% of the foreign students were from Western European countries. The UK and Germany, who accounted for 21% of all international students from Western Europe, were the top two destinations for these students.

There was a greater proportion of foreign students from outside the European Union than inside it in all the member states, excluding Austria, Denmark, Ireland and Italy. The greatest difference between European and other international students was in Portugal, where the ratio was one to five, although in absolute numbers France and Germany attracted the highest number of non-EU international students. Of the international spontaneous students, 23% were new entrants in the higher education system (i.e. they had not registered at a university in their home country before going to a university in a foreign country). The main motivation for these students appears to have been a desire to circumvent restrictive admissions conditions, either in terms of education requirements or place availability, within their home countries (Jallade *et al.*, 2001). The data presented by Jallade *et al.* (2001) was incomplete in terms of postgraduate students' international mobility, as data was only available for 11 of the EU states. However, it was estimated that 22% of the spontaneously mobile students in these countries were postgraduates.

The international spontaneous mobility of university students has resulted in a situation where some countries are net gainers of these students while others are net losers. Within the context of the European

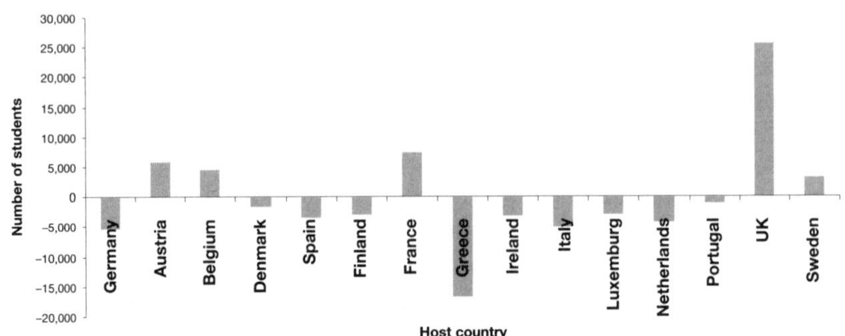

Figure 5.2 Balance of incoming and outgoing spontaneously mobile students in the European Union in 1993/94 and 1992/93

Notes: 1. Excluding incoming students from Austria, Finland, and Sweden. 2. Excluding incoming students into Portugal for whom data is not available by country of origin.
Source: Jallade *et al.* (2001)

Union, Figure 5.2 shows the balance of incoming and outgoing students for each of the member states. It demonstrates that, in the mid 1990s, the UK gained the most students as a result of spontaneous student mobility, while France, Austria, Belgium and Sweden were the other net importing nations. In contrast, the largest net exporter was Greece, followed by Germany, both of whom had very high export levels. There was no specialisation of the host countries in particular fields of study but in each country there were favourite subjects chosen by large numbers of international students. These ranged from medicine and social sciences in Belgium, to arts and humanities in France, to law in Italy and language in Greece. Despite the Greek case, language is generally not the main reason why spontaneously mobile students decide to study in a particular country (Jallade *et al.*, 2001). Import–export imbalances of European Union students in the UK continued to widen throughout the 1990s, doubling between 1992 and 1998, and costing the country approximately £100 million a year (Tysome, 1998). In Australia research has been undertaken which illustrates that higher education by international students generates substantial economic benefits for the host country at a national level (see Exhibit 5.3).

Exhibit 5.3

Economic impact of overseas university students in the Australian higher education sector

By Brent Ritchie

Although some studies illustrate the economic impact of foreign university students on the local or regional economy (see McKay & Lewis, 1993; Musca & Shanka, 1998; Michael *et al.*, 1999), few have examined the impact at the national level associated with international education or the higher education sector in particular. However, the growth of offshore education and the move by Western countries toward a post-industrial economic base has provided the impetus for increased research on the value of international education and the higher education sector. This exhibit discusses research undertaken in 1997 in Australia which examined the economic impact and value of higher education at a national level. Where appropriate, comparisons are made with a similar survey undertaken in 1992. This illustrates the value of this form of educational tourism, but also illustrates how the research was implemented and what economic attributes were measured which may be of benefit to destination managers and researchers.

A total of 1705 interviews were undertaken to examine the characteristics, perceptions and economic impact of international education in Australia. For the purposes of this exhibit only the results concerning higher education income and expenditure are discussed. A total of 928 higher education interviews were undertaken in 1997 out of the total of 1705 respondents (the remainder included ECLIOS, vocational and secondary school education). The sample was a random stratified sample based upon student origins and study location in Australia. Respondents were recruited via a mail-out to nearly 9000 students but only 807 interviews in total were undertaken for all types of international education. This low response rate from individuals was supplemented by a snowball sample where students gave contact details for other students who were then screened and, where appropriate, were surveyed (AIEF, 1998). Respondents were interviewed by way of a personal interview by experienced market researchers, with the average interview lasting approximately 47 minutes. Measurement of income and expenditure

Table 5.1 Income categories for respondents in Australian International Education Survey

Sources	*Income categories*
Within Australia	• Income from paid employment • Income from a business or partnership • Rent from property investments • Dividends or interest earned • Income from an Australian employer • An Australian government scholarship • An Australian university or school scholarship or cadetship
From overseas	• Income from family or friends • Income from other sources • Income from the sale of personal possessions • Income from an overseas government • Income from an overseas employer • Income from overseas family members or friends • Income from other overseas sources

Source: Modified from AIEF (1998: 23–24)

was based on the large number of categories listed in Tables 5.1 and 5.2. With respect to income, any from a spouse or partner (residing in Australia but not studying) was also included but separately identified, as was information on money taken out of Australia or sent overseas (AIEF, 1998: 24). As can be seen from the tables, the income and expenditure categories were specific and exhaustive, providing accurate data on a sectorial basis.

Outliers in both income and expenditure were excluded as they exerted an influence on estimates of average expenditure. Examples included a student who received USA$927,000 from overseas family and friends, two students who brought or transferred USA$1.5 million and USA$310,000 to Australia, and a student who received a lump sum of USA$110,000 from overseas family members to pay for his/her course fees (AIEF, 1998: 26). The demographic characteristics of the higher education sample are illustrated in Table 5.3. The table illustrates that the majority of students were from Asian destinations and were aged between 20 and 24 years. However, as Carr discussed

Table 5.2 Expenditure categories for respondents in Australian International Education Survey

Expenditure category	*Component*
Housing	Rent, board, mortgage repayment, rates (including land, water, etc.), repairs or maintenance, house insurance, home contents insurance
Utilities	Electricity expenses, gas expenses
Telephone	Telephone expenses, public phone calls and phone cards
Health	Health insurance, Medibank private, health costs including dental not covered by private health insurance
Groceries	Food and groceries, toiletries and cosmetics, meals and snacks bought away from home
Alcohol and cigarettes	Alcoholic beverages, cigarettes and tobacco
Car	Car maintenance, petrol, purchase price minus selling price, registration, insurance
Daily transport	Daily transport (not including petrol), other transport costs (bus, train, taxi fares)
Recreation and entertainment	Entertainment, lottery tickets and gambling, books, newspapers and magazines, recreational and sporting equipment
Clothing, footwear and other personal effects	Clothing and footwear, jewellery and watches
Household goods	Household goods, hire of household goods
Travel	Overseas travel (including airfares)
Own course fees	Own school or course fees
Partner's course fees	Partner's school or course fees
Children's course fees	Children's school or course fees
Course-related expenses	Stationery, photocopying and faxing, purchase hire or use of personal computers or printers, timber or arts supplies, uniforms or protective clothing, course-related fieldwork, books and textbooks for the course, other course-related expenses
Other weekly expenses	Childcare, postal charges, other weekly expenses
Other major expenses	Gifts, travel within Australia, travel goods, other major expenses

Source: Modified from AIEF (1998: 25–26)

Table 5.3 Demographic characteristics of higher education respondents

Characteristics	*Percentages*
Gender	• 47% male • 53% female
Age	• 6% aged 18–19 years • 58% aged 20–24 years • 22% aged 25–29 years • 7% aged 30–34 years • 3% aged 35–39 years • 4% aged 40 years and over
Origins	• 19% from Malaysia • 17% from Singapore • 12% from Hong Kong • 11% from Indonesia • 11% from Other North Asia (India, China, Taiwan) • 8% from Other South Asia (Japan, Thailand, South Korea) • 7% from Americas • 3% from Oceania • 10% from other countries

Source: Modified from AIEF (1998: 30–33)

earlier in this chapter a significant number were over 30 years of age, illustrating that students in this sample did not all belong to the youth population.

Total income is illustrated in Table 5.4, which demonstrates the average weekly income by type for overseas students in the higher education sector in Australia. This indicates a total weekly income of AUS$660 ±$41 (due to the margin of error), up from AUS$536 in 1992. This was the highest average income for all types of international education surveyed, a reversal of trends in 1992 when higher education students received the lowest average income compared to other international students. The table illustrates a high reliance on overseas support and funding from students' families, friends, government and personal income to support their study. For income generated within Australia, employment provides the highest

Table 5.4 Average weekly income by type of income for higher education international students (AUS$)

Type of income	*1997*	*1992*
From an overseas family or friends	314	261
Money transferred to Australia	210	99*
From overseas government	40	26
From overseas sources	36	0*
From paid employment in Australia	17	21
From an Australian government scholarship	15	n/a
From an Australian university scholarship	8	n/a
From family and friends in Australia	7	n/a
From an overseas employer	5	7
From assistance given by an Australian employer	3	n/a
From other sources in Australia	2	2
From the sale of personal possessions	2	1
From rental property in Australia	1	3*
From dividends/interest in Australia	1	0*
From a business in Australia	0	2
Fee subsidy	n/a	114
Total	660	536

Notes: * Indicates that the two adjoining cells were not measured separately in 1992. n/a Indicates that this information was not collected.
Source: Modified from AIEF (1998: 100)

average weekly amount followed by Australian government scholarships. International students in Australia are permitted to undertake part-time employment throughout their studies, resulting in the important contribution of employment to income.

An examination of Table 5.5 illustrates the average weekly expenditure for overseas students studying in higher education in Australia. The table illustrates that, for all higher education students, course fees, housing and food are the main expenditure items. However, an average of USA$20 was spent per week on recreation

Table 5.5 Average weekly expenditure by cost components for higher education international students (AUS$)

Type of expenditure	*1997*	*1992*
Respondents' course fees	292	224
Housing	79	78
Food and groceries	59	55
Course-related expenses	27	n/a
Other major expenses	22	44
Telephone costs	21	19
Recreation/entertainment	20	16
Overseas travel	19	15
Clothing and footwear	14	n/a
Car costs	13	44
Household goods	10	n/a
Daily transport	7	5
Alcohol and cigarettes	7	4
Health costs	6	6
Other weekly expenses	5	4
Utility costs	5	5
Children's course fees	0	n/a
Total	599 ± 24	520

Note: n/a indicates that this information was not collected.
Source: Modified from AIEF (1998: 105)

and entertainment, while USA$19 per week was spent on overseas travel, indicating that overseas students in higher education may provide economic benefits to the tourism industry directly, as well as indirectly in their daily living costs. Comparisons between the 1997 and 1992 studies show a significant increase in the cost of course fees as well as a significant reduction in car costs without an increase in daily transport costs, perhaps indicating reliance on walking or cycling. According to further research undertaken, higher education students send significantly more money to their home countries than other overseas students (USA$56 on average per week). Also, a total of AUS$1.4 billion is estimated to have been spent by overseas students in Australian higher education (AUS$599 multiplied by an average 44 weeks stay), and comprised nearly one half of the total estimated international education expenditure (AIEF, 1998: 106). No downstream or value-added impacts were examined in this study, but further research was planned using econometric impact modelling procedures.

This research has illustrated the direct economic impact of overseas students in higher education in Australia and demonstrated a high level of expenditure on items other than course fees. As an ongoing research programme it is one of the few benchmarking studies undertaken at a national level which includes a margin of error associated with the estimates. These estimates are useful for examining the impacts of overseas education on individual states and territories in Australia, as well as on individual sectors, including travel- and tourism-related businesses.

Organised mobility

In addition to the increase in numbers of students engaging in spontaneous international mobility, a variety of governmental and public bodies around the world have placed increasing emphasis on facilitating organised mobility. One of the aims of this has been to increase cross-cultural understanding and provide students with an international dimension to their education. Within the context of the European Union the Belgian presidency stated in a note to the EU Education Committee in 1994:

> By making students mobile we give them an experience that will influence them throughout the whole of their lives. They will gain an awareness of other cultures and a propensity to understand other people better. When they start their working lives they will be better placed to benefit from their right to free movement [within the EU], to find their niche in employment markets and to give a European dimension to their professional activities.

The creation of study-abroad schemes, such as ERASMUS (the European Community Action Scheme for the Mobility of University Students), by the European Union, has provided students with the option to take part of their degree at a foreign university. Unlike the situation with regards to spontaneous mobility, these schemes aim to establish reciprocal mobility, whereby the number of students a country exports is balanced by the number it imports. ERASMUS was created in 1987 by the

European Community with the aim of building an extensive mobility scheme for higher education (Erasmus Student Network, 2002). In the mid 1990s ERASMUS became a sub-programme of SOCRATES, an organisation that incorporates most of the educational support programmes of the European Union (Maiworm, 2001).

ERASMUS is concerned with the development of exchanges of staff and students, dissemination of knowledge and creation of networks between member states, amongst other activities. The participating countries are the 15 member states of the EU, Iceland, Liechtenstein, Norway, Cyprus, Malta, and all the Associated Countries of the EU in Central and Eastern Europe (ERASMUS, 2002b). The ERASMUS scheme provides students with funds to cover the additional costs of studying in another country within the EU for a period of between three months and one year. It does not cover the costs of travel, additional living expenses abroad and any required language courses (Teichler, 1996). There is an increasing shortfall between ERASMUS grants and student costs that the students increasingly have to cover in the face of declining national grant schemes (Maiworm, 2001). This may explain why, since the end of student grants in the UK, there has been a decline in the number of British students taking part in the ERASMUS scheme. Despite this, the ERASMUS programme appears to be very successful from the viewpoint of the students who take part in it, with over 50% of the 1998/99 cohort rating their academic progress while studying abroad as 'better than they would have expected during a corresponding period at home' (Maiworm, 2001: 467).

Figure 5.3 shows that there has been a rapid growth in the number of students taking part in the ERASMUS exchange programme since its conception, to the point where, in the academic year 1999/2000, funding was provided to 110,134 students to study at a foreign university. In 1993/94 it was estimated that organised mobility accounted for 33% of the students studying at foreign universities within Europe. As in the case of spontaneous mobility, there are countries that are net importers and net exporters of students engaged in organised mobility through the ERASMUS programme. The UK, France and Ireland fall into the former category, while the other EU nations are net exporters. Unlike spontaneous mobility, organised mobility tends to be concentrated on specific areas of study with management (22%) and foreign languages (21%) accounting for the highest proportion of organised international students in the EU (Jallade *et al.*, 2001).

In a further move to increase student mobility between member states the European Union signed the Bologna Declaration in 1999. This

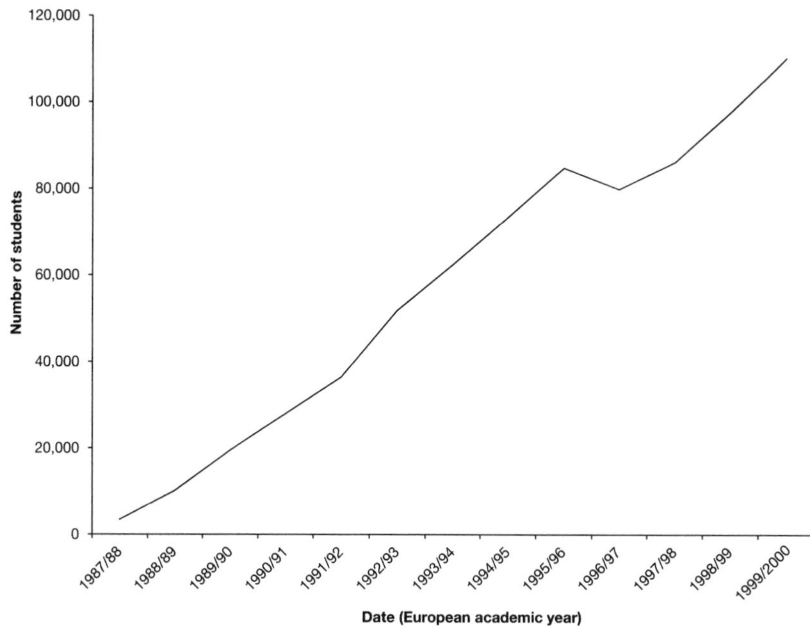

Figure 5.3 Number of ERASMUS students between 1987/88 and 1999/2000

Source: ERASMUS (2002a)

provided a significant step towards the creation of a European Higher Education Area by increasing the compatibility between different countries' university systems (Jobbins, 1999). This Declaration was also aimed at increasing the ability of EU universities to attract students from outside the EU (Van Der Wende, 2001). Similarly, in the UK the government launched an initiative in 1999 to attract more non-EU international students to British universities to increase institutions' earnings from international students' fees. The plan aimed to increase the number of international students studying in the UK by 50,000 by 2004/5 (Sanders & Brookman, 2001). This initiative appears to be working, with rapid growth in the number of students going to the UK from China in particular, as well as from India, Russia, Mexico and the Gulf States in the last couple of years (Paterson, 2002).

In addition to governmental and public bodies, individual universities are placing increasing emphasis on the development of organised international student mobility. This has led to the development of exchange programmes between partner universities in different countries. These relationships tend to be, like ERASMUS, based on the concept of reciprocation, which means there should be no net losers or gainers in terms of student numbers. Many tertiary institutions also view international students as a lucrative source of revenue in an era when universities find themselves forced to seek alternative incomes in the face of declining levels of funding from governments. This has led to the development of marketing policies designed to attract foreign residents to individual universities and non-reciprocal relations between institutions. A significant example of the latter is the establishment of relationships between universities in developed countries and institutions and/or governments in less developed nations, whereby students from the latter countries study for at least part of their degrees at universities in developed countries. This type of relationship provides economic benefits to participating universities in developed countries and increases access to high quality tertiary education for people from developing countries. Refer to Exhibit 5.4 for an example of the development of a university degree programme that encourages student mobility.

One result of an increasing focus on the monetary value of international students has been that, in an era of increasing student mobility, there has been a decline in the mobility of students from some developing countries. Indeed, it has been estimated that only 6% of students moving between Commonwealth countries were from the most disadvantaged member states. This is despite the fact that these countries comprise a significant proportion of the population of the Commonwealth (Bown, 2000). In particular, the ability of students from most African countries to participate in international mobility has declined since the end of the cold war. In addition, countries such as Iran, Iraq and Nigeria, which were major exporters of students in the 1970s, are no longer sources of large numbers of internationally mobile students. The decline in international mobility by students from some developing countries has the potential, according to the Council for Education in the Commonwealth and UKCOSA, to add to the intellectual and economic marginalisation of these nations (Jobbins, 2000).

Field trips

In addition to international mobility opportunities, many university students have the chance to participate in travel during their time in higher education through course-related field trips, which form an important part of the learning experience (see Exhibit 5.5). Excursions give

Exhibit 5.4

ITMC international internship programme

By Charlotte Vogels

The NHTV (Netherlands Institute of Tourism and Transport Studies) in Breda, which is a University of Professional Education, trains students for management positions in the fields of tourism and transport. Since the academic year 1994/95 the institute has offered the specialist area 'International Tourism Management & Consultancy' (ITMC). When completing the whole programme successfully, students will obtain the Dutch equivalent to a bachelor's degree. This undergraduate programme starts in the second academic year, preceded by a propaedeutic year in Dutch only. The ITMC courses are entirely taught in English, which enables foreign students from all over the world to register. Every year, the NHTV welcomes over 100 international students from all over the world. Due to exchange programmes with partner institutes, students from different countries are stimulated to study at the NHTV, which enhances cross-cultural relations between students.

The ITMC programme enables students to work in the international tourism industry and includes specific tourism modules, such as destination analysis, cross-cultural studies, tourism planning and development, while also focusing on principal business subjects, such as marketing, research and financial accounting. Together with computer and communication skills, and several languages, ITMC students gain a broad and solid knowledge of the international tourism industry, as well as key business and professional skills. In the third academic year, students have to fulfil an internship period and the final year comprises a graduation project, which generally includes writing a thesis. Because the educational system at the NHTV is very practice-oriented, students learn to work independently and have a problem-solving attitude; in brief, it creates self-starters ready for the professional field of tourism.

In the third academic year, students will conduct a 25-week internship period at a company in the tourism industry. In line with the international study programme, it is obligatory to fulfil this period abroad. ITMC students travel all over the world to conduct their internship period, for example in Europe, the Caribbean, Mexico,

Peru, South-Africa, Thailand and Australia. To be fully prepared, preparations start ahead of time, approximately a year before the commencement of the internship period itself. The placement office at the NHTV is largely involved in the process of training students prior to the start of the internship period abroad and assists in obtaining a suitable internship position for the students. Due to the ITMC programme being widely set up, students fulfil their internship period in a broad range of organisations, including government bodies and private sector companies. The most familiar are National Tourist Boards, accommodation suppliers, tour operators, consultancies and research firms.

When students have found a suitable internship position within a company in the tourism field, further contact can be established between the company and the student to examine the content of the internship, which will be stated in the internship contract. In general, next to the daily activities, students conduct a specific assignment during the internship period, most commonly in the field of marketing and market research. The student will be assigned a lecturer of the NHTV, who will assist the student from the institute's side by evaluation throughout and after the internship period, and help with problems that may arise. The student maintains contact with the assigned lecturer by sending interim reports every three weeks. The internship organisation needs to assign a supervisor, who will make the student acquainted with the organisation and its operations, provide work guidance, and evaluate the student by progress meetings and assessment at the end of the internship period. To learn the most from this experience abroad, students carry out an internship report, describing and evaluating all aspects of the internship period.

The ITMC programme is increasingly popular; in the initial year of the programme, the academic year 1994/95, the programme consisted of 51 students. This number expanded to 92 students in the academic year 1998/99. Evidently, the number of students participating in an internship period abroad also increased. In the academic year of 1998/99, 85 students conducted their internship period abroad. This increased to 109 students in the 2000/01 academic year. In concrete terms, each year, more than 90% of all ITMC students go abroad to carry out their internship period. Also, the independence of students has increased over the years; in the academic year 1998/99, 42 of the 92 ITMC students found an internship position by themselves. In the academic year 1995/96, only seven out of 44 students achieved this. Although many students find an internship position individually, the placement office still plays an active role in the process; it supports and advises students on the steps to take.

The international character of the internship programme of ITMC is rather unique, as it is generally not very common to fulfil an internship period in a foreign country. For instance, students who participate in one of the other specialist areas the NHTV has to offer are far less inclined to conduct an internship period abroad. As described above, the ITMC programme is increasingly participated in, and is likely to attract a growing number of students in the future. The profile of the international internship programme is in line with the ITMC programme due to its international character. The ITMC programme educates students to be professional experts in the global travel and tourism industry and, after graduating, students have the ability to work not only in their home country, but all over the world. By conducting the internship period abroad, students learn to work in the professional field in a cross-cultural environment as well as develop the skills and knowledge necessary to work in a foreign country.

students the opportunity to see and experience what they have been taught about in the classroom (Stainfield *et al.*, 2000). This form of experiential learning is designed to stimulate students' interest, aid their recognition of the links between theory and reality, and, as a result, help them engage in deep learning processes. The result can be a higher quality of learning and better graduates than would be the case without the presence of educational excursions in the curriculum (Wojtas, 1997). A wide variety of university disciplines, including geography, history, marine biology and tourism management, have a long history of offering excursions that tend to last anywhere between one day and a couple of weeks.

Traditionally, excursions tended to be funded by universities, allowing students to participate in them for free and enabling departments to make them an integral part of their degrees. Today, in a climate of increasing financial pressure on universities many departments are asking students to pay some or all of the costs of the excursions (Stainfeld, 2000; Stainfield *et al.*, 2000; Wojtas, 1997). In some instances this has meant that departments are no longer able to make excursions a compulsory part of the degree process, while in other institutions departments have ceased to

Exhibit 5.5

Field research projects in tertiary tourism education: Lessons from Vanuatu, Bali and Thailand

By Thomas G. Bauer

Introduction

This exhibit is based on the author's ten years of experience in teaching tourism at Victoria University of Technology in Melbourne, where the Bachelor of Business in Tourism Management programme was designed to provide graduates with opportunities to enter the tourism industry at middle management level. The course included a business core and a tourism specialisation consisting of a minimum of six compulsory subjects plus several electives.

From 'end-of-year-trip' to 'tourism field research project'

Early days in Vanuatu

Unlike in the physical sciences, where experiments in laboratories can be used to simulate an environmental setting, the breadth of tourism activities cannot easily be simulated in the classrooms of tertiary institutions. The author felt that, to round off student's tourism education, it was necessary to remove them from the classroom and to expose them to the realities of tourism in the field. In 1990 he explored the possibility of taking a group of 22 mainly final-year Tourism Management students to Vanuatu to experience a Pacific island destination and to study tourism on location. The initial response from the approving authority was negative and it took some time to convince them that field trips were more than holidays. The excursion lasted one week and included presentations by representatives of the local tourism industry, hotel inspections and a visit to a Custom village on the island of Tanna. There students came face to face with a group of semi-naked locals who performed dances for them and who sold them souvenirs – clearly an experience that could not be simulated in the classroom.

Field research project in Bali

In 1994 the author organised a field trip to Bali. The island is perceived by many to be an overdeveloped, polluted destination that is overcrowded and not worth visiting any more. Such negative images and newspaper articles with catchy titles like 'See Bali and cry' make a good starting point for an exploration of what tourism is really like on the island. Bali is also frequently cited in the tourism planning literature (see for example Inskeep, 1991: 390–396; Gunn, 1988: 43) and this provided credibility for the selection of the island for a study trip. Encouraged by the success of the 1994 field excursions, the author suggested that the 'end-of-year-trip' should be made into a full credit-earning subject. With the assistance of several colleagues the approval process was completed and the credit-bearing subject 'Tourism Field Research Project' was born.

In late 1997 the author again organised and guided a group of 22 students on a field research project trip to Bali, where the group inspected hotel properties, was addressed by executive managers of hotels and transport companies and exchanged ideas with their fellow students from the Bali Hotel and Tourism Training Institute. Students had the opportunity to observe the scenic beauty of the island but were also exposed to environmental degradation, polluted beaches, culturally insensitive resort developments and unsafe marine transport practices. During lectures in the tranquil setting of Puri Lumbum Cottages in Munduk, Singaraja Province, they learned in situ about responsible tourism development and about the impacts that tourism has on the culture of the Balinese people. By staying in remote, locally developed and owned and environmentally friendly accommodation, students had the opportunity to gain first-hand experiences in the management of one of the few true ecotourism developments.

To reflect the credit-bearing nature of the subject changes had to be made. Students enrolled in the subject had to attend regular preparatory pre-departure lectures that explored tourism development in Bali. They were required to select a research topic that covered one aspect of Balinese tourism and they had to complete their literature review and background reading for the required 4000-word paper prior to departure. During their stay in Bali students had to carry out primary research on their selected topic. The end result of their efforts was a compilation of their writings that was bound and placed in the university's library under the title *Tourism in Bali: The Good, The Bad and The Ugly.*

Thailand

Because of the success of the 1997 trip, the marketing of the 1998 project was much easier and relied mainly on word of mouth. Because the Field Research subject was now credit bearing and could also be taken as a summer school subject many students saw it as a great way of finishing their degrees. As a result 60 students enrolled in the 1998 Field Research Project to Thailand. During 1998 Victoria University had also become a member of the Network of Asia-Pacific Education and Training Institutes in Tourism (APETIT) that had just been established under the auspices of the UN-ESCAP. One of the major objectives of APETIT is the exchange of students and staff among its member institutions and, consequently, a visit to the Hotel and Tourism Training Institute (HTTI) was included.

There, students had the opportunity to interact with their local counterparts. The group was also addressed by speakers from the Tourism Authority of Thailand and, during an evening visit to the resort town of Pattaya, students were introduced to the 'darker' side of tourism in Thailand. To increase the social awareness of students, a visit to a World Vision project in the slums of Bangkok was also included. Students observed first hand what it means to be poor in an urban environment. By exposing the group to a diversity of experiences at a destination a much broader and deeper understanding of tourism was achieved.

In designing an itinerary for a study tour it is important to note that there has to be a balance between exposing students to poverty, pollution and negative impacts of tourism and showing them the beauty of the country and the friendliness of its people. Because of the multifaceted nature of Thailand's tourism product this objective was achieved by spending a few days on the tropical island of Ko Samed.

Conclusion

With the above in mind it can be concluded that field research projects are an important component of quality tertiary tourism education. There is only so much that students can learn about tourism from attending lectures and seminars in the confines of a university classroom and from reading textbooks and journal articles. Tourism is such a multifacetted, multidisciplinary field that, without going 'into the field' to experience first hand how tourism works, many will only see the theoretical side of the phenomenon. Field research projects complement what has been learned in the lectures. They provide students with the opportunity to travel and to see and experience how tourism operates and what impacts it has on the local population. The author strongly encourages all universities to incorporate field research projects into their tourism curriculum.

offer excursions. Even where excursions have been kept as an option their value to the learning experience is compromised, as they can no longer be fully integrated into the degree programme because some members of a degree cohort may not be able to pay to go on a particular excursion. The ability to offer students excursions is also coming under pressure as a result of increasing demands on university staff to assess and minimise potential risks relating to field trips. This time-consuming task can reduce the ability and willingness of lecturers to provide excursions for students (Adams, 1999).

A potential solution to at least some of the problems associated with field trips is the development of virtual reality programs that allow students to gain the benefits of excursions without leaving the university. Although a full-immersion virtual reality experience is still many years away, a variety of programs have already been created that provide students with access to international field sites from the comfort of their computer terminals (Stainfield, *et al.*, 2000). These programs offer students an affordable and risk-free alternative to actual excursions. Virtual reality field trips also provide students with the ability to make repeat visits to a destination and enable them to clearly see sites that in reality may be overcrowded, providing them with a higher quality visitor experience (Nowak, 1997; Wojtas, 1997). However, it is unlikely that virtual reality field trips will be able to replace real excursions, at least in the short to medium term. Indeed, in a study of university students, Spicer and Stratford (2001: 345) found that 'while students were extremely positive about the potential of VFT [virtual field trips] to provide valuable learning experiences . . . nearly all of the students were insistent that it could not, and should not, replace real field trips'. These findings support the view that one of the primary aims of virtual reality field trips should be to prepare students for real excursions, not replace them (Stainfield *et al.*,

2000). Until technology catches up with the complexities of reality the use of virtual field trips rather than real ones is likely to lead to a lower quality learning experience for the students, although they may be better than no excursions at all.

Conclusion: The Future of University and College Students' Tourism

The global university student population now represents a significant proportion of the world's general population. In addition, the number of young and mature people attending universities looks set to continue to grow. While the time and financial constraints of the student population remain relatively low, the economic pressure on students is likely to rise, leading to higher debt levels amongst students and larger numbers working during their degrees. Despite the increasing financial problems faced by students they continue to be a major segment of the tourist population, and this shows signs of continuing in the future as students appear willing to work and/or go into debt to fund their travel desires. Despite the significance of the student population's engagement in tourism the majority of tour operators are not trusted by students and fail to provide the holidays students desire. While companies, such as STA Travel, that cater specifically to students, may be doing a better job than more generalised operators, all tourism companies could do more to meet the needs of the student population. This is because students form a significant tourism population and one that, after graduation, has relatively high earning potential.

The number of students engaging in spontaneous and organised international mobility will carry on increasing with the support of student organisations, national governments, multinational institutions and universities (Musca & Shanka, 1998). Despite the growth in spontaneous and organised international mobility the vast majority of students still undertake and complete their degrees within their home country without engaging in international travel to a foreign university. Indeed, in 1993/94 it was estimated that only 2% of the total EU university student population of nine million undertook part or all of their studies at a foreign tertiary institution. This figure varies considerably at the national level, with less than 1% of the Mediterranean countries' student population consisting of internationally mobile students compared to 5.6% of the Austrian and 4% of the British (Jallade *et al.*, 2001). The eventual aim of ERASMUS is to enable 10% of all European students to engage in organised mobility (Teichler, 1996). It is, however, important that ERASMUS, and other organisations interested in the reciprocal exchange of students across countries, work to solve the current export–import imbalances that exist. There is also a need for these organisations to ensure that students in developing countries continue to have access to high quality tertiary education through international mobility programmes. All the stakeholders interested in developing international student mobility for primarily economic reasons have to be more cautious in the future. The impacts of the mid 1990s' economic recession in Southeast Asia have shown that the flow of international students to developed countries cannot be taken for granted. In addition, many of those countries that are currently net student exporters have recognised the economic need to provide students with domestic educational opportunities that minimise the need for international mobility. Long-term planning of universities based on income from international student fees may, therefore, be a flawed strategy.

Unlike other areas of university student tourism, field trips are in an increasingly unhealthy state. This is despite the recognition of the value of education outside of the classroom and experiential learning processes. Although virtual reality may aid the quality of field trip experiences it cannot replace real excursions. Therefore, to protect against the continued demise of field trips there is an urgent need for research into the value of excursions to students' learning experiences.

Case Study 5.1

Use and trust of tourism information sources amongst university students

By Neil Carr

Introduction

This case study examines the types of information sources utilised by university students when planning a vacation and the levels of trust they ascribe to them. The need for this research is related to the fact that, without a clear understanding of how students and people in general gain information about potential holiday destinations, it is impossible to accurately market products to them (Fodness & Murray, 1997; Swarbrooke & Horner, 1999). In addition, although university students represent a separate and significant part of the tourist population there is a paucity of research on the holiday experiences of this population (Chadee & Cutler, 1996; Sirakaya & McLellan, 1997).

A variety of information sources about holiday destinations are available to tourists. These may be divided into two groups, namely 'formal' and 'informal' sources. The first of these includes information from travel agents, travel brochures, newspapers, magazines and television. The other type of information stems from sources such as friends, relatives and personal experience. When planning their holidays people may utilise these sources to enhance the quality of their vacations and decrease the risk of having a negative holiday experience (McIntosh & Goeldner, 1990; Fodness & Murray, 1997).

Carr (1997) found that young people tend to rely on formal sources of information when travelling internationally and informal ones when holidaying at the domestic level. Furthermore, Wheatcroft and Seekings (1995: 14) have stated that the pre-packaged share of the youth market is rising, although they also state that this population's 'dominant source of travel information is word-of-mouth from other young people – often acquired during travel'. Similarly, Chadee and Cutler (1996) and Field (1999) reported that the majority of the university students they studied only used informal sources of holiday information.

Despite young people's apparent use of formal sources of information it appears that the informal sources are generally preferred 'because they are often credited with greater reliability and authenticity than more formal sources' (Laing, 1987: 275; Carr, 1997). However, Laing (1987) suggests that the use of informal sources by young people is constrained by their limited availability, making the use of formal sources an 'enforced' behaviour.

Methodology

The data used in this paper are based on a study of the holiday behaviour of British students enrolled at the University of Hertfordshire, England. A quantitative overview of students' use and trust of tourism information sources was collected using a questionnaire survey. In addition, a series of in-depth interviews that each lasted approximately one hour were conducted to gather qualitative data in order to understand why students use and trust holiday information sources. The use of multimethod approaches to data collection is not without precedence (e.g. Woodward *et al.*, 1988; Mowl, 1994; Carr, 1998) and provides a more detailed understanding of students' use and trust of information sources than would have been possible if only one method of data collection had

Table 5.6 Characteristics of the students who took part in the questionnaire survey and in-depth interviews (% of students in brackets)

		Questionnaire survey	*In-depth interviews*
Gender	Male	220 (44.53)	11 (34.38)
	Female	274 (55.47)	21 (65.62)
Year of study	First	103 (22.79)	10 (32.26)
	Second	298 (65.93)	11 (35.48)
	Final	51 (11.28)	10 (32.26)
Age (years)	25 and under	483 (96.41)	26 (81.25)
	Over 25	18 (3.59)	6 (18.75)

been used. Convenience samples of 494 and 32 students took part in the survey and in-depth interviews, respectively. The characteristics of the students in each sample are shown in Table 5.6.

Findings

Table 5.7 shows that each of the holiday information sources was used by the majority of students who took part in the questionnaire survey. However, it is worth noting that a fifth and a quarter of the students stated that they had never used a tourist information centre or the Internet as a source of holiday information, respectively. The pattern of use of information sources highlighted in Table 5.7 is similar to that reported by the students who took part in the in-depth interviews. These students indicated that they used multiple sources of formal and informal information when deciding where to go on vacation. For example, when asked which sources she had used Amanda stated, 'Well generally I speak to friends and family. Sometimes if more than one person tells me they've had quite a good experience in a particular resort I'll investigate it further either through brochures and Internet, books, articles, that kind of thing. And also I guess general knowledge as well.' The aim of using multiple formal and informal sources of information was explained by Samuel who stated, 'I do like to get more than one source of information. You know, just see if I can get word of mouth and media and then possibly get something else. Just so, you know, they don't all contradict each other.'

Figure 5.4 indicates that, overall, the students who took part in the questionnaire survey trusted informal sources more than the formal ones. The

Table 5.7 Students who had never used particular types of sources of information

Source of information	*% of students*	*No. of students*
Relatives	1.86	10
Friends	2.49	12
Previous visits	3.11	15
Travel agents	3.11	15
TV/radio	8.13	39
Newspapers/magazines	10.83	52
Tourist information centres	20.00	98
The Internet	27.77	134

source 'totally trusted' by the highest percentage of students was previous visits (71%). In contrast, only 0.6% of the students said they totally trusted the Internet as a source of holiday information. The students who took part in the in-depth interviews demonstrated a lack of trust in the formal sources similar to that indicated in the figure. For example, when asked how much she trusted this type of information Brenda replied, 'I'm happy to read, but I'd take it with a pinch of salt. There's a lot of over-marketing out there.' Similarly, when asked about his trust of travel agents Paul stated, 'It's mixed really because they must know a certain amount being a travel agent. But you hear so many stories of, you know, like bad hotels and things like that that you can only trust them so much. So you're best doing a lot of your own research in the first place because then you can say "yeah I want to go to that place" regardless.'

Even though most of the students used travel agents this did not mean they trusted them. Indeed, Claire, who always took package holidays booked through travel agents, stated that she did not really trust them. Rather, she claimed to use them because, 'having somebody else there, who's supposed to know what they're doing, kind of helps my confidence. And also if it goes wrong, there's someone else to blame.' In addition, Ben demonstrated a type of enforced behaviour when, in response to being asked about his trust of travel agents, he stated, 'Well you have to trust them really if you haven't got any other source of information to go on really.' Brenda also indicated the convenience of formal

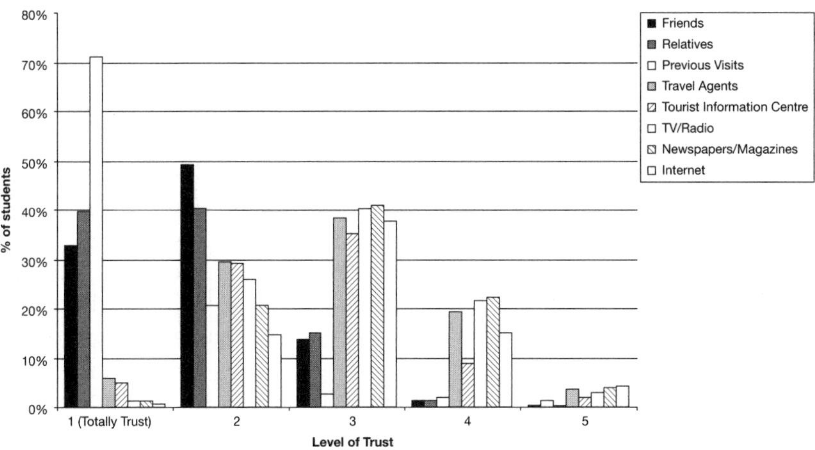

Figure 5.4 Students' trust of holiday information sources

sources when, in reply to being asked about her use of the Internet, she stated, 'I'm not desperately keen about giving out my visa details. But yes, I do. It's more that the convenience outweighs the danger.' In contrast, Tiffany was the only student interviewed who stated, 'Travel agents I trust a lot. But then we've never ever had a bad experience with them, bar one. That was recently.' Asked if this experience had reduced her trust of travel agents Tiffany replied, 'No, cause we're still going away with them this year.'

The interviewees demonstrated a higher trust of informal sources than formal ones. When asked to explain why this was the case Sarah stated that she trusted her friends as a source of holiday information more than formal sources, 'because they've experienced something that you couldn't really put in a brochure. A brochure can't really take in every aspect of the place, the atmosphere, the culture, the different places that you can go to that you might find off the track somewhere.' However, the students indicated that trust of informal sources was not uniform. For example, when ask about her trust of holiday information from friends, Patti stated, 'Um, it depends how close a friend they are. If it was just someone I met in . . . the coffee shop here [at university] saying "oh yes, I've been to so and so and it was really good" then no . . . If it's a close friend of mine and I know what sort of holiday they go on then yes, I would.'

Conclusion

The results of this study indicate that university students tend to use a combination of formal and informal sources of information when deciding where to go on holiday. This behaviour seems to be related to a desire to reduce the chances of making a decision based on inaccurate information. The use of travel agents is, at least partially, based on their perceived legitimacy as industry 'experts'. The use of formal sources may also be an enforced behaviour and/or a function of the convenience of this type of information. However, it is important to recognise that use of a source does not necessarily equate with trust in it. Furthermore, although the students tended to trust informal sources more than formal ones, this trust was not uniform.

This study indicates that the tourism industry has a lot of work to do to encourage students to use formal sources of information and feel that they can trust them. This is especially the case for the Internet, which, although often viewed as the future of tourism marketing, is currently the least used and trusted source of holiday information amongst a population with easy access to this formal source. Another potential problem for the tourism industry relates to the fact that most university students are young and their access to informal information sources is relatively limited. However, this may change as they and their friends take more vacations. This may lead to a reduction in the use of formal sources by this population. Further longitudinal research is required to validate this hypothesis, but the results of this study indicate that students increasingly organise their vacations by themselves as they become more experienced travellers.

Case Study 5.2

Comparing international and domestic university students

By Brent Ritchie and Mark Priddle

From a demand perspective, perhaps the largest markets involved in educational tourism are domestic and international university students, who comprise a valuable and accessible youth market (Field, 1999). According to Sirakaya and McLellan (1997) these students are a major economic force, with the importance of international students to the tourism industry illustrated by international visitor expenditure, where education is the third highest item of expenditure for international visitors travelling to Australia. Increasing attention is being paid to international university students and their travel and tourism behaviour as well as their economic contribution to the national, regional and local community (McKay & Lewis, 1993; Musca & Shanka, 1998; Michael *et al.*, 1999). According to Musca and Shanka (1998: 1), 'with the rapid globalisation and improving international access through transport and telecommunications, offshore education continues to represent a growing market for higher education institutions'.

Canberra is the National Capital of Australia and is heavily reliant on its function as the administrative capital and on the resulting public sector economy. However, more recent government policies have led to the cutting back and restructuring of the public sector which has impacted upon industry and employment in Canberra. Canberra has had to reduce its reliance on the public service as a major employer and diversify the economy with the help of the service sector, including education and tourism. Yet, despite the growing importance attached to offshore education and international university students in Canberra, little research has been conducted on this group of educational tourists. Nor has past research been undertaken which has directly examined and compared domestic and international university student motivations as well as their travel and tourism behaviour.

The international component of this study took place during the first university semester of 1999 after a pilot test in the second semester, 1998, while the domestic study took place during the second semester of 1999. The international study involved the assistance of the international offices at both the University of Canberra and the Australian National University, who supplied a list of approximately 1000 and 1200 international student names and addresses, respectively (all of their international students). A total target population of 1000 was randomly selected from the target population of 2200 using a random systematic method. The survey was mailed to all international students in the first semester, 1999, who were then asked to complete the survey and return it in the freepost envelope provided. A total of 275 usable self-completion surveys were returned by international students studying at both the Australian National University and the University of Canberra (from a total of 952 delivered surveys), indicating a 28.9% response rate.

The domestic sample was gathered through randomly selecting 1000 student identification numbers from a list of 1500 interstate students studying at the University of Canberra only. The student administration section of the University of Canberra printed name and address labels which were then used to mail a similar survey to that used in the international student research to the selected 1000 domestic students studying at the University during the second semester, 1999. The Australian National University was not used in the domestic study due to time restrictions and the nature of this project which was undertaken by a student at the University of Canberra. A total of 235 usable returns were received (from a total of 990 delivered surveys), indicating a 23.7% response rate. Due to limited funding and time it was decided that a follow-up procedure would not take place.

The results of the study illustrate that both domestic and international university students rated educational attributes as more important motivational factors than general destination and tourism attributes. In other words, they were highly motivated, not surprisingly, by the educational element of their trip. Despite the result, there were significant differences between the two samples, especially with respect to the importance of general and tourism attributes for undertaking an educational trip to Canberra (see Table 5.8). In particular, international students gave statistically more importance to destination safety, cultural experiences and climate than did domestic students, while domestic students were more motivated toward making friends, entertainment and nightlife. This illustrates that social factors are more important to domestic university students than external factors such as climate, culture and safety.

Other results illustrated that some tourism attributes were perceived as being more important for international students than domestic students, including quality of attractions, tourism facilities and tourism value for money. All other tourism attributes were rated similarly between the two samples as being neither important nor unimportant. Although tourism attributes were generally less important than educational attributes, a significant proportion of both international and domestic university students did participate in travel and tourism during their educational visit, with the majority taking part in both day trips and overnight trips within Australia. A similar proportion of international and domestic students undertook day trips during their time in Canberra (65% and 70%, respectively) and planned to undertake a day trip in the next 12 months (11.8% each). However, not surprisingly, a significantly greater number of domestic students had undertaken, and planned to undertake, an overnight trip within Australia (82% and 77% compared with 70% and 54% of international students). A significantly greater number of international respondents had undertaken an international trip and were planning to undertake a further international trip in the next 12 months (32% and 30%) often using local travel services.

Table 5.8 Motivations of international and domestic university students, Canberra, Australia

	Sample mean scores		*Significant differences**		
Attribute	***International***	***Domestic***	***t-value***	***df***	***p***
General					
Destination safety/security	3.97	3.39	5.829	502	.000
Relaxation	3.45	3.26			
Making friends	3.72	3.95	–2.641	497.190	.009
Cultural experiences	3.74	3.16	6.716	501	.000
Entertainment and nightlife	2.81	3.48	–6.649	503	.000
Climate	3.30	2.93	4.004	503	.000
Different social environment	3.48	3.54			
Destination value for money	3.60	3.40	2.071	502	.039
Tourism					
Range of attractions	3.35	3.20			
Quality of attractions	3.40	3.20	2.159	501	.031
Ease of travel	3.66	3.75			
Sporting facilities	3.21	3.38			
Tourism facilities	3.26	3.03	2.482	498.077	.013
Outdoor activities and adventure	3.41	3.38			
Tourism value for money	3.53	3.13	4.132	502	.000

Note: * Significant at the .01 level.

Tourist activity and attraction participation of both international and domestic students illustrated that a significant proportion of university students from outside Canberra participate in local attractions and activities, despite the lower importance attached to these activities. Most popular attractions visited by both samples tend to be the icon and national attractions related to Canberra as the National Capital of Australia. However, a greater proportion of international students had visited nature-based attractions, while domestic students appear to frequent many attractions in greater numbers than their international counterparts.

As well as activity and attraction participation, both international and domestic university students have time to entertain and host visiting friends and family, which may also contribute to the local economy in a positive way. A total of 86% of the domestic sample had an average of eight friends from interstate or overseas visit them for three days, while only 51% of international students had an average of four friends visit them from overseas or interstate for an average of 16 days. A total of 57.2% of the international sample had an average of three family members visit for 22 days on average. Figures for domestic family member visitation were not collected.

The survey attempted to ascertain the general living costs and economic impact on the local host community, rather than examine the economic impact generated by course fees. Table 5.9 illustrates that international students spend more than domestic students on a weekly basis during their time in Canberra, especially in the areas of shopping and souvenirs, study costs and other expenses. Whereas domestic students spend more on entertainment, perhaps related to the motivations toward social life and entertainment discussed previously. Past research has illustrated that students from higher educational institutions spent AUS$307 per week, excluding course fees, in Australia (AIEF, 1998). This is slightly higher than the study sample amount of AUS$278, and could perhaps be explained by the lower cost of living in Canberra compared to other cities in Australia.

International students arrive on average two weeks before their course begins and stay on average for four weeks after their 36-week course. Multiplying the average weekly expenditure by the length of stay (42 weeks) gives a total direct economic impact of AUS$11,717.58 for the study sample, or, when multiplied by the target population of international students at both the Australian National University and the University of Canberra (2200), AUS$25,778,676. Figures from AIEF (1998) show that higher education in the ACT contributed AUS$39 million to

Table 5.9 Average weekly expenditure by university students in Canberra, Australia (AUS$)

Economic sector	*International students*	*Domestic students*
Accommodation/lodgings	98.04	91.71
Groceries/food	46.89	39.12
Attractions and activities	18.69	16.02
Shopping and souvenirs	25.92	18.83
Entertainment	19.46	24.30
Travel	20.79	16.47
Study costs (excluding fees)	23.86	18.94
Other miscellaneous	25.34	17.49
Total	278.99	242.88

the local ACT economy in 1997. The difference between the two figures may consist of spending from overseas students in other higher educational institutions in Canberra. Domestic students arrive on average two weeks before their course begins and stay on average for two weeks after their 36-week course. Multiplying the average weekly expenditure by the length of stay (40 weeks) gives a total direct economic impact of AUS$9,715 for the study sample, or, when multiplied by the target population of domestic students at the University of Canberra (1500 students), AUS$14,572,800.

The research has illustrated that there are differences between the motivations of domestic and international university students, yet despite these differences and lower importance placed on tourism attributes, these educational tourists consume local, national and international tourism services and facilities. Moreover, they contribute a significant amount of direct expenditure while staying at a destination on such tourism-related services as attractions, activities, entertainment and travel. Further research is needed on the longer-term benefits of university educational tourists, including their repeat visitation, friends and family visitation, as well as on the links between offshore education and tourism generally.

Chapter 6

Destination Marketing, Regional Development and Educational Tourism

Introduction

As highlighted in Chapter 1, global trends, including a move in Western countries toward a post-industrial economic base and globalisation have meant that destinations are increasingly adjusting themselves structurally, with education and tourism becoming increasingly prominent industry sectors. The economic and social impacts of educational tourism have already been highlighted in Chapters 2 and 3, while Chapters 4 and 5 have initially stressed the regional development opportunities of schools' and university/college students' tourism. This chapter first outlines the growth of global trends and issues facing destinations, including the need for restructuring, and discusses the role that educational forms of tourism ('tourism first' and 'education first' types) can play in destination marketing and regional development. It then outlines some of the current problems related to the development and management of educational tourism and notes that the fragmentation and diversity of this market have led to a lack of coordination. Finally, the chapter discusses mechanisms to overcome this lack of coordination and fragmentation with emphasis on the development of networks and cooperative structures to link education and tourism providers. By collaborating and developing partnerships, organisations involved in educational tourism can maximise the marketing and regional development benefits that this form of tourism can provide.

Globalisation and Restructuring

At a global level many countries have been experiencing changes in their underlying economic and social structures and are subsequently facing a series of challenges and potential opportunities. The issue of political, economic and social restructuring is a widely debated issue because it has been apparent at both global and local levels throughout the industrialised world since the late 1970s (Clark *et al.*, 1992 in Jenkins *et al.*, 1998). Both urban cities and rural areas are facing restructuring and need to attract new economic activities to replace declining industries.

In rural areas one of the largest changes is declining agricultural production and a downturn in agricultural activities, which has not only impacted upon the local economy of countries but society in general. Furthermore, rural or regional areas (places that are peripheral or outlying) are the most vulnerable to this type of agricultural decline and restructuring. Many factors have led to this current situation, including:

- *Free trade and globalisation.* As Page and Getz (1997: 8) note, 'rural areas themselves are in a complex process of change' whereby governments are intervening less in protecting traditional industries as they implement free market policies, including deregulation and privatisation. The development of GATT and globalisation will allow this process to continue.
- *Industrialisation and mechanisation.* With the development and use of machinery such as harvesters and the use of herbicides and pesticides, productivity has increased at the expense of human labour, resulting in unemployment in rural regions. As Page *et al.* (2001: 352) state, 'changes in agricultural practice and policy (intensification and modernization) . . . have created unemployment, falling agricultural incomes and the economic marginalization of smaller farms'.
- *Boom/bust agricultural cycles.* Created due to changing weather patterns these produce inconsistent farm incomes, further increasing business closures and outmigration of local populations.

As noted above, the almost universal result of these factors has been a major outmigration of businesses, services and workers from rural areas to urban and coastal regions in search of employment (Welch, 1992; Lane, 1994). In the majority of such countries measures are sought to reduce outmigration or alternatively to introduce new economic activities to support existing rural populations and prevent their demise. According to Hall and Jenkins (1998) past and current government economic policies have compounded these difficulties, including reductions in community services such as railways, schools, banks and hospitals due to population change and decline. Not only has this affected the local economy, but also the nature and resilience of many of these rural communities. Rural areas need economic development and a consistent flow of people using local infrastructure for them to be sustainable in the long term. According to Lane (1996) these aspects are critical to the survival of rural areas, with destinations further declining unless they find replacement industries or innovative ways to redevelop traditional industries and market themselves to the global community.

Urban areas are also undergoing political, economic and social restructuring and are competing against each other to attract investment and people. Following the economic restructuring of urban cities and the subsequent loss of heavy industry in many industrial and waterfront areas in the 1970s and 1980s, tourism has been perceived as a mechanism to regenerate urban areas through the creation of leisure, retail and tourism space (Law, 1993). Examples were provided in Chapter 2 concerning the use of cultural heritage tourism to regenerate waterfront areas. Similarly, education and the development of 'clever cities', which link education with industry, have been heavily promoted and supported by government.

Destination Marketing and Investment

Service-based industries, such as tourism and education, have been heavily promoted by government at all levels to replace declining agricultural and manufacturing sectors as a move toward a more post-industrial economic base. Many countries have also taken advantage of the increasing tourist trade and have developed tourist products and marketing campaigns to attract visitors and the associated economic development for their countries and depressed rural regions. Hall (2000: 163) comments that:

> although destinations have long promoted themselves to potential visitors, there has been a qualitative change in the nature of place promotion since the early 1980s when shifts to reduce the role of the state in a globalising economy, otherwise known as 'Thatcherism' (UK), 'Reganomics' (USA) and 'Rogernomics' (New Zealand), occurred.

The need for marketing to attract global capital and investment for restructuring and regional development has become an important priority for destinations and this looks likely to continue in the future. Marketing is often associated with imaging, or in the case of some cities or rural regions, re-imaging. According to Kotler *et al.* (1993) we are living in a time of 'place wars', in which places are competing for their economic survival with other places and regions not only in their own country but throughout the world.

> All places are in trouble now, or will be in the near future. The globalization of the world's economy and the accelerating pace of technological changes are two forces that require all places to learn how to compete. Places must learn how to think more like businesses, developing products, markets, and customers. (Kotler *et al.*, 1993: 346)

An increasing number of cities and rural areas are developing educational tourism products to attract investment and economic and social development opportunities through developing offshore education, language schools and heritage tourism (see Case Study 6.1 and Exhibit 6.1). The development of educational tourism for regional development is not limited to the Western world. Ankomah and Larson (2002) note that educational tourism can provide alternative development strategies to mass tourism in sub-Saharan African countries. They comment that marketing and coordination between stakeholders will help maximise the benefits of educational tourism for sub-Saharan Africa. Warner (1999) notes the potential of educational heritage tourism and overseas students as a development option for North Cyprus. A total of six universities in North Cyprus host 20,000 overseas students and, 'as long as the Turkish higher education sector is unable to cope with demand, the number of foreign students in North Cyprus is likely to grow' (Warner, 1999: 137). However, Warner (1999) also notes that, although an increase in foreign students is perceived to be beneficial, negative impacts upon resident quality of life could occur, as well as conflict between students and residents, if ratios of students to locals rapidly increase.

The marketing of places, destinations and communities has several major implications for regional development. Not only may economic patterns change through increased investment and tourist expenditure, but social changes may also be evident as tourists and migrants are attracted, with resulting social and environmental consequences. Hall (2000) notes that little consideration of local residents occurs and they are often left out of the place-marketing frame of reference; while more integrated tourism planning involves a wider variety of stakeholders, it may not involve local communities specifically. Who actually benefits from this place-marketing and who controls how tourism or educational forms of tourism are implemented into marketing and regional development strategies? Case Study 6.1 highlights the case of Marmilla in Sardinia, where the use of educational tourism for regional development became highly politicised. Problems in collaboration between individual agencies and those involved in the project from England resulted in wasted resources and reduced benefit to the local population. There is a need for a wide range of stakeholders, including local residents, to work together in the planning, decision making and development of any marketing or regional development strategy for educational tourism so that the benefits are maximised.

Maximising Educational Tourism Marketing and Regional Development

Understanding stakeholders

As discussed in previous chapters there is a lack of recognition of educational tourism markets, especially the schools' and university student market. This coupled with the fragmented nature of the tourism and educational tourism market poses significant challenges to educational tourism marketers and planners. Stakeholders need to work together to create educational tourism products and market those products for the benefit of the destination and the benefit of educational tourists. According to Freeman (1984: 46), 'stakeholders are those group(s) or organisation(s) that can affect or are affected by the achievement of an organisation's objectives'. Sautter and Leison (1999: 326) note, 'if [tourism] players proactively consider the interests of all other stakeholders, the industry as a whole stands to gain significant returns in the long term'. Bramwell and Lane (2000) comment that stakeholder collaboration has the potential to build mutually supportive proposals concerning how tourism should be developed, thus increasing competitive advantage for organisations and destinations. The potential benefits and problems of stakeholder collaboration are outlined in Table 6.1 and, as Selin (2000: 129) rightly comments, partnerships and collaboration can be a force for good or bad.

Stakeholders can be internal (employees, managers, shareholders), external (other organisations, individuals, local community) or future stakeholders (such as future tourists and local residents). Stakeholders can also be further conceptualised as being primary and secondary. A primary stakeholder is 'one without whose continuing participation the corporation cannot survive as a going concern' (Clarkson, 1995: 106). Clarkson (1995) noted that an organisation is effectively a set of primary stakeholders with different interests, rights, objectives, expectations and responsibilities, whereas secondary stakeholders are 'those who influence or affect, or are influenced and affected by, the corporation and are not essential for its survival' (Clarkson, 1995: 107).

Issues concerning stakeholders and collaboration have recently emerged as thinking moves from the discussion of sustainable tourism to the implementation of sustainable tourism policies (Bramwell & Lane, 2000). The concept of stakeholders has been given increased prominence in the field of tourism planning. Hall and McArthur (1998) advocate a stakeholder and collaborative approach to heritage management and suggest that stakeholder recognition is important for the management of cultural and natural heritage, while Selin and Myers (1998) suggest that stakeholder management and collaboration are important for the development of marketing initiatives. Jamal and Getz (1995) note the importance of stakeholders and their collaboration for the solution of planning problems and management issues, particularly the social and environmental impacts of tourism (Bramwell & Lane, 2000). Other authors, such as Keogh (1990) and Marsh and Henshall (1987) also note the importance of understanding stakeholders and collaboration in tourism. Several steps in identifying and managing stakeholders are outlined in Table 6.2, and provide useful guidance to managers in identifying and understanding those stakeholders who may influence, or be influenced by, their actions. Understanding relevant stakeholder needs and collaborating with stakeholders in a formal or informal way are essential to the long-term survival of an organisation or destination. This is even more important as organisations become more aware of their interdependence and competition in a globalised world.

As outlined initially in Chapter 1 and discussed in Chapter 3, there are multiple stakeholders that combine to provide the adult educational tourism product, from public sector organisations through to private industry. Some have an educational mandate and are non-profit organisations (such as Elderhostel and alumni groups), while others are more commercially focused and profit-driven (such as tour operators and the tourism industry). However, stakeholders need to work together to provide and promote educational tourism products. Similarly, the schools' educational tourism market also consists of a variety of stakeholders, such as tour operators, teachers, students, educationalists and attractions, who provide opportunities for educational excursions and field trips. Again a collaborative approach by stakeholders is required if educational products are to be successfully developed and marketed, and benefits to educational tourists and the destination maximised.

The potential of educational tourism appears unrealised and untapped (Smith & Jenner, 1997a), with little recognition of the various market segments. This is because of the perceived difficulties in reaching the various educational tourism market segments and a lack of coordination amongst key providers and stakeholders. As noted in Chapter 4, the schools' market is suffering from many problems, including a lack of

Table 6.1 Potential problems and benefits of collaboration and partnerships in tourism planning

Benefits
• There may be involvement by a range of stakeholders, all of whom are affected by the multiple issues of tourism development and may be well placed to introduce change and improvement.
• Decision-making power and control may diffuse to the multiple stakeholders who are affected by the issues, which is favourable for democracy.
• The involvement of several stakeholders may increase the social acceptance of policies, so that implementation and enforcement may be easier to effect.
• More constructive and less adversarial attitudes might result in consequence of working together.
• The parties who are directly affected by the issues may bring their knowledge, attitudes and other capabilities to the policy-making process.
• A creative synergy may result from working together, perhaps leading to greater innovation and effectiveness.
• Partnerships can promote learning about the work, skills and potential of the other partners, and also develop the group interaction and negotiating skills that help to make partnerships successful.
• Parties involved in policy-making may have a greater commitment to putting the resulting policies into practice.
• There may be improved communication of the policies and related actions of the multiple stakeholders.
• There may be greater consideration of the diverse economic, environmental and social issues that affect the sustainable development of resources.
• There may be greater recognition of the importance of non-economic issues and interests if they are included in the collaborative framework, and this may strengthen the range of tourism products available.
• There may be the pooling of the resources of stakeholders, which might lead to their more effective use.
• When multiple stakeholders are engaged in decision-making the resulting policies may be more flexible and also more sensitive to local circumstances and to changing conditions.
• Non-tourism activities may be encouraged, leading to a broadening of the economic, employment and societal base of a given community or region.
Source: Adapted from Bramwell and Lane (2000: 7, 9)

Table 6.1 (continued)

Problems
• In some places and for some issues there may be only a limited tradition of stakeholders participating in policy-making.
• A partnership may be set up simply as 'window dressing' to avoid tackling real problems head-on.
• Healthy conflict can be stifled.
• Collaborative efforts may be under-resourced in relation to requirements for additional staff time, leadership and administrative resources.
• Actors may not be disposed to reduce their own power or to work together with unfamiliar partners or previous adversaries.
• Those stakeholders with less power may be excluded from the process of collaborative working or may have less influence on the process.
• Power within collaborative arrangements could pass to groups or individuals with more effective political skills.
• Some key parties may be uninterested or inactive in working with others, sometimes because they decide to rely on others to produce the benefits resulting from a partnership.
• Some partners might coerce others by threatening to leave the partnership in order to press their own case.
• The involvement of democratically elected government in collaborative working and consensus building may compromise its ability to protect the 'public interest'.
• Accountability to various constituencies may become blurred as the greater institutional complexity of collaboration can obscure who is accountable to whom and for what.
• Collaboration may increase uncertainty about the future as the policies developed by multiple stakeholders are more difficult to predict than those developed by a central authority.
• The vested interests and established practices of the multiple stakeholders involved in collaborative working may block innovation.
• The need to develop consensus, and the need to disclose new ideas in advance of their introduction, might discourage entrepreneurial development.
• Involving a range of stakeholders in policy-making may be costly and time-consuming.
• The complexity of engaging diverse stakeholders in policy-making makes it difficult to involve them all equally.
• There may be fragmentation in decision-making and reduced control over implementation.
• The power of some partnerships may be too great, leading to the creation of cartels.
• Some collaborative arrangements may outlive their usefulness, with their bureaucracies seeking to extend their lives unreasonably.

Table 6.2 Components in a stakeholder management audit

1.	Identification of stakeholders, identifying those that have a legitimate claim on the attention of managers.
2.	Examining stakeholders who should have their claims and demands attended to by management. Assessing whether stakeholders are primary or secondary.
3.	Determination of primary and secondary stakeholder interests, goals, priorities and values.
4.	Review of past stakeholder behaviour in order to assess their strategies relating to issues and the likelihood of them forming coalitions with other stakeholders.
5.	Estimation of the relative power (legal authority, political authority, financial, human and physical resources, access to media) of each stakeholder and stakeholder coalitions.
6.	Assessment of how well an organisation is currently meeting the needs and interests of stakeholders.
7.	Formulation of new strategies, if necessary, to manage relations with stakeholders and stakeholder coalitions.
8.	Evaluation of effectiveness of stakeholder management strategies, with revisions and readjustment of priorities in order to meet stakeholder interests.

Sources: After Roberts and King (1989); Clarkson (1995); Hall and McArthur (1996); Mitchell *et al.* (1997)

coordination due to its fragmented or diverse nature. The implications of this could result in restricted leveraging of educational tourism and regional development opportunities. Part of the reason for these problems is due to the partial industrialisation of tourism (Leiper, 1989, 1990) and educational tourism. Both tourism and education are not industries as such but an integrated system of sub-sectors, such as transport, accommodation, food and beverages, attractions and construction (as outlined in Chapter 1). The implications of this are noted by Hall (2000: 53), who comments:

> although we can recognise that many sectors of the economy benefit from tourism, it is only those organisations which perceive a direct relationship to tourists and tourism producers that become actively involved in fostering tourism development or in marketing.

Subsequently, partial industrialisation results in diversity and inherently a lack of coordination as only organisations that perceive themselves as part of the industry will collaborate or develop networks to facilitate or market educational tourism. This industry fragmentation and resulting lack of industry coordination has been noted in schools' tourism (see Cooper, 1999; Ritchie, 2001), language schools (Muñoz Gonzalez, 2001; Ritchie, 2001; Batchelor, 1998, 2000) and adult educational tourism (CTC, 2001; Ritchie, 2001). An obvious way to reduce this fragmentation, diversity and lack of coordination is through identifying relevant and potential stakeholders in educational tourism and through the development of cooperative structures and networks to facilitate greater stakeholder coordination and involvement. In time this may move towards clustering of organisations to provide greater opportunities for local growth and development through educational tourism.

Overcoming fragmentation: Stakeholder collaboration, cooperative structures and clustering

One way to overcome the fragmented or diverse nature of educational tourism is for the development of collaborative mechanisms to facilitate positive collaboration amongst stakeholders to resolve conflict and advance shared visions. Collaboration is 'a process of joint decision making among key stakeholders of a problem domain about the future of that domain' (Gray 1989: 11). Gray (1989) noted a number of characteristics critical to collaboration, including:

- stakeholders are independent;
- solutions emerge by dealing constructively with differences;
- joint ownership of decisions is involved;
- stakeholders assume collective responsibility for the future direction of the domain; and
- collaboration is an emergent process.

Collaboration is a three-step process according to McCann (1983) in Jamal and Getz (1995: 189):

- the first stage includes problem setting (identifying key stakeholders and issues);
- the second stage is concerned with direction setting (identifying and sharing future collaborative interpretations; appreciating a sense of common purpose); and
- the third stage is implementation, which may or may not be required depending on the nature and objective of collaboration.

A number of facilitating conditions and actions/steps help to determine a potential process for developing collaborative forms of tourism and are illustrated in Table 6.3. The table illustrates that shared power and values are essential facilitating conditions for the development of a collaborative process. Mechanisms such as networks and cooperative structures help link various stakeholders together in a collaborative framework and can assist in the implementation of a shared vision. Networking involves cooperation between potential competitors and other organisations linked through economic and social relationships and transactions (Hall, 2000: 175). Exchange of knowledge, innovation, ideas and expertise can lead to organisations working in a mutually beneficial and supportive way. Networks can operate at an international, supra-national, national, regional and local level and range from informal relationships through to formal contracts (Selin, 2000; Hall, 2000). Network development for tourism marketing and promotion often occurs between different private and public sector organisations. According to Selin (2000) collaboration and partnerships facilitated through network development can differ depending on:

- the formality of the network or collaboration (from partners voluntarily collaborating to the creation of legal entities or authorities and forced collaboration);
- the level of stakeholder participation in the process (from single agency control to multiple stakeholder control);
- the scale of organisational diversity and size (from a small number of homogeneous organisations to a large number of multi-sector organisations); and
- the geographic time scale required by the domain problem (from temporary collaboration to solve a short-term problem to a permanent longer-term structure).

Several types of inter-organisational networks have been identified by researchers and are illustrated in Table 6.4 along with potential examples from educational tourism market segments. Some structures are more formal than others and differ in size and scope. Some have been created to respond to a short-term problem or project (such as the Schools Educational Tourism Committee in Canberra, Australia), while others have a more permanent and long-term structure (such as IAATO). Obviously the resourcing and funding of network or collaborative structures are important considerations. In the case of the Schools Educational Tourism Committee in Canberra, this collaborative structure provided resources for initial research which was then used to lobby relevant authorities for

Table 6.3 Stages, facilitating conditions and actions for collaborative tourism planning

Facilitating conditions	*Actions/steps*
Stage I: *Problem-setting*	
• Recognition of interdependence • Identification of a required number of stakeholders • Perception of legitimacy among stakeholders • Legitimate/skilled convenor • Positive beliefs about outcomes • Shared access to power • Mandate (external or internal) • Adequate resources to convene and enable collaboration process	• Define purpose and domain • Identify convenor • Convene stakeholders • Define problems/issues to resolve • Identify and legitimise stakeholders • Build commitment to collaborate by raising awareness of interdependence • Balance power differences • Address stakeholder concerns • Ensure adequate resources available to allow collaboration to proceed with key stakeholders present
Stage II: *Direction-setting*	
• Coincidence of values • Dispersion of power amongst stakeholders	• Collect and share information • Appreciate shared values, enhance perceived interdependence • Ensure power distributed among several stakeholders • Establish rules and agenda for direction setting • Organise subgroups if required • List alternatives • Discuss various options • Select appropriate solutions • Arrive at shared vision or plan/ strategy through consensus
Stage III: *Implementation*	
• High degree of ongoing interdependence • External mandate • Redistribution of power • Influencing the contextual environment	• Discuss means of implementing and monitoring solutions, shared vision, plan or strategy • Select suitable structure for institutionalising process • Assign goals and tasks • Monitor ongoing progress and ensure compliance to collaboration decisions

Source: Based on Gray (1985, 1989) in Jamal and Getz (1995: 190)

substantial funding to develop the NCETP for promoting schools' tourism to Canberra in 2001, the Centenary of Federation for Australia. This funding was also used to evaluate the success of their project and whether it helped achieve the shared vision for Canberra of attracting 200,001 school students in the year 2001 (see Exhibit 4.2).

Although the concept of network development to assist innovation and collaboration is not new, the development of networks for tourism and educational tourism is a more recent phenomenon. Network development and the development of cooperative structures may reduce the problems that educational tourism may face through fragmentation and an inherent lack of coordination. Networks can facilitate regional development and improve the economic benefits of educational tourism through increasing linkages between industry sectors, thus creating a greater economic multiplier. They may also reduce marketing and product development costs as individual organisations work collaboratively toward common goals or the solution of common problems. Goals may include the promotion and marketing of educational tourism, the development and packaging of new products for educational tourists, and the undertaking of research and monitoring at an international, supra-national, national, regional or local level. According to Hall (2000), for the benefits of networks to be maximised relationships should move from dyadic relationships and organisation sets between a small number of organisations towards action sets and networks. Hopkins and Michael (2001: 4) note that collaboration in the form of formal strategic alliances may not be suitable for small-scale tourism development due to a number of problems, including goal incongruity, high transaction costs, issues of trust and commitment, and historical/parochial rivalries. They suggest that clusters can lead to the acceleration of benefits for organisations due to economies of scale and scope. Clusters may also have few formal arrangements and reduce the costs associated with formal alliances.

Therefore, government at a local, regional and national level should promote the benefits of educational tourism action sets, networks and clusters for organisations across the education and tourism sector, so that marketing and regional development opportunities are maximised and so that a mutually beneficial relationship can be developed between educational providers and the tourism industry. Ankomah and Larson (2002) call for collaboration in developing educational tourism in sub-Saharan Africa through universities and government collaborating with tourism stakeholders to produce workable education programmes integrating classroom and on-site experience. The authors advocate regional blocs or supra-national organisations taking the lead role in developing

Table 6.4 Network categorisations: using educational tourism examples

Inter-organisational relationship	*Market segment*	*Specific examples*
Dyadic linkages		
Formed when two organisations find it mutually beneficial to collaborate in achieving a common goal.	Schools' tourism	• Primary/secondary schools' attraction (e.g. museum, art gallery) works with a specialist schools' tour operator to promote an educational tourism experience.
	Adult educational tourism	• An attraction working with Elderhostel to develop an educational package for a group of adults.
Organisation sets		
Inter-organisational linkages that refer to the clusters of dyadic relations maintained by a focal organisation.	Schools' tourism	• British Council provide information and develop individual relationships with language school providers.
	University/college students' tourism	• University placement team makes and maintains industrial placement contacts for students.
	Adult educational tourism	• Canadian Tourism Commission provides information on educational tours.
Action sets		
A coalition of interacting organisations that work together in order to achieve a specific purpose.	Schools' tourism	• A local tourism body works with local attraction operators to produce an excursion planner for school teachers.
	University/college students' tourism	• Local tourism promotional body works with Universities to provide familiarisation material and maps to foreign students during their induction week.
	Adult educational tourism	• The Nepean Hawkesbury Wine and Grape Growers Association (NHWGGA), who market wine as an educational tourism product (see Case Study 3.1).
Networks		
Used in a narrow formal sense, refers to a group of organisations that share common organisational ties and can be recognised as a bounded inter-organisational system.	Schools' tourism	• Schools Educational Tourism Committee and the National Capital Education Tourism Project (NCETP) for Canberra, Australia (see Exhibit 4.2).
	University/college students' tourism	• International Student Travel Confederation (ISTC) who bring several associations together to work collectively to facilitate student, youth and academic travel (see Exhibit 5.1).
	Adult educational tourism	• The International Association of Antarctica Tour Operators (IAATO) (see Case Study 3.2).

Source: Modified after Harper (1993) and Hall (1998, 2000)

educational tourism product. Organisations include the Economic Community of West African States (ECOWAS), the East African Cooperation (EAC) and the Southern African Development Community (SADC). Similarly, the CTC (2001: 45) believe that alliances and collaboration could assist educational tourism in Canada through:

- allowing funds to be leveraged and primary research to be conducted that will define the size and scope of the learning travel market;
- creating outlets for product development training workshops that could educate and unite local tourism and educational providers at the community and regional levels;
- helping package a wide range of learning vacations;
- creating partnerships that value resource-respectful commerce and manage the cultural and natural heritage; and
- destination marketing organisations (DMOs) providing support for a collaborative marketing campaign for educational tourism.

As illustrated in Table 6.4 collaboration is occurring at various other levels within different educational tourism market segments. Further examples are provided in Exhibits 6.1 and 6.2. However, the future sustainable development of educational tourism is dependent upon further collaboration and network development between the education and tourism industries. Furthermore, it should be noted that collaboration is not without its problems with certain stakeholders are often able to influence the nature of collaboration and benefits through their relative power and influence (see Table 6.1).

Conclusion

This chapter has outlined the changing nature of both urban and rural destinations through the process of globalisation and resulting social and economic restructuring. This in turn has led to the need for destinations to market themselves as commodities in order to attract investment and regional development benefits to assist in the restructuring process. Both education and tourism have received heightened attention in helping with the restructuring process. However, as this chapter has noted, both tourism and education, and educational forms of tourism, are highly fragmented because the industry consists of multiple stakeholders and organisations. Understanding stakeholders is critical for overcoming some of the barriers to the effective and efficient development and promotion of educational forms of tourism, and failure in this could be one

Exhibit 6.1

Collaboration and network development for educational tourism: The case of offshore education in New Zealand

The recent focus toward offshore education in New Zealand has led to a number of initiatives at national and local levels to facilitate and promote educational forms of tourism. Network partnerships have been developed at the national level between Education New Zealand (a national body to promote New Zealand education) and Trade New Zealand (a body to promote and develop international trade). The two organisations have joined forces to promote and facilitate the development of offshore education and educational forms of tourism to New Zealand. This has led to the growth of local partnerships between organisations at a city level, such as Education Wellington International and Education Dunedin, which attempt to attract students to their particular region by taking advantage of the national marketing of New Zealand education. They also use the contacts and support of both Education New Zealand and Trade New Zealand in promoting local education services to potential overseas markets.

In the case of Education Wellington International, this partnership brings together a total of 45 education providers and is funded by local government and member organisations. Its mission is to ensure visiting students receive high-quality education in a safe, positive environment and to develop Wellington as the education capital of New Zealand. With this in mind Education Wellington International has used its location as capital of New Zealand as a unique selling point, and is attempting to brand Wellington as the 'education capital'. Education Wellington International has members from a range of educational providers, including:

- high schools (including private or state schools, single-sex or co-educational schools and boarding schools);
- private language schools;
- tertiary education (including polytechnics, universities, teacher training and institutes of technology); and
- private training institutions (including arts, drama and business schools).

Dunedin is also known as a centre for education and learning and was one of the first cities to develop a partnership network to attract offshore students. Despite its isolated location in the South Island of New Zealand, Dunedin has moved towards becoming post-industrial through the development of service sectors such as education and tourism (Kearsley, 1995). Education Dunedin is a charitable trust with members including the city's tertiary institutions – University of Otago, Dunedin College of Education, Otago Polytechnic and the Otago Language Centre – plus 11 Dunedin secondary schools, Telford Rural Polytechnic, a group of Otago rural schools and the local government body, the Dunedin City Council (DCC).

Education Dunedin is mainly concerned with the marketing of Dunedin as an educational destination in order to provide economic benefits and exposure for Dunedin. This is illustrated by the coordination of the organisation within the Economic Development Unit of the local DCC. Education Dunedin has instituted a variety of marketing projects to encourage students to study in the city, and used the marketing slogan 'teaching a world of students'. Some of the specific marketing projects include:

- The development of a database of video footage, photographic images, information about Dunedin and New Zealand, the Kiwi lifestyle, tourism and local education facilities. This allows for swift creation of custom-made promotional presentations relevant to a particular market. The database is not just for the Trust's use; each of its member institutions has access for their individual marketing promotions.
- A generic brochure about Dunedin's education opportunities that has been translated into Spanish, Portugese, Korean, Chinese and Vietnamese, as has a brochure giving a broad range of information about the city. Education Dunedin has also hosted a number of journalists from a range of countries who have been gathering research for articles about education opportunities in New Zealand.
- Missions to countries where a potential market is identified, which form a big part of the drive to bring international students to Dunedin. In 2001 missions were undertaken to Brazil, Argentina and China. Trips are organised in conjunction with Trade New Zealand staff on an itinerary which includes

visiting education agents and institutions and making public presentations.

For some target markets Education Dunedin is drawing on other strengths of the city, such as its strong rugby union sporting tradition. This is particularly important for the South American and Argentinian market who are interested in Dunedin as an English language and rugby training centre. A promotional package was developed with the Otago Rugby Football Union to help attract coaches and teams to Dunedin for education and training opportunities, promoting Dunedin as the 'Rugby City'. Education Dunedin representatives talked to the Buenos Aires Rugby Football Union, clubs, schools and education agents about combining language learning and sport. Education Dunedin's range of promotions are also designed to reach beyond young students to mature students with children and teachers who may wish to improve their skills. For instance, postgraduates with children are appealed to by demonstrating that Dunedin's primary schools are able to provide education for children who do not speak English (one school has children of around 45 nationalities on its roll).

The success of initiatives at both national and local levels is attributed to shared partnership and the development of networks which allow individual organisations to work together collaboratively to represent education interests in cities such as Wellington and Dunedin. By including representatives from the different education sectors a commitment to education is demonstrated to potential target markets, and organisations are able to pool and share resources to market efficiently to overseas markets. As the importance of language learning, university study and short courses increases, so too will the need for organisations to realise their interdependence and work together towards a shared vision which will benefit both the education and tourism industry in their respective cities.

Sources: Dunedin City Council (2002); Education Wellington International (2002)

Exhibit 6.2

ARELS membership in Britain

ARELS (the Association of Recognised English Language Services) is the leading association of independent English language teaching establishments in Britain. It represents the majority of the accredited sector (over 210 organisations). The association's key objectives are:

- to encourage high professional standards among members and throughout the industry;
- to represent the interests of members and students to government and other relevant bodies; and
- to promote as widely as possible the benefits of learning English in Britain.

Members of ARELS become part of a highly influential and respected organisation. Formed in 1960, ARELS is the longest-established English language teaching association in the world. Membership entitles organisations to the support of Britain's leading ELT association on educational, management, welfare and promotional matters, and organisations also benefit from representation to national and international government bodies and other opinion formers. ARELS also works with the British Council and BASELT to run the English in Britain Accreditation scheme.

Services to members

Membership provides numerous benefits, including the services of a team of 11 full-time London-based staff who, in addition to handling thousands of enquiries throughout the year, act on behalf of the whole membership in pursuit of the above objectives. Principal benefits include:

- free listing in the Association's leaflet 'Learn English in Britain with ARELS', which is distributed worldwide to British Tourist Authority and British Council offices and to language travel agents, as well as through key UK-based outlets such as embassies, libraries and international corporations;
- a comprehensive website, www.arels.org.uk, with hyperlinks to all schools and International Language Fair information;

- a monthly newsflash that includes business data, forthcoming events and updates on the Association's activities, etc.;
- representation to government departments and other key organisations, including the British Council;
- promotion and publicity through a range of publications and representation at international language fairs and academic conferences;
- a quarterly magazine, ARENA, covering a range of issues related to British ELT;
- advice and information on education and welfare issues;
- general marketing support;
- promotional and editorial opportunities, including 'familiarisation trips' to schools; and
- commission on sales of the ARELS Worldtalk phonecard to students, who can save up to 70% on the cost of overseas calls (ARELS members only), and other business benefits.

In addition, the following services are offered to members at a substantial discount:

- participation at the annual ARELS International English Language Fair;
- the Annual Conference (ARELS members only);
- annual conferences for teachers, directors of studies, welfare officers and social organisers;
- training seminars, courses and conferences for academic welfare and management staff, including the ARELS Diploma in ELT Management; and
- a range of publications, including the Welfare Manual, the Health and Safety Manual, the Care of Juniors Manual and student and host family advice booklets.

Source: ARELS (2002)

reason for the lack of research and acknowledgement of educational forms of tourism to date.

Collaboration and the development of networks, partnerships and clusters between the tourism and education industry and private and public sectors at international, supra-national, national, regional and local levels could help facilitate the sustainable growth and management of educational tourism. A number of partnerships have developed as educational forms of tourism grow and the demand for offshore education, training and lifelong learning opportunities increases. Those destinations which are able to facilitate and encourage the development of collaborative partnerships, networks and clusters, often involving those organisations that may not perceive themselves as part of the educational tourism industry, may find themselves with improved opportunities to use educational tourism for marketing and regional development. Pooling resources may enable organisations and destinations to undertake research, develop new products and market educational tourism more efficiently in an integrated way.

Case Study 6.1

The development of adult educational tourism in Marmilla, Sardinia

The Sardinian context

Sardinia has the lowest population density of Southern Italy with approximately 69 inhabitants per square kilometre. It also has an ageing population and migration to urban and coastal centres in search of work (ROP, 2001), while unemployment has also been a major issue in Sardinia associated with the restructuring process. In the last 15 years unemployment has fluctuated between 18% and 21%, and in 2000 a total of 22.1% of the population of Sardinia were unemployed (ROP, 2001). Sardinia also has problems concerning its capacity for agricultural activity which limit the potential regeneration of the agricultural sector. For instance, in 1996 the agricultural industry employed 11.4% of the working population but only produced 6.3% of the regional added value due (ROP, 2001).

Regional development agencies have recognised the potential of tourism, especially the potential of the natural and cultural resources of

Sardinia for developing alternative forms of tourism. Currently the majority of the tourist product and experience is concerned with marine and seaside tourism and subsequently restricted to the summer months of July and August. Similar to other summer destinations this seasonality problem restricts tourist movement to key coastal and urban centres and reduces the efficiency and productivity of hotel and tourism facilities which are not fully used at other times of the year. International visitation to Sardinia is also low, with over 80% of visitors from Italy, nearly half of Italy as a whole (ROP, 2001).

Subsequently, for rural communities tourism, and certain tourism products in particular, may be considered as a means to overcome low incomes and provide employment and economic development opportunities for interior destinations. This could help reduce inequality between regions within Sardinia and between Sardinia and mainland Italy and Europe as a whole. Moreover, rural tourism does not often require large-scale investment in infrastructure or facilities. According to Lane (1994), special interest tourism products often help disperse visitors to rural regions and may provide opportunities for rural tourism development without the negative impacts often associated with mass tourism. Furthermore, cultural and nature-based tourism often rely heavily on existing resources and on those that can further promote cultural understanding and social cohesion, a goal of the European Union. Independent cultural tourists and groups of educational tourists from organisations such as Elderhostel provide an opportunity to strengthen local tradition and culture while providing much needed social and economic development to rural regions in Sardinia, such as Marmilla.

The regional development project

A project funded under the European Commission's LEADER II programme to assist regional development in Europe was implemented to develop cultural educational tours to Marmilla, a rural part of southern Sardinia. The project was run by a non-profit British-based organisation called 'Education for Development' (consisting mostly of adult educators and trainers), in collaboration with the Centre for Cultural Tourism (in the region within Sardinia) and the OC (organising committee in the local region including local government and industry). The aims of the project were to train local residents to deliver information, and in time educational packages to cultural tourists, and in doing so to achieve the following two main objectives:

- to assist with the celebration and promotion of Sardinian culture and create international understanding and friendship; and
- to create economic development opportunities for rural parts of Sardinia, especially the Marmilla region, and to impart knowledge and expertise to the local population.

Thus, the aims of the project were to use educational tourism to create regional, social and economic development for a region that is currently undergoing restructuring (see Plate 6.1). A team of local people had been trained as interpreters to deliver study tours to groups of cultural tourists, and the topics explored on these educational tours included:

- *The geology and geography of the area.* Marmilla is characterised by large basalt plateaus as part of its intense volcanic activity and history.
- *The archaeology and anthropology of the area.* A nuraghic civilisation inhabited the island from the Bronze Age through to the late Iron Age and many artefacts and megalithic tombs are scattered throughout the area. A museum displaying many of the artefacts

Plate 6.1 Regional development programmes such as the LEADER Programme have provided funds to rejuvenate traditional Marmillan homes which are also being used to accommodate educational tourists

Source: B. Ritchie

has recently opened in Villanovaforru, Marmilla, funded by the European Union.

- *The art and architecture of the area.* The region has a number of small romanesque churches which house renaissance panel paintings. Architecture ranges from Roman and Spanish to Gothic styles, illustrating the rich history of Sardinia.
- *The gastronomy of the area.* Sardinia is well known for its food and wine, and particularly its cheese.
- *The oral/local history of the area.* The above points were to be related by local interpreters and in travel guides developed for independent and group travellers.

Plate 6.2 Marketing information developed to facilitate educational tourism in Marmilla, Sardinia. An integrated tourism itinerary has been developed for a wide range of thematic areas, drawing on the strengths and resources of the Marmilla region

The project target market were individual adults interested in integrating learning and education with travel, as well as more specialist groups such as Elderhostel and University of the Third Age who organise adult study tours. Training has now been completed for local tour guides and several of the local tourism operators, while interpretative materials, guide books and the like have also been created and contact made with universities and other key target markets (see Plate 6.2). However, the project had many problems associated with it including:

- Delays in completing the project due to political problems. Difficulties exist in satisfying all of the local government areas and tourism industry involved in the project, which often have conflicting views and agendas. This delayed the implementation and resulting regional development benefits of the project.
- Difficulties for Education for Development in trying to supervise project staff caused by language barriers and geographical barriers between England and Sardinia.
- Problems in appointing adequate staff from the Marmilla region to be trained as interpreters and tour guides for cultural tourists. This point is related in part to the first problem and the difficulties in hiring suitable people due to the migration of a young educated workforce from the Marmilla region.
- Problems in persuading the local population that other people would be interested in their region, as they have been perceived to undervalue their local culture (Jones, 2001).

These problems slowed the project with only one successful tour being implemented, although the training and development of materials and brochures has been completed, and linkages established between the region and potential target market and organisations. The above discussion suggests that, although cultural educational tourism can provide a useful tool for assisting with the restructuring process of rural areas and developing countries, problems may exist in translating ideas into reality through the LEADER II programme for regional development. This is in part due to the politicisation of tourism, but also to language and distance barriers between the project leaders and staff in Marmilla. However, cultural educational tourists do have the potential to provide economic and social development opportunities for peripheral regions that are facing difficulties, such as Marmilla, and to help spread the regional development opportunities more widely than coastal areas. The challenge is for the people of Marmilla to use the materials and experience from the

LEADER II project to further develop and promote educational tourism to key target markets. Further assistance and support for this process is necessary from local businesses, the European Union and outsiders.

Chapter 7

Conclusions and Reflections: The Future of Educational Tourism

Introduction

As illustrated in this book, educational tourism consists of many different market segments and sub-segments. This diversity of markets is combined with a variety of organisations involved with educational tourism who are not visibly part of the educational tourism market system. This is perhaps one of the reasons why little study and attention has been devoted to this form of tourism. This chapter summarises the key underlying themes concerning the demand, supply and management of educational tourism segments. The chapter then examines the potential future development of educational tourism by considering the impact of technology, the role of quality and issues concerning product development. The chapter concludes with a discussion of the role of cooperative structures and some future research avenues for educational tourism.

Reflections: Towards Understanding and Managing Educational Tourism

Very little information is collected on educational tourists, especially their education and learning needs. A number of authors report the demand and the growing provision for this market, but empirical research and evidence is scarce. As Chapter 2 identified, many of the active definitions of ecotourism involve some component of study or learning, often through the use of interpretation. Similarly, cultural heritage tourism may also involve some form of learning or education. However, research has questioned whether in fact ecotourists and indeed cultural heritage tourists learn a great deal from their visits, as the underlying motivations may be social rather than the cognitive acquisition of knowledge. Some authors have noted that the consumption of tourist experiences, including the cultural and natural environment, is part of a search for exotic and postmodern experiences. Little discussion or examination has occurred considering the education and learning needs of educational tourists and how these may be best incorporated into the development of suitable tourism experiences. Research outlined in Chapter 2 suggests that there are specific segments of ecotourists and cultural heritage tourists who seek more active and educationally orientated experiences during their holidays. Although some segments have been identified and their characteristics discussed these studies are limited in size and geographic scope.

The growth of the seniors' educational tourism market is due in part to an ageing population and an increasing interest in experiencing life, engaging in special interest holidays and enjoying active leisure time. The growth of the *Socially Aware* and similar market segments in countries such as the USA, Canada and New Zealand also illustrates the growing interest in learning, self-discovery and education amongst consumers. The combination of these factors has resulted in interest in educational holidays and the integration of learning within holiday experiences, leading to the development of small-scale commercial tour operations catering for geological, cultural and wine tourism excursions. Furthermore, a range of organisations, often with a non-profit or educational mandate, have also been developed to cater for the seniors' market, including Elderhostel, University of the Third Age and university extension and study tour programmes. The economic value of the seniors' market has also been acknowledged, with seniors often having both discretionary income and time to undertake holidays, often in the off-tourist season, thus helping to reduce seasonality.

The growth of education and learning vacations to cultural and natural heritage sites poses problems with many sites under environmental pressure. If the growth of tourism to these sites increases, then the impacts of these sites may be severe. Chapter 2 outlined the growth of tourism to the Galapagos Islands and the problems in managing educational tourism to this fragile destination. Similar issues were outlined in Chapter 3 concerning Antarctica; despite the development of codes of conduct and a strict management regime negative impacts still occur. This issue is likely to grow as tourism demand expands and experiences such as ecotourism broaden appeal to a growing mass market. This places more emphasis on the need for interpretation and incorporation of education into tourist experiences in order to modify tourists' on-site behaviour and instil conservation values. Yet disagreement exists over what form this interpretation should take and who is ultimately responsible for the education of tourists.

A lack of research into 'education first' market segments such as schools and universities is also evident, reducing the understanding of these segments and their travel behaviour and needs. As highlighted in Chapter 4, the growth in school students in Western countries appears to be in decline and is likely to reduce further as birth rates fall, as opposed to developing countries such as Africa and Asia where growth is predicted. However, as noted in Chapter 4, the ability of educational authorities or parents to fund school trips in these countries is limited, and the relevance of school trips is also being questioned despite the reported educational benefits. Economic considerations provide a real constraint to school excursions which may be out of the control of destination marketers. However, methods such as subsidy schemes can be implemented to reduce financial constraints, as in the case of Canberra, Australia although effective marketing of such schemes has also been illustrated as important.

A similar economic situation exists in the university and college student market. Although university student numbers have rapidly increased, so too have the financial burdens placed upon students, with many faced with rising tuition fees, student loans and overdrafts. Nevertheless, university/college students are able to borrow to fund their holidays or use savings from part-time employment. Furthermore, they have the discretionary time in vacations to undertake travel. Chapter 5 illustrated that university students have a high travel propensity, and this market segment is now a multi-billion dollar industry with an increasing number of providers targeting the student market. Similar to school excursions, university and college student tourism can be curriculum- or non-curriculum-related. The travel motivations of students in non-curriculum travel appear to be centred around escape motives and the desire for rest, relaxation and in many cases hedonistic activity. With respect to curriculum-related travel, a growing number of students now travel to foreign countries to complete a component of their studies (ranging from industrial placements or internships, to exchange partnerships lasting from a semester to several years, to field trips). Curriculum-based travel may be organised by internal university placement personnel or through arrangements created at an institutional or a supra-national level, such as the ERASMUS programme currently in place in the European Union.

Safety issues are also highlighted with respect to school excursions, language schools and university/college students' tourism. Destination safety and security are important considerations for foreign students and, as illustrated in Case Study 5.2, may influence overseas student destination choice. Educational providers who do not offer social activities for language school students may encourage them to congregate in town centres, exposing them to crime and criminal activity. As discussed in Chapter 4, a number of criminals are targeting international students, and police in some destinations are providing resources to deal with these threats to student security. The growing number of reports of school excursion accidents and deaths have created debate in some countries concerning the value and need for such educational excursions. Although risk is an accepted part of school excursions, reports of sexual activity, alcohol consumption, accidents and death may result in litigation for schools and teachers who plan such trips (Lacey, 2001). This potential litigation could reduce the number of planned school excursions and, as Chapter 4 notes, could rob students of the opportunity to take part in school trips and experience the educational benefits associated with them.

Seasonality is another issue associated with the demand of 'education first' educational tourism. Chapter 4 illustrates that, because the majority of demand for language schools is in the summer vacation market, the growth of this form of tourism can be highly seasonal. This, coupled with the location of language schools in a number of heritage cities or coastal resorts in England, has created congestion and pressure on housing for local residents and on tourist accommodation (Grant *et al.*, 1998). Despite the reported benefits of language schools in reducing tourism seasonality it appears that in some destinations language school tourism has merely exacerbated seasonality problems, potentially constraining future increases in language school tourism in some destinations due to the growth of the summer vacation market. More discussion and analysis of mechanisms to promote and facilitate all-year language school tourism is required to reduce the congestion and potential displacement of traditional summer tourists. School excursions have also been noted to spread the seasonality of tourism, often for attraction providers at destinations. However, as noted in Chapter 4, school excursions are often constrained by curriculum, school timetabling and climate, with the reality being that many are undertaken at particular times of the year, mainly during summer and spring months. This is even more evident in non-curriculum school trips which may include recreational activities held in winter (such as skiing) or are best conducted in summer (such as boating and camping trips). The challenge for providers and marketers is to facilitate school trips in the off or shoulder season through the use of timely information and marketing, and also discounts and subsidies. As Chapter 4 notes, understanding the nature of school constraints and how excursions are planned is critical for the educational tourism industry.

The economic importance of educational tourism has been discussed in many of the preceding chapters. In Chapter 6 it was noted that education and tourism are two important industries for urban and rural destinations, primarily because of their export earnings and economic impact. Educational tourism enables destinations to market themselves, attract new industry and create employment opportunities for the resident population. The importance of language school students for export and the tourism industry was noted in Chapter 4 and, although the school excursion market may not be lucrative, it can be economically important and a vital part of the market for many tourist attractions. Similarly, the growing numbers of university/college students have been targeted by many destinations for their export earnings potential. In all market segments there is an opportunity to showcase the destination to a potentially important and influential market segment. The opportunity to create a favourable experience and perceptions for school excursion students, language students and university or college students can result in visits from friends and families of students, an increase in repeat visits at a later stage, positive word of mouth and even potential migration of students to host destinations. In short, school and university students can become ambassadors for a destination. However, to date there has been little empirical research undertaken on these factors.

Future Directions for Educational Tourism

One of the largest impacts upon the future of tourism and educational forms of tourism is technology. Technological advancements and the increased diffusion and use of technology in everyday life will have a major impact upon both tourist and educational experiences. As discussed in Chapter 4, the Internet appears to have the potential to offer an alternative to school field trips and may overcome some of the safety issues currently impacting upon school excursions. Once the technology has been purchased it is often cheaper than school excursions and offers the chance to interact with other nationalities without the requisite costs to students or parents. Despite these benefits, Chapter 4 notes that the Internet fails to really allow students to experience living in another country and the lack of immersion leads to a poorer quality learning experience. Chapter 5 also discusses how virtual reality may replace some university and college student field trips, although, as with school trips and the Internet, the ability of virtual reality to replace travel is uncertain. However, it is difficult to argue against the implementation of such technology when there is a lack of current evidence pertaining to the educational benefits of student field trips.

Distance education and the predicted growth of e-learning may have a dramatic impact upon offshore forms of educational tourism, including travel to universities, colleges and language schools. The ability to source information through the Internet, including video and audio conferencing, will impact upon the future of educational programmes and the provision of courses and study. Kurzweil (1999: 191–193) in a vision of the future suggests that:

> students of all ages typically have a computer of their own, which is a thin tablet-like device ... most textual language is created by speaking. Learning materials are accessed through wireless communication ... learning at a distance is commonplace ... by 2019 most learning is accomplished using intelligent software-based simulated teachers.

Kurzweil (1999) paints an interesting if not slightly chilling picture of the future of learning and education but one which illustrates the potential of technology. According to Stallings (2001), e-education is evolving into a growth industry with implications for a wide number of stakeholders, including universities, students, government and destinations. Stallings (2001: 4) believes that 'most communicating and learning in the future will be done at a distance'. Drucker (1995) believes that online continuing education is the future and is a market worth hundreds of billions of dollars, facilitated by the growth and promotion of lifelong learning by government and a desire to keep ahead in a knowledge economy.

Technology may also impact upon 'tourism first' forms of educational tourism as discussed in Chapter 2 and has been introduced into both cultural heritage sites, such as museums and galleries, and national parks and visitor centres. The debate outlined in Chapter 2 is concerned with the impact of technology on visitor experiences. To what extent does the use of technology in museums and galleries turn the visitor experience into a theme park or form of leisure entertainment rather than an educative experience? Or can entertainment and education coexist? Although it is recognised that mindlessness can occur when visitors are exposed to a lack of sensory, visual or interactive material (Moscardo, 1996), there is the potential for some technology to simplify interpretation and result in a theme park experience (Griffin *et al.*, 2000) rather than an educative one. The use of technology is a challenge for attraction and site managers as it can help them expand their educational mandate to a broader section of society by making information more accessible and engaging, but they can also be criticised for becoming too commercial and entertainment-focused.

The provision of quality and sometimes consistent educational tourist experiences is also noticeable as a growing trend and one that is likely to increase as educational tourism and competition grow. In 'tourism first' experiences this has seen the development and implementation of accreditation programmes for ecotourism operators despite problems with defining and acknowledging what constitutes an ecotourism experience. The implementation of certification programmes for tour guides can also ensure quality interpretation is provided to educational tourists, resulting in improved service quality. Quality product is also a goal for 'education first' forms of tourism. The language schools' sector has implemented an accreditation scheme for language school providers in many countries. As discussed in Exhibit 4.4, while schemes in Britain are not compulsory the majority of language school students are attracted to accredited organisations, even though accredited providers are in the minority compared to unaccredited organisations. The issue of quality provision and experiences is important and is linked to positive word of mouth, return visitation and favourable destination image, and the value of such programmes will continue to be debated in the future.

Careful product development and packaging is required for educational tourism as the market is a specialist area comprising niche markets. Chapter 3 noted that packaging and promotional activities undertaken by adult educational providers differ depending on the type of provider involved and the nature of the educational tourism experience. There is a variety of learning vacations on the market and a diverse range of products and services on offer. Diversity is also found in the provision of language schools' tourism. In both instances providers need to understand the market and may have to work together to package educational forms of tourism. This may mean educational providers, including language schools, working closely with the tourism industry to develop social activities and field trips for school students. Similarly, for the adult educational tourism market, this could mean the tourism industry working closely with educational providers or non-profit organisations such as museums and universities, which may not all see themselves as part of the tourism industry as such.

Successful educational tourism providers have worked together toward a shared vision or goal. In some cases, as outlined in Chapter 6, organisations have developed collaborative arrangements for specific short-term purposes or projects such as marketing. Other organisations have developed networks and clusters related to educational tourism for more permanent collaboration to promote or facilitate the development of educational tourism. Examples were provided in Chapter 6 and illustrate that organisations may have to overcome different agendas, perspectives and past rivalries to share power and work collaboratively. It is expected that as educational tourism grows more collaboration will occur between organisations at local, regional, national, supra-national and international levels. The result of this collaboration will be a sharing of innovation and resources so that educational tourism will be better marketed, developed, managed and researched, thus providing a better quality product and visitor experience, and economic and social benefits to host destinations.

The lack of research in many areas related to educational tourism is a major underlying theme of this book and the major reason for its completion. In particular, there is:

- The need to assess and evaluate the educational needs of school teachers, school students, ecotourists, cultural heritage tourists and the adult educational tourist market.
- The need to understand the scale and nature of educational tourism. How big is this market segment and resulting sub-segments? What are the drivers and inhibitors of this form of tourism? What policies or methods would be best to overcome some of the problems of this form of tourism?
- A need to understand the impacts of educational tourism, including the economic, social, environmental, marketing and long-term personal benefits of educational forms of tourism.

In short, more empirical research is required, as understanding the nature of educational tourism and its impacts upon society will result in better management and planning. It is hoped that this book has made a small contribution to the understanding of educational tourism, promoting a systems-based and integrative approach. It is also hoped that this book will be a starting point to encourage more research, so that more informed decision making and better management of educational forms of tourism will occur.

References

Adams, J. (1999) Don't trip on the red tape. *The Times Higher Education Supplement* (online accessed 4/6/99).

Adams, M. (1997) *Sex in the Snow: Canadian Social Values at the End of the Millennium.* Toronto: Viking.

Admin, C. (2001) High cost of international school excursions. *Achieve Online Australia.* http://www.achieveonline.com.au/article/articleeview/100/ (online accessed 16/5/02).

Ali-Knight, J. and Charters, S. (1999) Education in a west Australian wine tourism context. *International Journal of Wine Marketing* 11 (1), 7–18.

The All England Lawn Tennis and Croquet Club (2002) *Guide: About the Museum.* http://www.wimbledon.org/about/lawn.html (online accessed 24/6/02).

Ankomah, P. K. and Larson, R. T. (2002) *Education Tourism: A Strategy to Sustainable Tourism Development in Sub-Saharan Africa.* http://unpan1.un.org/intradoc/groups/public/documents/idep/unpan002585.pdf (online accessed 15/6/02).

Anonymous (1994) School trips. *Leisure Management* March, 80–82.

Anonymous (1998) International Exchange. *Travel Journal International: News Highlights.* http://www2.tjnet.co.jp/intl/news/980511–25/ (online accessed 16/5/02).

Anonymous (2002) Special report: Why schools go overseas for school trips, and overseas school trip market virtually untapped. *Travel Journal International.* http://www2.tjnet.co.jp/intl/news/990308–22/specialreport.html (online accessed 16/5/02).

Anonymous (2002a) Student debt triples in three years. *The Guardian* (online accessed 22/4/02).

Anonymous (2002b) Will company collapse wreck my holiday? *The Observer* (online accessed 3/2/02).

Arsenault, M. (1998) Typologies and the leisure learner. *Ageing International* 15, 64–74.

Association of Recognised English Language Services (ARELS) (2002) *ARELS Membership Information.* http://www.arels.org.uk/info_pages/non_members/non_mem_info.html (online accessed 16/6/02).

Australian Bureau of Statistics (2002) *Education and Training: Higher Education.* http://www.abs.gov.au/ausstats/abs@.nsf/94713ad445ff1425ca25682000192af2/d0ec838b86413ffca256b3500187316!OpenDocument (online accessed 2/7/02).

Australian International Education Foundation (AIEF) (1998) *International Student Survey 1997/1998.* Canberra: Canberra Government Publisher.

Ayala, H. (1995) From quality product to eco-product: Will Fiji set a precedent? *Tourism Management* 16 (1), 39–47.

Ayala, H. (1996) Resort ecotourism: A master plan for experience management. *Cornell Hotel and Restaurant Administration Quarterly* 37 (5), 46–53.

Babin, B. and Kim, K. (2001) International students' travel behavior: A model of the travel-related consumer/dissatisfaction model. *Journal of Travel and Tourism Marketing* 10 (1), 93–106.

Backman, S. J. and Crompton, J. L. (1989) Discriminating between continuers and discontinuers of two public leisure services. *Journal of Park and Recreation Administration* 7, 56–71.

Baig, E. (1994) Vacations that put your mind to work. *Business Week* April (4), 112–113.

Baker, M. (2001) Second thoughts about school outings. *BBC News*. http://news.bbc.co.uk/hi/english/education/features/mike_baker/newsid_1426000/1426203.stm (online accessed 6/7/01).

BASELT (2002) *List of Members*. http://www.baselt.org.uk/ (online accessed 18/2/02).

Batchelor, R. (1998) Does British English rule okay? *Insights* March, A-121.

Batchelor, R. (2000) *What You Need to Know about Marketing English Language Courses*. London: The British Council.

Baty, P. (2000) Dependence on foreign fees poses threat to UK research. *The Times Higher Education Supplement* (online accessed 4/8/00).

Bauer, T. G. (2001) *Tourism in the Antarctic: Opportunities, Constraints and Future Prospects*. Binghamton: Haworth Hospitality Press.

BBC News. (1998) *Schools Explore the Great Indoors*. http://news.bbc.co.uk/hi/english/education/newsid_170000/170960.stm (online accessed 12/9/98).

BBC News. (1999) *EU Birth Rates Drop*. http://news.bbc.co.uk/hi/english/health/newsid_278000/278653.stm (online accessed 4/6/02).

BBC News. (2002) *Fresh School Safety Review Pledged*. http://news.bbc.co.uk/hi/english/education/newsid_1862000/1862840.stm (online accessed 8/3/02).

Beaumont, N. (2001) Ecotourism and the conservation ethic: Recruiting the uninitiated or preaching to the converted? *Journal of Sustainable Tourism* 9 (4), 317–341.

Benedict, J. (1995) Disney Institute: A new concept in vacation resorts. *Travel-ASSIST Magazine* 5. http://www.travelassist.com/mag/a106.html (online accessed 24/4/01).

Blamey, R. K. (1997) Ecotourism: The search for an operational definition. *Journal of Sustainable Tourism* 5, 109–130.

Blamey, R. K. and Braithwaite, V. A. (1997) A social values segmentation of the potential ecotourism market. *Journal of Sustainable Tourism* 5 (1), 29–45.

Blamey, R. K. and Hatch, D. (1998) *Profiles and Motivations of Nature-based Tourists Visiting Australia*. BTR Occasional Paper 5. Canberra: Bureau of Tourism Research.

Blangy, S. and Epler Wood, M. (1992) *Developing and Implementing Ecotourism Guidelines for Wildlands and Neighbouring Communities*. Vermont: The Ecotourism Society.

Bloch, S. (1998) The future for children's museum galleries. *Insights* March, D1–D7.

Bodger, D. (1998) Leisure, learning and travel. *Journal of Physical Education, Recreation and Dance* 69 (4), 28–31.

Bonink, C. and Richards, G. (1992) *Cultural Tourism in Europe.* ATLAS Research Report. London: University of North London.

Bown, L. (2000) The give-and-take case for overseas students. *The Times Higher Education Supplement* (online accessed 23/6/00).

Bramwell, B. and Lane, B. (2000) Collaboration and partnerships in tourism planning. In B. Bramwell and B. Lane (eds) *Tourism Collaboration and Partnerships* (pp. 1–19). Clevedon: Channel View Publications.

Brandon, K. (1996) *Ecotourism and Conservation: A Review of Key Issues.* Environmental Department Paper No. 23. Washington, DC: The World Bank.

Brause, D. (1992) The challenge of ecotourism: Balancing resources, indigenous people and tourists. *Transitions Abroad* November/December, 29–31.

British Council (2000) *EIBAS Handbook, 2002. Section 1: The English in Britain Accreditation Scheme.* http://www.britishcouncil.org/english/handbook.htm (online accessed 18/2/02).

British Council (2002) *English in Britain Accreditation Scheme – Why Choose an Accredited Centre?* http://www.britishcouncil.org/english/courses/infostu.htm (online accessed 18/2/02).

British Tourist Authority (2001) *BTA Britain at its Best.* http://www.visitbritain.com/news/pr_0066.htm (online accessed 8/11/01)

Britton, S. (1982) The political economy of tourism in the Third World. *Annals of Tourism Research* 9 (3), 331–358.

Brueggemann, W. (1987) *Hope Within History.* Atlanta: John Knox Press.

Bryd, T. (1998) Tourist-hungry Disney Institute shifts gears: Will appeal to non-Disney fans help? http://www.icopyright.com/1.1655.95221 (online accessed 24/4/01).

Buckley, R. (1994) A framework for ecotourism. *Annals of Tourism Research* 31 (3), 661–665.

Budowski, G. (1976) Tourism and conservation: conflict, coexistence or symbiosis. *Environmental Conservation* 3 (1), 27–31.

Bull, A. (1995) *The Economics of Travel and Tourism* (2nd edn). Melbourne: Addison Wesley Longman.

Burkart, A. J. and Medlik, S. (1981) *Tourism: Past, Present and Future.* London: Heinemann.

Burns, P. and Holden, A. (1995) *Tourism: A New Perspective.* London: Prentice Hall.

Butler, R. (1991) Tourism, environment and sustainable development. *Environmental Conservation* 18 (3), 201–209.

Bywater, M. (1993a) Market segments: The youth and student travel market. *Travel and Tourism Analyst* 5 (3), 35–50.

Bywater, M. (1993b) The market for cultural tourism in Europe. *Travel and Tourism Analyst* 6, 30–46.

Callender, C. and Kemp, M. (2000) *Changing Student Finances: Income, Expenditure and the Take-up of Student Loans among Full and Part-time Higher Education Students in 1998/99.* London: Department for Education and Employment.

Canadian Tourism Commission (CTC). (2001) *Learning Travel: 'Canadian Ed-Ventures' Learning Vacations in Canada: An Overview.* Ontario: Canadian Tourism Commission.

Carlson, J. and Widaman, K. (1988) The effects of study abroad during college on attitudes toward other cultures. *International Journal of Intercultural Relations* 12 (1), 1–17.

Carlson, J. *et al.* (1990) *Study Abroad: The Experiences of American Undergraduates in Western Europe and the United States.* Westport: Greenwood Press.

Carr, N. (1997) The holiday behaviour of young tourists: A comparative study. Ph.D. Thesis, University of Exeter.

Carr, N. (1998) Gendered differences in young tourists' use of leisure spaces and times. *Journal of Youth Studies* 1 (3), 279–294.

Carr, N. (2001a) 'Tourist culture' or 'tourist cultures' in an age of globalization. Paper presented at the New Zealand Geographical Society and the Institute of Australian Geographers Joint Conference, Dunedin, New Zealand.

Carr, N. (2001b) An assessment of the use and trust of different tourism information sources amongst university students. Paper presented at the Council for Australian University Tourism and Hospitality and Education (CAUTHE) Annual Conference, Canberra, Australia.

Carr, N. (forthcoming, a) Poverty and university students' leisure: A passing relationship? In F. Lobo (ed.) *Ambivalent Legacies and Rising Challenges in Leisure.*

Carr, N. (forthcoming, b) University students' holiday behaviour: A case study from New Zealand. In C. Michael Hall (ed.) *Introduction to Tourism in Australia: Impacts, Planning and Developments* (4th edn). South Melbourne: Pearson Education.

Cater, E. (1993) Ecotourism in the third world: Problems for sustainable tourism development. *Tourism Management* April, 85–90.

Cater, E. (1994) Tourism in the third world: Problems and prospects for sustainability. In E. Cater and G. Lowman (eds) *Ecotourism: A Sustainable Option?* (pp. 69–86). Chichester: John Wiley.

Canadian Environmental Advisory Council (CEAC) (1992) *Ecotourism in Canada.* Ottawa: Minister of Supply and Services.

Ceballos-Lascuráin, H. (1987) Estudio de prefactibilidaad socioeconómica del turismo ecológico y anteproyecto asquitectónico y urbanístico del Centro de Turismo Ecológico de Sian Ka'an, Quintana Roo. Study completed for SEDUE, Mexico.

Chadee, D. and Cutler, J. (1996) Insights into international travel by students. *Journal of Travel Research* 35 (2), 75–80.

Charters, S. and Ali-Knight, J. (2002) Who is the wine tourist? *Tourism Management* 23 (3), 311–319.

Chickering, A. (1969) *Education and Identity.* San Francisco: Jossey-Bass.

Christie, H. and Munro, M. (2001) Making ends meet: Student incomes and debt. *Studies in Higher Education* 26 (3), 363–383.

CIEE (2002) *About CIEE and Membership.* Council on International Educational Exchange. http://www.ciee.org/about_ciee.cfm?subnav=ciee (online accessed 2/7/02).

Clark, N. and Clift, S. (1994) A survey of student health and risk behaviour on holidays abroad. *Travel, Lifestyles and Health Working Papers.* Christchurch, New Zealand: Canterbury University.

Clarkson, M. (1995) A stakeholder framework for analyzing and evaluating corporate social performance. *The Academy of Management Review* 20, 92–117.

Cleaver, M. and Muller, T. E. (2001) The socially aware baby boomer: Gaining a lifestyle-based understanding of the new wave of ecotourists. Unpublished working paper. Gold Coast: School of Marketing and Management, Griffith University.

Coelho, G. (1962) Personal growth and educational development through working and studying abroad. *Journal of Social Issues* 18, 55–67.

Cohen, E. (1985) The tourist guide: The origins, structure and dynamics of a role. *Annals of Tourism Research* 12 (1), 5–29.

Cohen, E. (1988) Authenticity and commoditization in tourism. *Annals of Tourism Research* 15, 371–386.

Commonwealth Department of Tourism (1994) *National Ecotourism Strategy*. Canberra: Commonwealth Government Publishing Service.

Consumer Research Group (1996) *New Zealand Towards 2000: A Consumer Lifestyles Study*. Dunedin, New Zealand: Department of Marketing, University of Otago.

Conter, R. (1994) Measuring the economic impact of older adult education/travel expenditures. Paper presented at the 3rd Global Classroom Conference, Educational Tourism and the Needs of Older Adults, Montreal, Canada.

Cooper, C. (1999) The European school travel market. *Travel and Tourism Analyst* 5, 89–106.

Cooper, C. and Latham, J. (1985) *The Market for Educational Visits to Tourist Attractions in England and Wales*. Poole: Dorset Institute of Higher Education.

Cooper, C. and Latham, J. (1988) English educational tourism. *Leisure Studies* 9 (4), 331–334.

Cooper, C. and Latham, J. (1989) School trips: An uncertain future? *Leisure Management* 9 (8), 73–75.

Cooper, C. and Latham, J. (1990) Educational visits to tourist attractions. *Insights* 6, 1–10.

Coughlan, D. and Ritchie, B. W. (1998) Educational tourism: An insight into the motivations and perceptions of these special interest travellers. Paper presented at the New Zealand Tourism and Hospitality Research Conference, Akaroa, New Zealand, 1–4 December.

Coughlan, D. and Wells, J. (1999a) Educational tourism: The case for marketing to schools. Paper presented at CAUTHE, 9th National Research Conference, Adelaide, Australia.

Coughlan, D. and Wells, J. (1999b) Investing in the future: The nature and potential of the schools market. In E. Arola and T. Mikkonen (eds) *Tourism Education and Industry Symposium* (pp. 174–186). Jyvaskyla: Jyvaskyla Polytechnic.

Coughlan, D., Ritchie, B., Tsang, A. and Wells, J. (1999) *Schools Educational Tourism Project Research*. Unpublished report commissioned by the Schools Educational Tourism Committee, Canberra, Australia.

Coventry, N. (1996) New Zealand lures Asian families. *PATA Travel News: Asia Pacific* July, 18–19.

Craik, J. (2001) Cultural heritage tourism. In N. Douglas, N. Douglas and R. Derrett (eds) *Special Interest Tourism: Contexts and Cases* (pp. 113–137). Brisbane: John Wiley.

Crawford, D. W. and Godbey, G. (1987) Reconceptualizing barriers to family leisure. *Leisure Science* 9 (2), 119–127.

Crocombe, R. (1984) Education, enjoyment and integrity in tourism. *Contours* 1 (8), 10–14.

Crompton, J. L. (1979) Motivations for pleasure travel. *Annals of Tourism Research* 6, 408–424.

Cross, K. (1981) *Adults as Learners*. San Francisco: Jossey-Bass.

Dann, G. (2001) Senior tourism. *Annals of Tourism Research* 28 (1), 235–238.

Davies, E. and Lea, S. (1995) Student attitudes to student debt. *Journal of Economic Psychology* 16 (4), 663–679.

Deutsch, S. (1970) *International Education and Exchange: A Sociological Analysis*. Cleveland: The Case Western Reserve University Press.

Devlin, P. (1993) Outdoor recreation and environment: Towards an understanding of the use of the outdoors in New Zealand. In H. Perkins and G. Cushman (eds) *Leisure, Recreation and Tourism* (pp. 84–98). Auckland: Longman Paul.

DFES (2001) *Education and Skills – Delivering Results: A Strategy to 2006*. www.dfes.gov.uk/delivering-results (online accessed 6/2/02).

Dietl, J. (2002) Trends in birth statistics in Europe. *Zeitschrift Für Geburtshilfe und Neonatologie* 206 (2), 48–50.

Dowling, R. (1997) Plans for the development of regional ecotourism: Theory and practice. In C. M. Hall, J. Jenkins and G. Kearsley (eds) *Tourism Planning and Policy in Australia and New Zealand: Cases and Issues* (pp. 110–126). Sydney: Irwin.

Drucker, P. (1995) *Managing in a Time of Great Change*. New York: Dutton.

Duffus, D. and Dearden, P. (1990) Non-consumptive wildlife orientated recreation: A conceptual framework. *Biological Conservation* 53, 213–231.

Dunedin City Council (2002) *Our Education on the Market*. http://www.cityofdunedin.com/city/?page=Education_Dn (online accessed 22/6/02).

Eagles, P. (1997) *International Ecotourism Management: Using Australia and Africa as Case Studies*. Albany, Australia: IUCN World Commission on Protected Areas, Protected areas in the 21st century: From islands to networks.

Eastbourne Borough Council (1998) *Eastbourne Tourism Study*. Eastbourne: Eastbourne Borough Council.

Ecotourism Association of Australia (2002) *EcoGuide Program*. http://www.ecotourism.org.au/Eaa_guidecert.htm (online accessed 4/2/02).

The Ecotourism Society (1993) *Ecotourism Guidelines for Nature Tour Operators*. North Bennington: The Ecotourism Society.

Eden Project (2001) *The Eden Effect: A Snapshot of Economic Impact Locally and Regionally*. http://www.edenproject.com (online accessed 17/12/01).

Education and Training Export Group (1998) The British Institute of English Language Teaching and its role. *Exporting Education* Winter, p. 13.

Education Wellington International (2002) *Education Wellington International* http://www.ewi.org.nz/ (online accessed 23/6/02).

Encyclopaedia.com (2002) *Colleges and Universities*. Encyclopaedia.com. http://www.encyclopaedia.com/html/section/collsnun_universities.asp (online accessed 22/3/02).

Environmetrics (1991) *Needs and Expectations of Tourists Aged over 55 Years*. Sydney: New South Wales Tourism Commission.

ERASMUS Student Network (2002) *Erasmus Student Network: Students Helping Students*. http://www.esn.org (online accessed 22/3/02).

ERASMUS (2002a) *Statistics, Chart: Timeseries Erasmus Students*. http://europa.eu.int/comm/education/erasmus/stat.html (online accessed 22/3/02).

ERASMUS (2002b) *SOCRATES–ERASMUS: The European Community Programme in the Field of Higher Education*. http://europa.eu.int/comm/education/erasmus.html (online accessed 23/4/02).

Euromonitor (1998) *European Marketing Data and Statistics*. London: Euromonitor.

European Commission (2001) *DG XXII, Eurodyce European Unit*. Brussels: European Commission.

European Union (2001) *Lifelong Learning*. http://europa.eu.int/comm/education/life/ (online accessed 3/2/02).

Farrell, B. and Runyan, D. (1991) Ecology and tourism. *Annals of Tourism Research* 18 (1), 26–40.

Fennell, D. (1999) *Ecotourism: An Introduction*. London: Routledge.

Fennell, D. (2001) A content analysis of ecotourism definitions. *Current Issues in Tourism* 4 (5), 403–421.

Fennell, D. and Eagles, P. (1990) Ecotourism in Costa Rica: A conceptual framework. *Journal of Park and Recreation Administration* 8 (1), 23–34.

Field, A. (1999) The college student market segment: A comparative study of travel behaviours of international and domestic students at a southeastern university. *Journal of Travel Research* 37 (May), 375–381.

Figgis, P. (1993) Eco-tourism: Special interest or major direction? *Habitat Australia* (February), 8–11.

Fodness, D. and Murray, B. (1997) Tourist information search. *Annals of Tourism Research* 24 (3), 503–523.

Ford, P. (1981) *Principles and Practices of Outdoor/Environmental Education*. New York: John Wiley.

Forestell, P. H. (1993) If Leviathan has a face, does Gaia have a soul? Incorporating environmental education in marine eco-tourism programs. *Ocean & Coastal Management* 20 (3), 267–282.

Freeman, R. E. (1984) *Strategic Management: A Stakeholder Approach*. Boston: Pitman.

French, C., Craig-Smith, S. and Collier, A. (2000) *Principles of Tourism*. French's Forest, Australia: Pearson Education.

Gardom, T. (1996) Playing clever. *Attractions Management* June, 51–52.

Garrod, B. and Fyall, A. (2000) Managing heritage tourism. *Annals of Tourism Research* 27 (3), 682–708.

Gee, C., Makens, J. C. and Choy, D. J. L. (1997) *The Travel Industry* (3rd edn). New York: Van Nostrand Reinhold.

Giannecchini, J. (1993) Ecotourism: New partners, new relationships. *Conservation Biology* 7 (2), 429–432.

Gibson, H. (1998) The educational tourist. *Journal of Physical Education, Recreation and Dance* 69 (4), 32–34.

Glyn-Jones, F. (2001) We can see the future and it speaks English. *The Eastbourne Society* Winter, 145.

Gmelch, G. (1997) Crossing cultures: Student travel and personal development. *International Journal of Intercultural Relations* 21 (4), 475–490.

Godbey, G. (1990). Presentation to the special sessions on leisure constraints research. Sixth Canadian Congress on Leisure Research, University of Waterloo.

Goldberg, E. (1996) Educational tourism: Travel that exercises the mind. Unpublished Diploma in Tourism dissertation, Centre for Tourism, University of Otago, Dunedin, New Zealand.

Goodal, B. and Ashworth, G. (1988) *Marketing in the Tourism Industry: The Promotion of Destination Regions*. London: Routledge.

Goodale, T. L. (1992) Constraints research: Performing without a net next time. Featured speaker, Psychological/Social Psychological Aspects of Leisure Behaviour, Part I, NRPA Symposium on Leisure Research, Cincinnati, Ohio.

Goodwin, H. (1996) In pursuit of ecotourism. *Biodiversity and Conservation* 5 (3), 277–291.

Graddol, D. (1997) *The Future of English? A Guide to Forecasting the Popularity of the English Language in the 21st Century*. London: The English Company.

Grant, M., Human, B. and Le Pelley, B. (1998) Language schools and destination management. *Insights* November, A-81.

Gray, B. (1989) *Collaborating: Finding Common Ground for Multiparty Problems*. San Francisco: Jossey-Bass.

Gray, H. (1970) *International Travel – International Trade*. Lexington: Heath Lexington.

Greater Western Sydney Economic Development Board (2000) *Western Sydney Profile*. http://www.gws.org.au/ (online accessed 30/7/00).

Griffin, D., Saines, C. and Wilson, R. (2000) *Ministry for Culture and Heritage Special Report on Issues Relating to the Museum of New Zealand Te Papa Tongarewa*, June.

Gunn, C. (1988) *Tourism Planning* (2nd edn). New York: Taylor & Francis.

Halbertsma, N. F. (1988) Proper management is a must. *Naturopa* 59, 23–24.

Hall, C. M. (1995) *Introduction to Tourism in Australia: Impacts, Planning and Development* (2nd edn). Melbourne: Longman.

Hall, C. M. (1998) *Introduction to Tourism: Development, Dimensions and Issues* (3rd edn). Melbourne: Pearson Education Australia.

Hall, C. M. (2000) *Tourism Planning: Policies, Processes and Relationships*. London: Pearson Education.

Hall, C. M. and Jenkins, J. (1998) The policy dimensions of rural tourism and recreation. In R. Butler, C. M. Hall and J. Jenkins (eds) *Tourism and Recreation in Rural Areas* (pp. 19–42). Chichester: John Wiley.

Hall, C. M. and McArthur, S. (1996) Strategic planning: Integrating people and places through participation. In C. M. Hall and S. McArthur (eds) *Heritage Management in Australia and New Zealand: The Human Dimension* (pp. 22–36). Melbourne: Oxford University Press.

Hall, C. M. and McArthur, S. (1998) *Integrated Heritage Management: Principles and Practice*. London: The Stationery Office.

Hall, C. M., Cambourne, B., Macionis, N. and Johnston, G. (1997) Wine tourism and network development in Australia and New Zealand: Review, establishment and prospects. *International Journal of Wine Marketing* 9 (2/3), 5–31.

Hansel, B. (1988) Developing an international perspective in youth through exchange programs. *Education and Urban Society* 20 (2), 177–195.

Hardwick, H. (2000) Educational travel: Factors influencing traveller choices. Paper presented at the 14th Annual Conference for Non-profits in Travel, Washington, DC.

Harper, D. A. (1993) *An Analysis of Interfirm Networks*. Wellington: New Zealand Institute of Economic Research.

Harrison, M. (1970) *Learning Out of School*. London: Ward Lock Educational.

Headland, K. (2001) *Protected Areas in the Antarctic Treaty Region*. Cambridge: Scott Polar Institute. http://www.spri.cam.ac.uk/bob/protect.htm#cc (online accessed 20/7/01).

Helber, L. E. (1988) The roles of government in planning in tourism with special regard for the cultural and environmental impact of tourism. In D. McSwan (ed.) *The Roles of Government in the Development of Tourism as an Economic Resource* (pp. 17–23, Seminar series No. 1). Townsville: Centre for Studies in Travel and Tourism, James Cook University.

Hibbert, C. (1987) *The Grand Tour.* London: Methuen.

Hinch, T., Jackson, E. L. and Hickey, G. (1998) Tourism seasonality and leisure constraints. In J. Kandampully (ed.) *Advances in Research.* Proceedings of the 3rd Biennial New Zealand Tourism and Hospitality Research Conference, Lincoln University, New Zealand.

Hobson, J. S. P. and Josiam, B. (1992) Spring break student travel: An exploratory study. *Journal of Travel and Tourism Marketing* 1 (3), 87–97.

Hobson, J. S. P. and Josiam, B. (1995) Spring break student travel: A longitudinal study. *Journal of Vacation Marketing* 2 (2), 137–150.

Holdnak, A. and Holland, S. (1996) Edu-tourism: Vacationing to learn. *Parks and Recreation* 3 (9), 72–77.

Hollander, G., Threlfall, P. and Tucker, K. (1982) *Energy and the Australian Tourism Industry.* Canberra: Bureau of Industry Economics.

Hopkins, K. and Michael, E. (2001) Tourism clusters: Towards a theory for regional development. In J. Ruddy and S. Flanagan (eds) Proceedings of ATLAS 10th Anniversary Conference (n.p.). Dublin, Ireland, 4–6 October.

Hsu, C. and Sung, S. (1997) Travel behaviours of international students at a midwestern university. *Journal of Travel Research* 36 (1), 59–65.

Hughes, H. (1987) Culture as a tourist resource: A theoretical consideration. *Tourism Management* 8, 205–216.

Hunter, C. and Green, H. (1995) *Tourism and the Environment: A Sustainable Relationship?* London: Routledge.

Hurd, D. (1997) Novelty and its relation to field trips. *Education* 118, 29–36.

Inskeep, E. (1991) *Tourism Planning: An Integrated and Sustainable Development Approach.* New York: Van Nostrand Reinhold.

Institute of International Education (1998) *Open Doors: Foreign Students in HE in USA.* Online: http://www.opendoorsweb.org/foreign.xls (accessed 12/4/01).

The Interpreter (1985) *Interpreting to School Groups.* Special issue, Summer.

Irish Tourist Board (1988) *Inventory of Cultural Tourism Resources in the Member States and Assessment of Methods Used to Promote Them.* Brussels: European Commission DG VII.

Iso-Ahola, S. E. (1983) Towards a social psychology of recreational travel. *Leisure Studies* 2, 45–56.

ISTC (2002) *About ISTC.* International Student Travel Confederation. http://www.aboutitsc.org/about.html (online accessed 2/7/02).

Jackson, E. L. and Scott, D. (1999) Constraints to leisure. In E. L. Jackson and T. L. Burton (eds) *Leisure Studies at the Millennium.* State College, Pennsylvania: Venture.

Jallade, J. P., Gordon, J. and Lebeau, N. (2001) *Student Mobility Within the European Union: A Statistical Analysis.* http://europa.eu.int/comm/education/erasmus/statisti/index.html (online accessed 15/2/02).

Jamal, T. B. and Getz, D. (1995) Collaboration theory and community tourism planning. *Annals of Tourism Research* 22 (1), 186–204.

Jenkins, J., Hall, C. M. and Troughton, M. J. (1998) The restructuring of rural economies: Rural tourism and recreation as a government response. In R. Butler,

C. M. Hall and J. Jenkins (eds) *Tourism and Recreation in Rural Areas* (pp. 43–68). Chichester: John Wiley.

Jenner, P. and Smith, C. (1992) *The Tourism Industry and the Environment*. London: Economist Intelligence Unit.

Jobbins, D. (1999) Europe aims for greater student mobility. *The Times Higher Education Supplement* 25/6/99.

Jobbins, D. (2000) Where the flow goes. *The Times Higher Education Supplement* 30/6/00.

Jones, D. (2001) Seeing Sardinia. In D. Jones and G. Normie (eds) *2001: A Spatial Odyssey* (pp. 116–126). Nottingham: Continuing Education Press.

Jones, G. and Copley, J. (1997) Students to pay £1,000 tuition fees. *The Daily Telegraph* 17/7/97.

Josiam, B. M., Clements, C. J. and Hobson, J. S. (1994) Youth travel in the USA: Understanding the spring break market. In. A. V. Seaton (ed.) *Tourism, The State of the Art* (pp. 322–331). Chichester: John Wiley.

Kale, S. H., McIntyre, R. P. and Weir, K. M. (1987) Marketing overseas tour packages to the youth segment: An empirical analysis. *Journal of Travel Research* 26 (4), 20–24.

Kalinowski, K. and Weiler, B. (1992) Educational travel. In C. M. Hall and B. Weiler (eds) *Special Interest Tourism* (pp. 15–26). London: Belhaven.

Kearsley, G. W. (1993) Changing patterns of international visitor flows through New Zealand. Paper presented at the XIVth New Zealand Geographical Society Conference, Christchurch, New Zealand.

Keeley, P. (1993) The school visits market. *Insights* November, A133–A139.

Kennedy, M. (2001) This is the favourite exhibit in the world's favourite museum of modern art. *The Guardian* 12/5/01.

Keogh, B. (1990) Public participation in community tourism planning. *Annals of Tourism Research* 17, 449–465.

Kidd, J. (1973) *How Adults Learn*. Chicago: Follett.

Kimmel, J. R. (1999). Ecotourism as environmental learning. *The Journal of Environmental Education* 30 (2), 40–44.

Knight, J. (2000) Students learn a hard lesson about debt. *The Daily Telegraph* 8/10/00.

Knudson, D. M., Cable, T. T. and Beck, L. (1995) *Interpretation of Cultural and Natural Resources*. State College, Pennsylvania: Venture.

Kotler, P., Haider, D. H. and Rein, I. (1993) *Marketing Places: Attracting Investment, Industry, and Tourism to Cities, States, and Nations*. New York: The Free Press.

Krippendorf, J. (1982) Towards new tourism policies: The importance of environmental and socio-cultural factors. *Tourism Management* 3 (3), 135–148.

Krippendorf, J. (1987) *The Holiday Makers: Understanding the Impact of Leisure and Travel*. Oxford: Heinemann Professional.

Kulich, J. (1987) The university and adult education: The newest role and responsibility of the university. In W. Leirman and J. Kuilich (eds) *Adult Education and the Challenges of the 1990s* (pp. 170–190). New York: Croom Helm.

Kurzweil, R. (1999) *The Age of Spiritual Machines: When Computers Exceed Human Intelligence*. New York: Penguin.

Kutay, K. (1989) The New Ethic in Adventure Travel. *Buzzworm: The Environmental Journal* 1 (4), 31–34.

Lacey, H. (2001) Foreign tongues. *The Guardian* 29/5/01.
Lai, K. C. (1999) Freedom to learn: A study of the experiences of secondary school teachers and students in a geography field trip. *International Research in Geographical and Environmental Education* 8 (3), 239–255.
Laing A. N. (1987) The package holiday: Participant, choice and behaviour. Unpublished Ph.D. Thesis, Hull University.
Lane, B. (1994) What is rural tourism? *Journal of Sustainable Tourism* 2 (1/2), 7–21.
Lane, B. (1996) Rural tourism. Seminar given at the Invermay Agriculture Centre, July, Dunedin, New Zealand.
Larman, J. G. and Durst, P. (1989) Nature, travel and tropical forests. FREI Working Paper Series. Southeast Center for Forest Economics Research, Raleigh, North Carolina State University.
Law, C. M. (1993) *Urban Tourism: Attracting Visitors to Large Cities*. London: Mansell.
Leiper, N. (1989) *Tourism and Tourism Systems*. Occasional Paper No. 1. Palmerston North, New Zealand: Massey University.
Leiper, N. (1990) Partial industrialization of tourism systems. *Annals of Tourism Research* 17, 600–605.
Leman, G. (2002) Has technology made foreign language visits passé? *Online Latest*. Department of Education and Employment. http://wwwdfee.gov.uk/teacher/teachmag/data/online/data/passe_08.htm (online accessed 24/5/02).
Lennon, J. and Foley, M. (2000) *Dark Tourism*. London: Continuum.
Leopold, T. (2001) Memorials or tourist attractions? The case of former German Nazi concentration camps. Unpublished BA (Hons) dissertation in International Tourism Management, School of Service Management, University of Brighton.
Levinson, D. (1996) *The Seasons of a Woman's Life*. New York: Knopf.
Lew, A. (1998) The Asia-Pacific ecotourism industry: Putting sustainable tourism into practice. In C. M. Hall and A. Lew (eds) *Sustainable Tourism: A Geographical Perspective* (pp. 92–106). Harlow: Addison Wesley Longman.
Lifelong Learning Policy Bureau (2002) *Number of University Students (F.Y. 1984–2001)*. Ministry of Education, Culture, Sports, Science and Technology: Japan. http://www.jin.jcic.or.jp/stat/stats/16EDU59.html (online accessed 2/7/02).
Lightfoot, L. (2001) Alarm as pupils claim to have sex on school trips. *The Telegraph* 24/5/01.
Little, A. (2001) *2001 Wimbledon Compendium*. London: The All England Lawn Tennis and Croquet Club.
Loverseed, H. (1997) Market segments: The post-war generation and the North American travel industry. *Travel and Tourism Analyst* 3, 44–59.
Macionis, N. and Cambourne, B. (1998) Wine tourism: Just what is it all about? *Australia & New Zealand Wine Industry Journal* 13 (1), 41–47.
MacKenzie, A. and White, R. (1982) Fieldwork in geography and long-term memory structures. *American Educational Research Journal* 19 (4), 623–632.
Maiworm, F. (2001) ERASMUS: Continuity and change in the 1990s. *European Journal of Education* 36 (4), 459–472.
Major, L. E. (2002a) Tuition fees not benefiting universities. *The Guardian* 29/1/02.
Major, L. E. (2002b) Student numbers continue to rise. *The Guardian* 8/4/02.

Manning, R. (1983) *Studies in Outdoor Recreation: Search and Research for Satisfaction.* Oregon: Oregon State University Press.

Markwell, S., Bennett, M. and Ravenscroft, N. (1997) The changing market for heritage tourism: A case study of visits to historic houses in England. *International Journal of Heritage Studies* 3, 95–108.

Marsh, N. R. and Henshall, B. D. (1987) Planning better tourism: The strategic importance of tourist–resident expectations and interactions. *Tourism Recreation Research* 12, 47–54.

Martin, W. and Mason, S. (1987) Social trends and tourism futures. *Tourism Management* 8 (2), 112–114.

Masberg, B. A. and Savige, M. (1996) Incorporating ecotourist needs data into the interpretive planning process. *The Journal of Environmental Education* 27 (3), 34–40.

Mathieson, A. and Wall, G. (1982) *Tourism: Economic, Physical and Social Impacts.* London: Harlow.

McCallen, B. (2000) *ELT Competitor Analysis.* London: The British Council.

McCannell, D. (1976) *The Tourist: A New Theory of the Leisure Class.* London: Macmillan.

McCannell, D. (1993) *Empty Meeting Grounds.* London: Routledge.

McIntosh, R. and Goeldner, C. (1986) *Tourism: Principles, Practices, Philosophies* (5th edn). New York: John Wiley.

McIntosh, R. and Goeldner, C. (1990) *Tourism: Principles, Practices, Philosophies* (6th edn). New York: John Wiley.

McIntosh, R., Goeldner, C. and Ritchie, J. R. B. (1995) *Tourism: Principles, Practice, Philosophies* (7th edn). New York: John Wiley.

McKay, D. and Lewis, D. (1993) *Expenditure by International University Students at the University of Wollongong.* Economics Department, University of Wollongong: Wollongong.

Mewhinney, D., Herold, E. and Maticka-Tyndale, E. (1995) Sexual scripts and risk-taking of Canadian university students on spring break in Daytona Beach, Florida. *The Canadian Journal of Human Sexuality* 4 (4), 273–288.

Michael, I., Patel, A., Armstrong, A. and King, B. (1999) The impact of overseas students on the tourism industry of Victoria. Paper presented at the Australian Tourism and Hospitality Research Conference, Adelaide, Australia, 10–13 February.

Middleton, V. and Clarke, J. (1998) *Sustainable Tourism: A Marketing Approach.* Oxford: Butterworth-Heinemann.

Middleton, V. and Clarke, J. (2001) *Marketing in Travel and Tourism* (3rd edn). Oxford: Butterworth-Heinemann.

Mill, R. C. and Morrison, A. M. (1985) *The Tourism System: An Introductory Text.* Englewood Cliffs: Prentice Hall.

Milne, S. (1990) The impact of tourism development in small Pacific island states. *New Zealand Journal of Geography* 89, 16–20.

Ministry of Education, Culture, Sports, Science and Technology (1996) *1994 Academic Survey on the State of International Exchange in Senior High Schools: Press Release.* http://www.mext.go.jp/english/news/1996/04/960406.htm (online accessed 27/5/02).

Mitchell R. D. (1999) 1999 New Zealand winery visitors' survey: National summary report. Unpublished report.
Mitchell R. D. and Hall, C.M. (2001) The influence of gender and region on the New Zealand winery visit. *Tourism Recreation Research* 26 (2), 63–75.
Mitchell, R. K., Agle, B. R. and Wood, D. J. (1997) Toward a theory of stakeholder identification and salience: Defining the principle of who and what really counts. *The Academy of Management Review* 22 (4), 853–886.
Mitchell, R. D., Hall, C. M. and McIntosh, A. (2000) Wine tourism and consumer behaviour. In C. M. Hall, L. Sharples, B. Cambourne and N. Macionis (eds) *Wine Tourism Around the World: Development, Management and Markets* (pp. 115–135). Oxford: Butterworth-Heinemann.
Morrison, M., O'Leary, J., Hsieg, S. and Li, C. (1994) Identifying educational opportunities for older adults using the Canadian Travel Survey. Paper presented at the 3rd Global Classroom Conference: Educational Tourism and the Needs of Older Adults, Montreal, Canada.
Moscardo, G. (1996) Mindful visitors: Heritage and tourism. *Annals of Tourism Research* 23, 376–397.
Moser, H. and Kaspar, C. (1990) Private schools: Impact on the Swiss tourist economy. *St Galler Beitrage zum Fremdenverkehr und zur Verkehrswirtschaft Reihe Fremdenverkehr.* 20, 39–46.
Mowl, G. (1994) *Gender, Place and Leisure: Women's Leisure in Two Contrasting Areas of Tyneside.* Departmental Occasional Papers. New Series No. 10. Division of Geography and Environmental Management, University of Northumbria at Newcastle.
Muller, T. E. and Cleaver, M. (2000) Targeting the CANZUS baby boomer explorer and adventurer segments. *Journal of Vacation Marketing* 6 (2), 154–169.
Muloin, S. (1992) Wilderness access for persons with a disability: A discussion. In *Ecotourism: Incorporating the Global Classroom International Conference Papers* (pp. 20–25). Christchurch, New Zealand: Canterbury University.
Muñoz Gonzalez, S. (2001) The role of English language schools in Eastbourne's tourism industry and economy. Unpublished BA (Hons) dissertation in International Tourism Management, School of Service Management, University of Brighton.
Murphy, P. E. (1985) *Tourism: A Community Approach.* New York: Methuen.
Musca, J. and Shanka, T. (1998) Travel industry: Why aren't we marketing to international students? In J. Kandampully (ed.) Proceedings of New Zealand Tourism and Hospitality Research Conference (n.p.). Akaroa, New Zealand, 1–4 December.
National Capital Educational Tourism Project (NCETP) (2001) *National Capital Educational Tourism Project Homepage.* http://www.nationalcapital.gov.au/edtourism/home.htm (online accessed 23/3/02).
National Foundation for Educational Research (NFER) (1991) *Charging for School Activities.* Slough: NFER.
Nespor, J. (2000) School field trips and the curriculum of public spaces. *Journal of Curriculum Studies* 32 (1), 25–43.
Newberry, E. (1996) *Learning on Location.* Chichester: Newberry and England.
Nowak, P. F. (1972) Education in and about our environment. In G. W. Donaldson and O. Goering (eds) *Perspectives on Outdoor Education.* Dubuque: Wm. C. Brown.

Nowak, S. (1997) From a rock to a soft place in QuickTime. *The Times Higher Education Supplement* 01/1/97.

NSF (2002) *Comparison of Nationalities 1994/1995–2000/2001.* National Science Foundation. http://www.iaato.org (online accessed 7/2/2002).

OECD (2000) Organization for Economic Cooperation and Development. http://www.oecd.org/EN/home/0,,EN-home-26-nodirectorate-no-no-26,00.html (online accessed 14/11/00).

OECD (2001) *Cities and Regions in the New Learning Economy.* http://www.oecd.org/_els_pdfs_ED (online accessed 24/6/02).

Office of National Statistics (1996) *1996 International Passenger Survey.* London: The Stationery Office.

Olding S. (2000) Funding heritage. *Insights* July, pp. A9–A12.

Orams, M. (1995a) Towards a more desirable form of ecotourism. *Tourism Management* 16 (1), 3–8.

Orams, M. (1995b) Using interpretation to manage nature-based tourism. *Journal of Sustainable Tourism* 4 (2), 81–94.

Orams, M. (1997) The effectiveness of environmental education: Can we turn tourists into 'greenies'? *Progress in Tourism and Hospitality Research* 3, 295–306.

Orams, M. B. and Hill, G. J. E. (1998) Controlling the ecotourist in a wild dolphin feeding programme: Is education the answer? *The Journal of Environmental Education* 29 (3), 33–38.

Overseas Students' Advisory Committee (1999) Minutes of meeting held on Tuesday 23 November 1999, Gold Room, Winter Gardens, Eastbourne.

Page, S. (1995) *Urban Tourism.* London: Routledge.

Page, S. (1999) *Transport and Tourism.* London: Addison Wesley Longman.

Page, S., Brunt, P., Busby, G. and Connell, J. (2001) *Tourism: A Modern Synthesis.* London: Thomson.

Page, S. and Dowling, R. (2002) *Ecotourism.* Harlow: Pearson Education.

Page, S. and Getz, D. (1997) The business of rural tourism: International perspectives. In S. Page and D. Getz (eds) *The Business of Rural Tourism: International Perspectives* (pp. 3–37). London: Thomson.

Pasquier, B. (1994) ESL field trips: Bringing the world to the world. *The Clearing House* 67 (4), 192.

Paterson, N. (2002) How UK can sell more '1st class tickets for life'. *The Times Higher Education Supplement* 22/2/02.

Pearce, D. (1989) *Tourist Development* (2nd edn). Harlow: Longman Scientific and Technical.

Pearce, P., Morrison, A. and Routledge, J. (1998) *Tourism: Bridges Across Continents.* Sydney: McGraw-Hill.

Pearce, P. L. (1982) *The Social Psychology of Tourist Behaviour.* Oxford: Pergamon.

Piirto, R. (1991) *Beyond Mind Games: The Marketing Power of Psychographics.* Ithaca: American Demographic Books.

Poon, A. (1993) *Tourism, Technology and Competitive Strategies.* Wallingford: CAB International.

Prentice, R. (1993) *Tourism and Heritage Attractions.* London: Routledge.

Pritchard, A. and Morgan, N. J. (1996) Sex still sells to generation X: Promotional practice and the youth package holiday market. *Journal of Vacation Marketing* 3 (1), 69–80.

Read, S. (1980) A prime force in the expansion of tourism in the next decade: Special interest travel. In D. Hawkins, E. Shafer and J. Rovelstad (eds) *Tourism Marketing and Management Issues* (pp. 193–202). Washington, DC: George Washington University.

Regional Operating Programme (ROP) (2001) *Councillorship of the Programming Budget, Credit and Order of the Territory*. Regional Center of Programming. http://www.regionone.sardenga.it/programmazione/por-06–2000/por06–2000-indice.htm (online accessed 28/8/01).

Riedmiller, S. (1991) *Environmental Education in Zanzibar: Proposals for Action*. Zanzibar: Department of Environment, FINNIDA.

Riedmiller, S. and Cooksey, B. (1995) *Science Teaching in Government Secondary Schools in Mainland Tanzania – A Situational Analysis*. Consultancy report, GTZ–University of Dar es Salaam.

Revell, P. (2002) Trips that end in tragedy. *The Guardian* 11/3/02.

Richards, G. (1996) Production and consumption of European cultural tourism. *Annals of Tourism Research* 23 (2), 261–283.

Richards, G. (1999) *Developing and Marketing Crafts Tourism*. Tilburg: ATLAS.

Richards, G. (2000) Creative tourism as a factor in destination development. In J. Ruddy and S. Flanagan (eds) Proceedings of ATLAS 10th Anniversary Conference (n.p.), Dublin, Ireland, October 4–6.

Richards, G. (2001) The development of cultural tourism in Europe. In G. Richards (ed.) *Cultural Attractions and European Tourism* (pp. 3–29). Wallingford: CAB International.

Richardson, J. (1993) *Ecotourism and Nature-based Holidays*. Sydney: Simon and Schuster.

Richardson, J. (1997) Women travellers: Potentially a huge growth market in ecotourism. *Tourism & Hospitality Update* 55, 4.

Ritchie, B. W. (2001) Educational tourism: An innovative opportunity for regional development? In J. Ruddy and S. Flanagan (eds) Proceedings of ATLAS 10th Anniversary Conference (n.p.), Dublin, Ireland, October 4–6.

Ritchie, B. W. and Priddle, M. (2000) International and domestic university students and tourism: The case of the Australian capital territory. Paper presented at the Australian Tourism and Hospitality Research Conference, Mt Buller, Australia, 2–5 February.

Roberts, A. (1986) *Escorting Travel and Tourism Students on Visits out of College*. London: College for the Distributive Trades.

Roberts, N. C. and King, P. J. (1989) The stakeholder audit goes public. *Organizational Dynamics* 17 (3), 63–79.

Robertson, E. (2001) Risk needs to be managed, not feared. *Geographical* 73 (2), 78.

Roppolo, C. (1996) International education: What does this mean for universities and tourism? In M. Robinson, N. Evans and P. Callaghan (eds) *Tourism and Cultural Change* (pp. 191–201). Sunderland: Centre for Travel and Tourism and Business Editorial Press.

Ross, K. (1998) A preliminary report on the size of the US market for educational travel. Report prepared for the Canadian Forum on Cultural Learning Travel, Ottawa, Canada.

Roy Morgan (1996) *Roy Morgan Value Segments Holiday Tracking Research*. Sydney: Roy Morgan Research.

Roy Morgan (1997) *Roy Morgan Value Segments*. http://www.roymorgan.com.au/products/values (online accessed 10/10/00).

Roy Morgan (2000) *National Top-10 Television Programs*. http://www.roymorgan.com.au/tv-top-ten/ (online accessed 10/10/00).

Ruys, H. and Wei, S. (2001) Senior tourism. In N. Douglas, N. Douglas and R. Derrett (eds) *Special Interest Tourism: Contexts and Cases* (pp. 407–429). Brisbane: John Wiley.

Ryan, C. (1991) *Recreational Tourism: A Social Science Perspective*. London: Routledge.

Ryan, C. (1995) *Researching Tourist Satisfaction*. London: Routledge.

Ryan, C. and Robertson, E. (1997) New Zealand student-tourists: Risk behaviour and health. In S. Clift and P. Grabowski (eds) *Tourism and Health: Risks, Research and Responses*. London: Pinter.

Ryan, C., Hughes, K. and Chirgwin, S. (2000) The gaze, spectacle and ecotourism. *Annals of Tourism Research* 27 (1), 148–163.

Ryan, C., Robertson, E., Page, S. J. and Kearsley, G. (1996) New Zealand students: Risk behaviours while on holiday. *Tourism Management* 17 (1), 64–68.

Sanders, C. and Brookman, J. (2001) Analysis: Struggle to reverse student immobility. *The Times Higher Education Supplement* 3/8/01.

Sautter, E. T. and Leison, B. (1999) Managing stakeholders: A tourism planning model. *Annals of Tourism Research* 26 (2), 312–328.

Schieven, A. (1988) A study of cycle tourists on Prince Edward Island. Unpublished Masters Thesis, University of Waterloo.

Schouten, F. (1995) Improving visitor care in heritage attractions. *Tourism Management* 16 (4), 259–261.

Scott, A., Lewis, A. and Lee, S. (2001) Introduction. In A. Scott, A. Lewis and S. Lee (eds) *Student Debt: The Causes and Consequences of Undergraduate Borrowing in the UK*. London: The Policy Press.

Seekings, J. (1998) The youth travel market. *Travel and Tourism Analyst* 5, 1–20.

Selin, S. and Myers, N. (1998) Tourism marketing alliances: Member satisfaction and effectiveness attributes of a regional initiative. *Journal of Travel and Tourism Marketing* 7 (3), 79–94.

Selin, S. (2000) Developing a typology of sustainable tourism partnerships. In B. Bramwell and B. Lane (eds) *Tourism Collaboration and Partnerships* (pp. 129–142). Clevedon: Channel View Publications.

Shackley, M. (1993) The land of Lo, Nepal/Tibet: The first eight months of tourism. *Tourism Management* 15 (1), 17–26.

Silberberg, T. (1995) Cultural tourism and business opportunities for museums and heritage sites. *Tourism Management* 16 (5), 361–365.

Singapore Tourist Promotion Board (1996) *Tourism Statistics*. Singapore: Singapore Tourist Promotion Board. http://www.Ionn.com/tourism/html/tourmkt4.html (online accessed 4/6/96).

Sirakaya, E. and McLellan, R. (1997) Factors affecting vacation destination choices of college students. *Anatolia* 8 (3), 31–44.

Smeaton, G., Josiam, B. and Dietrich, U. (1998) College students' binge drinking at a beach-front destination during spring break. *Journal of American College Health* 46 (6), 247–254.

Smith, C. and Jenner, P. (1997a) Market segments: Educational tourism. *Travel and Tourism Analyst* 3, 60–75.

Smith, C. and Jenner, P. (1997b) Market segments: The senior's travel market. *Travel and Tourism Analyst* 5, 43–62.

Smith, R. (1982) *Learning How to Learn*. Chicago: Follett.

Smith, S. (1988) Defining tourism: A supply-side view. *Annals of Tourism Research* 15 (2), 179–190.

Smithers, R. (2001) Blame culture 'could end trips'. *The Guardian* 2/8/01.

Sofield, T. (2000) Forest tourism and recreation in Nepal. In X. Font and J. Tribe (eds) *Forest Tourism and Recreation* (pp. 225–247). Wallingford: CAB International.

Sogno-Lalloz I. (2000) Branding strategy for museums and galleries. *Insights* September, A33.

Spicer, J. and Stratford, J. (2001) Student perceptions of a virtual field trip to replace a real field trip. *Journal of Computer Assisted Learning* 17, 345–354.

STA Travel (2002) *Corporate Stuff*. http://www.statravel.com.au/allaboutus/corporate.php (online accessed 22/3/02).

Stainfeld, J. (2000) Fields of dreams. *The Times Higher Education Supplement* 27/10/00.

Stainfield, J., Fisher, P., Ford, B. and Solem, M. (2000) International virtual field trips: A new direction? *Journal of Geography in Higher Education* 24 (2), 255–262.

Stallings, D. (2001) The virtual university: Organizing to survive in the 21st century. *Journal of Academic Librarianship* 27 (1), 3–14.

Stebbins, R. (1982) Serious leisure: A conceptual statement. *Pacific Sociological Review* 25, 251–272.

Stebbins, R. (1996) Cultural tourism as serious leisure. *Annals of Tourism Research* 23, 958–960.

Steinecke, A. (1993) The historical development of tourism in Europe. In W. Pompl and P. Lavery (eds) *Tourism in Europe: Structures and Developments* (pp. 3–12). Wallingford: CAB International.

Stitsworth, M. (1988) The relationship between previous foreign language study and personality change in youth exchange participants. *Foreign Language Annals* 21 (2), 131–137.

Sung, S. and Hsu, C. (1996) International students' travel characteristics: An exploratory study. *Journal of Travel and Tourism Marketing* 5 (3), 277–288.

Swarbrooke, J. (1995) *The Development and Management of Visitor Attractions*. Oxford: Butterworth-Heinemann.

Swarbrooke, J. (1996) Towards a sustainable future for cultural tourism: A European perspective. In M. Robinson, N. Evans and P. Callaghan (eds) *Tourism and Cultural Change* (pp. 227–255). Sunderland: Centre for Travel and Tourism and Business Editorial Press.

Swarbrooke, J. and Horner, S. (1999) *Consumer Behaviour in Tourism*. Oxford: Butterworth-Heinemann.

Tal, R. (2001) Incorporating field trips as science learning environment enrichment: An interpretative study. *Learning Environments Research* 4, 25–49.

Te Papa (2001) *Press Releases 1998/99*. http://www.tepapa.govt.nz/communications/press_archive.html (online accessed 8/10/01).

Teichler, U. (1996) Student mobility in the framework of ERASMUS: Findings of an evaluation study. *European Journal of Education* 31 (2), 153–179.

Theobold, W. (1998) *Global Tourism: The Next Decade* (2nd edn). Oxford: Butterworth-Heinemann.

Thinesse-Demel, J. (2001) Education as a tool for the arts: Museum and the art as placement for public education. In D. Jones and G. Normie (eds) *2001: A Spatial Odyssey* (pp. 226–236). Nottingham: Continuing Education Press.

Tilden, F. (1967) *Interpreting Our Heritage* (rev. edn). Chapel Hill: University of North Carolina Press.

Times Higher Education Supplement (2002) Higher education trends: Number of students in the UK. *The Times Higher Education Supplement* 25/3/02.

Tourism Queensland (2001) *Market Insights*. http://www.qttc.com.au/research/trends/issue16/insights.htm (online accessed 6/12/01).

Towner, J. (1996) *An Historical Geography of Recreation and Tourism in the Western World, 1540–1940*. Chichester: John Wiley.

Turner, R., Miller, G. and Gilbert, D. (2001) The role of UK charities and the tourism industry. *Tourism Management* 22, 463–472.

Tysome, T. (1998) Peers attack foreign study policy. *The Times Higher Education Supplement* 5/6/98.

Uhlig, R. (1999) Children becoming 'softies' as red tape halts adventure. *The Telegraph* 31/5/99.

UNESCO (2002) *Enrolment by Level of Education*. UNESCO: Institute for Statistics http://www.uis.unesco.org/en/stats/stats0.htm (online accessed 21/5/02).

UNESCO–UNEP (1988) *International Strategy for Action in the Field of Environmental Education and Training for the 1990s*. Moscow, Paris and Nairobi: Congress on Environmental Education and Training.

United Nations (2001) *UN Population Ageing 1999*. http://www.un.org/popin/wdtrends/a99/a99cht1.htm (online accessed 18/12/01).

Urry, J. (1990) *The Tourist Gaze: Leisure and Travel in Contemporary Societies*. London: Sage.

Uysal, M., Jurowski, C., Noe, P. and McDonald, C. (1994) Environmental attitudes by trip and visitor characteristics. *Tourism Management* 15, 284–294.

Valentine, P. (1993) Ecotourism and nature conservation: A definition with some recent developments in Micronesia. *Tourism Management* 14 (2), 107–115.

Van Der Wende, M. (2001) The international dimension in national higher education policies: What has changed in Europe in the last five years? *European Journal of Education* 36 (4), 431–441.

Van Miert, M. (1998) Asian recruitment crash is self-inflicted. *The Times Higher Education Supplement* 24/4/98.

Var, T., Schlutter, R., Ankomah, P. and Lee, T. (1989) Tourism and world peace: The case of Argentina. *Annals of Tourism Research* 16 (3), 431–433.

Wallace, G. N. and Pierce, S. M. (1996) An evaluation of ecotourism in Amazonas, Brazil. *Annals of Tourism Research* 23 (4), 843–873.

Warner, J. (1999) North Cyprus: Tourism and the challenge of non-recognition. *Journal of Sustainable Tourism* 7 (2), 128–145.

Watt, R. (2000) Students can't bank on Lloyds TSB. *The Daily Telegraph* 22 November 2000.

Weaver, D. (1998) *Ecotourism in the Less Developed World*. Wallingford: CAB International.

Weaver, D. (1999) Magnitude of ecotourism in Costa Rica and Kenya. *Annals of Tourism Research* 26 (4), 792–816.

Weaver, D. (2000) Tourism and national parks in ecologically vulnerable areas. In R. Butler and S. Boyd (eds) *Tourism and National Parks: Issues and Implications* (pp. 107–124). Chichester: John Wiley.

Weaver, D. (2001a) Introduction to ecotourism. In D. Weaver (ed.) *The Encyclopaedia of Ecotourism* (pp. 1–36). Wallingford: CAB International.

Weaver, D. (2001b) *Ecotourism*. Brisbane: John Wiley.

Weaver, D. and Lawton, L. (2002) Overnight ecotourist market segmentation in the Gold Coast hinterland of Australia. *Journal of Travel Research* 40 (4), 270–280.

Weaver, D. and Oppermann, M. (2000) *Tourism Management*. Brisbane: John Wiley.

Wei, S. and Ruys, H. (1998) *Seniors and Industry Perception Survey*. Report prepared for the Seniors Card Office, Brisbane, University of Queensland.

Weiler, B. and Davis, D. (1993) An exploratory investigation into the roles of the nature-based tour leader. *Tourism Management* 14 (2), 91–98.

Weiler, B. and Hall, C. M. (1992) *Special Interest Tourism*. London: Belhaven.

Weiler, B. and Ham, S. (2001) Tour guides and interpretation. In D. B. Weaver (ed.) *The Encyclopaedia of Ecotourism*. Wallingford: CAB International.

Weiler, B. and Kalinowski, K. (1990) Participants of educational travel: A Canadian case study. *The Journal of Tourism Studies* 1 (2), 43–50.

Welch, R. V. (1992) Capitalist restructuring and local economic development: Perspective from an ultra-peripheral city-economy. *Regional Studies* 27 (3), 237–249.

West Country Tourist Board (n.d.) *Marketing to Schools Manual*. Exeter: West Country Tourist Board.

Western, D. (1993) Defining Ecotourism. In K. Lindberg and D. E. Hawkins (eds) *Ecotourism: A Guide for Managers and Planners* (pp. 7–11). North Bennington: The Ecotourism Society.

Wheatcroft, S. and Seekings, J. (1995) *Europe's Youth Travel Market*. London: European Travel Commission.

Wheeller, B. (1992) Alternative tourism: A deceptive ploy. In C. Cooper (ed.) *Progress in Tourism, Recreation and Hospitality Management* (pp. 140–146). Chichester: John Wiley.

Wheeller, B. (1993) Sustaining the ego. *Journal of Sustainable Tourism* 1 (2), 121–129.

Wheeller, B. (1994) Egotourism, sustainable tourism and the environment: A symbiotic, symbolic or shambolic relationship? In A. Seaton (ed.) *Tourism: The State of the Art* (pp. 647–654). Chichester: John Wiley.

Whelan, T. (1991) *Nature Tourism: Managing for the Environment*. Washington, DC: Island Press.

Wight, P. A. (1993) Ecotourism: Ethics or eco-sell? *Journal of Travel Research* 29, 40–45.

Wight, P. A. (1996) North American ecotourists: Market profile and trip characteristics. *Journal of Travel Research* 36 (4), 2–10.

Wight, P. A. (2001) Ecotourists: Not a homogeneous market segment. In D. Weaver (ed.) *The Encyclopaedia of Ecotourism* (pp. 37–62). Wallingford: CAB International.

Winetitles (2000) *The Australian Wine Industry: An Overview.* http://www.winetitles.com.au/overview/ (online accessed 22/7/00).

Wojtas, O. (1997) VR field trips come step closer. *The Times Higher Education Supplement* 13/6/97.

Wood, C. (2001) Educational tourism. In N. Douglas, N. Douglas and R. Derrett (eds) *Special Interest Tourism: Contexts and Cases* (pp. 188–211). Brisbane: John Wiley.

Woodward, D., Green, E. and Hebron, S. (1988) Research note: The Sheffield study of gender and leisure: Its methodological approach. *Leisure Studies* 7, 95–101.

World Tourism Organization (WTO) (1985) *The Role of Recreation Management in the Development of Active Holidays and Special Interest Tourism and Consequent Enrichment of the Holiday Experience.* Madrid: World Tourism Organization.

World Tourism Organization (WTO) (1993) *Tourism at World Heritage Cultural Sites: The Site Manager's Handbook.* Washington, DC: ICOMOS.

World Tourism Organization (WTO) (1999) *Tourism: 2020 Vision – Executive Summary.* Madrid: World Tourism Organization.

World Tourism Organization (WTO) (2001) *Rising Popularity of the Cruise Industry.* World Tourism Organization. http:www.world-tourism.org/newsroom/Releases/more_releases/february2001/ICAO.htm (online accessed 24/2/01).

World Travel and Tourism Council (WTTC) (2001) *Travel and Tourism's Economic Perspective.* USA: World Travel and Tourism Council.

Yale, P. (1992) *Tourism in Britain.* Huntingdon: ELM Publications.

Zell, L. (1992) Ecotourism of the future: the vicarious experience. In *Ecotourism Incorporating the Global Classroom International Conference Papers* (pp. 30–35). Christchurch, New Zealand: Canterbury University.

Ziffer, K. (1989) *Ecotourism: The Uneasy Alliance.* Working Paper No. 1, Washington, DC: Conservation International.

Zukin, S. (1992) *Landscapes of Power: From Detroit to Disney World.* Berkeley: University of California Press.

Index